Teaching Public History

Teaching Public History

....

EDITED BY
JULIA BROCK
EVAN FAULKENBURY

The University of North Carolina Press Chapel Hill

This book was published with the assistance of the Anniversary Fund of the University of North Carolina Press.

© 2023 The University of North Carolina Press
All rights reserved
Set in Charis by Westchester Publishing Services
Manufactured in the United States of America

Library of Congress Cataloging-in-Publication Data
Names: Brock, Julia, editor. | Faulkenbury, Evan, editor.
Title: Teaching public history / edited by Julia Brock and Evan Faulkenbury.
Description: Chapel Hill : The University of North Carolina Press, [2023] | Includes bibliographical references and index.
Identifiers: LCCN 2022058213 | ISBN 9781469673295 (cloth ; (alk. paper)) | ISBN 9781469673301 (pbk. ; (alk. paper)) | ISBN 9781469673318 (ebook)
Subjects: LCSH: Public history—Study and teaching—United States.
Classification: LCC D16.163 .T43 2023 | DDC 907.1—dc23/eng/20221214
LC record available at https://lccn.loc.gov/2022058213

Contents

List of Illustrations, vii

Introduction, 1
JULIA BROCK AND EVAN FAULKENBURY

1 Reflective Practice, 13
Public History's Signature Pedagogy, Course Design, and Student Engagement
PATRICIA MOONEY-MELVIN

2 The Great Syllabus Swap, 36
LINDSEY PASSENGER WIECK AND REBECCA S. WINGO

3 The Big Picture Goals of Public History, 57
EVAN FAULKENBURY

4 Upbuilding an Inclusive Future, 75
A Semester of Reciprocal Learning
TORREN GATSON

5 Digital Restorative Justice in the Public History Classroom, 93
Data Literacy and Archival Literacy in Mapping Violence
JIM McGRATH

6 The Real Trick Is Holding On to That Energy and Not Collapsing, 120
Teaching Undergraduate Public History on the Verge of the Pandemic
ABIGAIL GAUTREAU

7 Imaginemos Cosas Chingonas, 143
Building the Other Football Public History Project
ROMEO GUZMÁN

8 Seven Weeks of Heaven, 168
Teaching an Undergraduate Introduction to Public History Course in Half a Semester
JENNIFER DICKEY

9   Keeping the Tensions Present in the Public History Classroom, 189
    JULIA BROCK

10 A Journey at the Center of Public History, 201
    THOMAS CAUVIN

11 Do Public Historians Need Grades?, 225
    Ungrading during a Pandemic
    KRISTEN BALDWIN DEATHRIDGE

    Contributors, 253

    Bibliography, 255

    Index, 269

Illustrations

Whiteboard discussion of museums, 127
Jaime Ramirez trading card, front and back, 159
Group photo from tournament-fundraiser, 162
Public His'tree, 203

Teaching Public History

Introduction

JULIA BROCK
EVAN FAULKENBURY

In the last two decades, scholars have written many books about public history, historical memory, museum studies, historic preservation, and allied fields, but few have focused on *teaching* public history. After public history emerged as a subfield within academia in the 1970s (typically referred to at the time as "applied history"), it remained a specialized category for the rest of the century, with few universities offering coursework. As a result, we now face a dearth of pedagogy on the teaching of public history, even at a time when courses are soaring in popularity within history departments. Public history courses in colleges and universities are in demand, not only because they reveal career options to students with a history degree but also because they teach "marketable" skills, such as web design, collaboration, problem-solving, audience engagement, focused research, and concise writing. Recently, public historians have authored practice-based textbooks, coinciding with the mission of the National Council on Public History (NCPH) to create best practice guides for graduate, undergraduate, and K–12 education.[1] There are also recent works that include reflection on pedagogy in digital public history practice and queer public history practice.[2] These textbooks are valuable, but we need more accounts of classroom instruction. All the while, colleges and universities are adding more public history courses, with over two hundred institutions now offering graduate and undergraduate options.[3]

This volume is a collection of eleven first-person essays that go behind the scenes to explore a full college semester inside public history courses. The authors share their journeys of teaching public history, including reflections on their thought processes, class preparation, course sessions, interactions with students, assignments, evaluations, student projects, and community partner relationships. These are reflective essays that admit successes and failures. Instead of offering the reader unsolicited advice, authors recount what they did and why. Teaching can be exhilarating, stressful, and at times lonely, and public history courses are no exception. These essays provide entry into the mindset of public historians who are teaching, struggling, and making mistakes, but also finding inspiration in their students and the public history classroom. We hope that educators, in reading these narratives, will find encouragement, pedagogical strategies, bold ideas, and renewed confidence in their own abilities.[4]

What exactly is public history? Few other fields exist within the historical profession that have so often debated definition. Practitioners agree that the term refers to public-facing history (rather than history written for academic audiences)—whether the outcomes might be museum exhibits, oral history projects, historic landmarks, walking tours, monuments, and so on—but the problem of definition remains. The NCPH offers a broad summary: "Public history describes the many and diverse ways in which history is put to work in the world. In this sense, it is history that is applied to real-world issues."[5] Rather than debate what does or does not "count," Alexandra M. Lord recently urged the NCPH and its members "to broaden the definition of public history itself."[6] Similarly, Jennifer Dickey (a contributor to this volume) imagines public history as a "big tent," encompassing numerous forms of community-facing history.[7] We offer this collection to help get to the heart of public history practice. As public history educators, we continually push the boundaries of our practice by what we accomplish with our students. The range of avenues by which we communicate and co-create history with general audiences means that our practice is ever-evolving and expanding. It is not insignificant, too, that we do so within the context of twenty-first century universities and colleges, which present institutional and structural possibilities and limitations. As each of these essayists demonstrates, public history is not a static field but one that we as educators shape through our methods of training.[8]

By reflecting on a semester in the classroom, the historians in this collection showcase the value of public history, though not without critical reflection on practice. Public history students can hone skills they do not necessarily receive in traditional history courses, such as working on a team, translating historical research for public consumption, considering audience responses, problem-solving for a partner, and building a public-facing project that lasts beyond the semester. Classroom work that goes off-campus comes with risk for both the instructor and students, but these essays illustrate that students find productive challenges, increase their capacity for empathy, and learn firsthand that public history, in its ideal form, is about service and conscientious application of historical skills. And for the wider community, the value of public history at a local college or university is that programs and courses can offer support to groups that are already sharing and preserving the nearby past. Public history is not insular but instead can reach beyond campus to build careful connections with community partners. Teaching public history, then, is not only about the students but also about supporting community members, however defined, and fostering a shared appreciation for local and regional histories, lifeways, and cultures.

These characteristics differentiate public history pedagogy from that explored in service learning and community engagement (SLCE) literature. There is common ground, to be sure, and the educator who embarks on a public history project may find helpful resources and support in institutional service learning programs. But generally, service learning is focused foremost on student needs—credits, credentials, and development—and, as some critics charge, outputs instead of outcomes that show the impact of engagement.[9] SLCE literature, by and large, focuses on the non-humanities fields, such as education, public health, and STEM; two historians who note the gap suggest that it is indicative of a lingering question in SLCE: "What relevance or worth does the study of the humanities have in the world outside the academy?"[10] Though public history educators are devoted to student support and development, we are practicing the principles and ethics defined by a wider field, one that finds space beyond institutions of higher education. Our standards require us, for example, to incorporate reflective practice, coauthorship and collaboration, and multivocal historical production. We apply these practices to the classroom rather than draw solely from the pedagogy of higher education.

Though we share common issues with engaged curriculum in other fields, public historians face unique challenges in the classroom. With the often tense relationship between town and gown, the expectations of a shared authority, and the goals that necessitate that student work be made accessible to audiences and stakeholders beyond the classroom, public history asks more of its students and teachers than do typical humanities courses. Students in a public history course have their work judged not only by the professor but also by the larger community, a situation that can create additional anxiety for both students and teachers. The stakes are high in public history courses as professors risk their professional and community reputations on how well they prepare their students to research, empathize, and make connections between the past and the present. Many of us, no doubt, put too much pressure on ourselves to meet everyone's expectations, but this often understated reality of public history pedagogy persists. With this volume, we spotlight these exceptional challenges within our field and share ideas for how to better manage our semesters without cracking before finals week.

At the same time, we envision these essays to be useful to educators within other humanities disciplines. Adjacent fields to public history, such as museum studies, historic preservation, and library science, may find this volume particularly useful. Practitioners in other areas, from anthropology to urban planning, may also discover helpful strategies. A common thread that connects public history to a variety of other fields is its commitment to pushing past the boundaries of academia. Public history exists to make the past useful to general audiences, similarly to how a related field, archival studies, strives to connect collections with people beyond their climate-controlled walls.

This volume points toward a collective vision for the future of historical study as action oriented. More than ever before, history departments are looking to public history to bolster a more traditional curriculum, which means that public history will push departments to increasingly embrace community-facing historical work. NCPH and practitioners have long understood the relationship between history and community service, and as public history continues its rise in popularity within departments, students will come to appreciate, even demand, this connection as part of their basic historical training. The educators in this volume signal that public history is on the cusp of becoming a major field within the profession, not just a sub-field. This service-based approach to historical inquiry should be welcome news to students, professors, departments, and public historians alike. In a political and cultural landscape where facts and evidence can be so easily dismissed, public history can offer an inclusive, community-focused platform to explore how and why the past shapes the present. By arguing why these classes matter for our students and our communities, we are also making the case for increased resources and institutional support. As professors in public history, we are laying a foundation for an action-oriented study of history.

Public history exists beyond the confines of a college classroom. How, then, should educators teach public history in a semester-long course on campus? In this collection, the authors explore this contrast by placing themselves as the bridge between classroom instruction and public history beyond academe. The field of public history situates itself between the worlds of academia and community-based practice. Within academia, some historians have perceived public history as trivial and non-scholarly (although this prejudice is dissipating as public history courses become more common within departments). At the same time, nonacademics who work as public historians through nonprofits, government services, or private organizations sometimes view the scholarly world of public history as too theory-laden and impractical for general audiences. These essays traverse the gap, demonstrating how college courses in public history can meaningfully engage with local communities beyond campus and, at the same time, ground students in the fundamentals of public history.

Educators with different backgrounds will glean unique insights from this collection. Veteran public history instructors may imagine new possibilities for their courses after reading through their peers' accounts. Historians who have not formally trained in public history yet include public history activities or projects within their semester will benefit from these stories. Department chairs and administrators should find these perspectives illuminating, perhaps enabling them to better understand the support needed to launch a public history program. But those who stand the most to gain are new teachers, just beginning to wade into the world of public history. Historians may be unfamiliar with public history pedagogy and yet may find themselves tasked with teaching such a course to accommodate departmental needs. Graduate students in the job market may not have had the opportunity to teach a public history course, but perhaps a job advertisement prefers candidates with knowledge of public or digital history methods. As more and more departments add public history coursework, fewer and fewer public history scholars will be left to fill the demand. Thus, this book acts as a primer for anyone about to teach their first public history class. This volume is not a replacement for an advanced degree in public history theory and methodology, but it is a jump start that can quickly and efficiently prepare an instructor to lead a class of students forward.

Themes that emerge across these eleven essays will guide new educators in constructing their courses. Many of the authors, for example, recognize the ways that institutional structures define the possibilities of the public history classroom. The semester is an arbitrary unit of time for community partners, whose needs can go beyond fifteen weeks. Institutional funding (or lack thereof) shapes travel, research, and production, and can bolster or stymie off-campus work. Partnerships with community organizations can be challenged by differing expectations and lack of trust, and public history instructors must carefully labor to sustain ethical and reciprocal relationships. Within the classroom, instructors work to offer a comprehensive introduction to public history in readings and assignments, while also meeting project needs and maintaining a commitment to a pedagogy that reflects the ethics of the field—a sometimes heavy load for the public historians herein. Instructors must face the reality, too, that student effort alone cannot meet project needs and that sometimes there will be work to be done at the end of the semester to bridge the gap between student production and a final, polished project. In addition, several of these writers were deeply affected by the COVID-19 pandemic in 2020 and 2021, and some explicitly address its impact on their teaching and course projects. In all, the experiences of contributing authors suggest what resources and strategies are required for the public history class: departmental support for class field trips or class projects, planning with community partners well in advance of the semester, and scaffolding student work so that students can blend principles with practice by the end of the semester.

The volume begins with insight from a longtime public history educator and ends with a reflection on the head-spinning shifts required for instruction during the pandemic. The first essay is by Patricia Mooney-Melvin, an associate professor of history and graduate program director at Loyola University Chicago. Her argument is clear from the start: "Reflective practice represents public history's signature pedagogy, which distinguishes it from other curricular design and course structures in the field of history." Before going through her fall 2019 graduate course Public History: Method and Theory, Mooney-Melvin explores the historiography of public history and teaching practice from the late 1970s onward. As a longtime leader within the field and the NCPH, Mooney-Melvin provides a contextual overview of public history education. Connecting this long history to her fall 2019 semester, she explains her department's relationship with the Rogers Park/West Ridge Historical Society and the class project. She then leads readers through a week-by-week appraisal of class sessions, readings, and goals through the end of the semester. Mooney-Melvin concludes by reemphasizing what she means by reflective practice and how, even if students do not always understand it in the moment, they internalize these lessons as they move through Loyola's graduate program in public history and into their careers.

Next, Lindsey Passenger Wieck and Rebecca S. Wingo recorded and edited a conversation they shared about their ongoing syllabus swap. Wieck, an associate professor of history at St. Mary's University in San Antonio, Texas, and Wingo, an assistant professor of history at the University of Cincinnati, both direct public history programs but struggle with impostor syndrome for not having formally trained in public history. After becoming friends during graduate school, they continued to rely on each other as public history professors and directors in an innovative "syllabus swap" in which they exchanged syllabi for their introduction to public history courses. According to Wieck and Wingo, the swap happens "with the understanding that the other will improve the readings and assignments before returning it. With this swap, we essentially double the speed with which we can improve our syllabi and, by proxy, our students' experience. We're basically the backwoods backpackers of academia: packing out the other person's rubbish to leave the syllabus better than we found it." They offer a lively account of the public history syllabus as a collaborative and intellectual undertaking.

Halfway through Evan Faulkenbury's fall 2019 introduction to public history course, he shifted gears and began emphasizing students' Big Picture Goals. Faulkenbury is an associate professor of history at SUNY Cortland who teaches the public history class that all history majors must take to graduate. In addition to surveying public history's multiple formats, such as museums, historic sites, and oral histories, Faulkenbury facilitated a partnership between his class, the Cortland County Historical Society, and the local tourism bureau. Their joint project used the digital platform Clio to create entries on fifty of Cortland County's roadside historic markers. As the project began, Faulkenbury began shifting the purpose of his class to focus on everyone's Big Picture Goals. Having just read a book about teaching, Faulkenbury started devoting time every class session to stressing how the information they were processing about public history and the skills they were developing through their project could help students achieve their personal career goals. Faulkenbury was surprised to see how this pedagogical strategy opened his students' eyes to seeing public history not only as a subject to be studied but as something relevant to their own lives and potential futures. The project itself concluded with both successes and failures, but the larger goal of making students aware of how public history can be a vehicle for accomplishing their own professional goals transformed the class in a positive way. The point of teaching public history to undergraduates should not necessarily be to introduce them to public history as a career path but to expose them to the skills of public history that can translate into any vocation. Remarkably, Faulkenbury discovered, "Public history . . . does this almost intrinsically, but professors have to be the ones to help students see the forest through the trees."

Torren Gatson, an assistant professor at the University of North Carolina, Greensboro, commits his public history courses to exploring and advancing inclusivity and equity in the public history field. In the fall of 2019, he taught a museum and historic site interpretation course in which he and students partnered with the Historic Magnolia House, a hotel that was included in *The Negro Motorist Green Book* and played a central part in the civil rights struggle in Greensboro. Gatson, an African American scholar and public historian, led a class of predominantly white students through uncomfortable discussions to help connect their rhetorical commitments to inclusivity to an applied practice via the work of community partnership and exhibit building. Gatson facilitated his course as an exercise in scholarly consciousness raising; in his words, students left the course with an "awareness of issues of authority and culturally responsive pedagogy, as well as an awareness of white privilege and tearing down barriers within museums, which allows for professionals to begin dismantling colonized spaces toward a more inclusive narrative." Awareness, he contends, is only a beginning but a necessary one as students move into their professional lives in a field that is only now confronting long-standing issues of inequity.

Jim McGrath considers public history pedagogy in the context of digital restorative justice work. With scholar Monica Muñoz Martinez, McGrath co-taught a Mapping Violence course for undergraduates at Brown University in the spring of 2020. McGrath, now a part-time lecturer at Northeastern University, underlines his essay with a question he and Martinez grappled with in the course: "How do we teach and reckon with long histories of state-sanctioned racial violence in the United States with students and with publics beyond the classroom?" Instructors and students worked on the "Mapping Violence" digital public history project begun by Martinez as an extension of her scholarship on racial violence in Texas between 1900 and 1930. McGrath and Martinez intentionally framed the course for students who were not enrolled in public history or public humanities certificates, and throughout the course of the semester, they worked to build a database of incidents of racial violence. In reflecting on the semester, McGrath notes that public history instructors "must reflect on how these pasts [of racial violence] and our relationships to them impact our pedagogical approaches in the present. Humanities instructors who work with data and archives in any context should think carefully about how their readings, lessons, and assignments acknowledge the colonial and violent legacies of data collection and the creation of archives." The course he and Martinez built charts a path for public historians engaging with the violent legacies we inherit and intentionally or unintentionally perpetuate.

Abigail Gautreau, an assistant professor of history at Grand Valley State University in Michigan, kept a daily journal of her class sessions for her winter/spring 2020 public history course. This record of her thought process is invaluable, as it allows readers to feel her emotions day by day in the course. Gautreau's writing is honest as she recounts what went well, what bombed, and the quotidian drudgery of actually managing a class. She pulls aside the curtain to allow readers to experience the hard labor of teaching public history, balancing her public history course load with two other classes on a multisite campus. Her class partnered with the Lowell Area Historical Museum for a project, but the COVID-19 pandemic cut their collaboration short. Up until that point, however, Gautreau led class sessions on historic preservation, the National Register, archives, and more, and took field trips to local museums. Gautreau's in-depth analysis of these class discussions reveals the difficulty in translating public history topics for student consideration, how they can easily go wrong, but also how they hold tremendous potential for opening students' eyes to the power of public history. Even when class sessions did not always pan out as she hoped, teaching this public history class more often than not rejuvenated Gautreau during a trying semester. As Gautreau writes, "What I really want to share . . . is that so often I leave my public history class with more energy than when I walked in. It's a special feeling, because I don't always feel that way when I leave class."

Romeo Guzmán, an assistant professor of history at Claremont Graduate University, writes in the style of creative nonfiction to illustrate how *fútbol* (soccer) enabled his students to become working public historians. While working as an assistant professor at California State University, Fresno, Guzmán taught Fútbol: A Local and Global History of the Beautiful Game during the spring semesters of 2018, 2019, and 2020. In his essay, Guzmán explores his own evolution as a public historian, followed by a detailed map of his course. He then shares how he and his students became part of a special movement to celebrate fútbol through a local professional club in Fresno while using the tools of public history to involve the community in their own regional history. The benefits of such an involved multi-semester project, according to Guzmán, "allowed us to have fun, to enjoy fútbol, and to engage an eager public. It also granted us a lot of credibility with the Central Valley soccer community and made it easier for me to pitch the significance of public history to my students and university." By designing trading cards, staffing tables, organizing events, printing T-shirts, attending games, and playing fútbol, Guzmán engineered a comprehensive public history project that, while not without its challenges, succeeded in bringing together the larger Fresno community.

Compressing an introduction to public history course from a traditional semester into just seven weeks is nothing new to Jennifer Dickey, a professor of history and coordinator of the public history program at Kennesaw State University. In this thoughtful and introspective essay, Dickey reports on the accomplishments of her fall 2019 class, which partnered with an old railroad depot in the nearby town of Tate, Georgia, to conduct research and propose exhibit panels. Knowing she was working with students just learning about public history (and in a seven-week course, no less), Dickey had no illusions about expecting too much, but she considers her ambitious schedule as a positive for her class. Dickey acknowledges that her "philosophy is that even if the students cannot complete a project that is ready for prime time, I am teaching them the process. Doing public history work is collaborative and iterative, and it is something that may take them years to master. My classes are the beginning of that process." Week by week, Dickey leads readers through her thought process, decision-making, and evaluation of students. Dickey reveals what worked and what did not, and considers how throwing students into public history headfirst has many more pros than cons.

Julia Brock outlines what she calls her "all-in approach" to the introduction to public history classroom, which, like similar courses discussed in the collection, includes seminar-style reading and discussion, visits by practitioners, field trips, and a final applied project. She also considers how public history teaching and practice are shaped by the institutions in which we teach, and what's at stake in extending the university "beyond the university."[11] She reflects on three ways that she asked students to engage with the power dynamics of the classroom and field in the fall of 2019: through examination of campus history, interrogation of the policies and practices that define what from the past is preserved, and a class project framed by the changing ethics of the field. The class partnered with the Old Cahawba Archaeological Park near Selma, Alabama, where students researched Reconstruction-era Black life in the former capital of Alabama. Brock concluded that the work outside the classroom was especially important in situating students in ethical practice, even as she acknowledges the limits of an intensive all-in course model.

Public history can verge on the whimsical. Thomas Cauvin embraces public history's weirdness in his essay about his students creating wall panels for public restrooms. Cauvin, an associate professor of public history at the University of Luxembourg, writes about teaching an undergraduate "Practices of Public History" course at Colorado State University during the fall 2019 semester. The first portion of the course centered around defining public history, overviewing topics, and listening to guest speakers. Then, Cauvin explains, he guided his students into two public history projects. Two separate projects may seem overly ambitious, but according to Cauvin, "My goal is for my students to leave the class not only with new knowledge and skills but also with something more concrete that they can show, share, discuss, and be proud of." One project involved a collaboration with the campus radio station creating short podcasts about the history of the university. The second required students to design wall panels about the history of Fort Collins and approach businesses around town to ask permission to mount panels in their restrooms. "Due to the special—some would say strange—location," Cauvin writes, "students had to be very careful and thoughtful about the contents and design. It also forced them to work outside their comfort zone, as they would be engaging with a specific but anonymous public." Cauvin explores the challenges of teaching public history, noting the importance of hardship (both for the professor and the students) to create worthwhile public history projects that last beyond the semester.

In this volume's sole essay on an online semester deep into the COVID-19 pandemic, Kristen Baldwin Deathridge, an associate professor of history at Appalachian State University, "ungraded" her spring 2021 introduction to digital history course. Deathridge guides readers through her semester in diary entries, written in present tense just after each class session ended. Jotting down her thoughts in the moment allowed Deathridge to record thoughtful observations about class sessions, Zoom calls, student progress, and the act of teaching public history through a screen. Due to the challenges of the pandemic and teaching online, Deathridge helped students create individual websites and digital projects rather than group work. She assesses the positives and negatives of this approach, and she considers the relationship between public history and digital history. To evaluate her students' work, Deathridge followed an "ungrading" pedagogical model that allowed her students to progress at their own pace, write critical self-examinations of their work, and shape their digital history projects in styles unburdened by traditional grading methods. Deathridge found this approach to be useful, though not without its challenges, writing at the start of the semester, "It is a bit scary . . . if I'm honest. But I think that allowing students to estimate their own grade for the class will help them to take ownership of their part of the work required for learning, which is an essential skill for both public and digital history."

As we enter into the twenty-first century's third decade, public history's rise within both academia and communities is unprecedented. Through our teaching, we will not only facilitate this ascent but also shape public history's usefulness to our students, departments, and local areas. Public history is about action—doing history out in the world. Through these eleven essays, we hope our passion for and critical assessment of public history enlightens those educators entering the public history classroom.

Notes

1. To see the NCPH's set of educational guides, visit the "For Public History Educators" webpage, https://ncph.org/publications-resources/educators. Public history textbooks include Cauvin, *Public History*; Lyon, Nix, and Shrum, *Introduction to Public History*. Related works include Kean and Martin, *The Public History Reader*; Gardner and Hamilton, *Oxford Handbook of Public History*; Sayer, *Public History*; Wingo, Heppler, and Schadewald, *Digital Community Engagement*; Smulyan, *Doing Public Humanities*.

2. See Wingo, Heppler, and Schadewald, *Digital Community Engagement*; Rosenthal, *Living Queer History*; Stein, *Queer Public History*.

3. See the complete list on the NCPH's guide to public history programs at https://ncph.org/program-guide/.

4. The only other comprehensive set of essays that focused on the teaching of public history was published in 1987. See the twelve essays in Johnson and Stowe, "Field of Public History."

5. See "How Do We Define Public History?" National Council on Public History, https://ncph.org/what-is-public-history/about-the-field/.

6. Lord, "Finding Connections," 11.

7. Dickey, "Public History and the Big Tent Theory."

8. For a brief historiography of public history's definitions and meanings, see Kelley, "Public History"; Grele, "Whose Public? Whose History?"; Achenbaum, "Public History's Past, Present, and Prospects"; Frisch, *A Shared Authority*; Appleby, "Should We All Become Public Historians?"; Liddington, "What Is Public History?"; Stanton, "What Is Public History? Redux"; Weible, "Defining Public History"; Meringolo, *Museums, Monuments, and National Parks*; Gardner and Hamilton, *Oxford Handbook of Public History*, introduction. For more complete bibliographies of public history's origins, meanings, and historiography, see Cauvin, *Public History*, 22–25; Gardner and Hamilton, *Oxford Handbook of Public History*, 19–22.

9. Stoecker, *Liberating Service Learning*.

10. Straus and Eckenrode, "Engaging Past and Present," 255. Historians have argued for the importance of history in service-learning curriculum; see Donovan and Harkavy, *Connecting Past and Present*.

11. Harney and Moten, *Undercommons*, 37.

1 Reflective Practice

Public History's Signature Pedagogy, Course Design, and Student Engagement

PATRICIA MOONEY-MELVIN

Although training and practice in what has increasingly fallen under the general designation of public history predates the use of the term "public history," the inauguration of *The Public Historian* in 1978 stimulated vigorous discussion about the ways that history works in the world outside the academy and the nature of graduate training in history. Whereas traditional training in history emphasized the discipline, public history training demanded the integration of theory, knowledge, and praxis in ways that contemporary programs did not address but were believed necessary to produce the "new type of professional person" G. Wesley Johnson called for in the inaugural issue of *The Public Historian*.[1] What was needed, a group of public history educators agreed, were new ways of thinking about graduate history education—overall curricular design as well as individual course structure—to meet the needs of students enrolled in public history courses or programs. Reflective practice emerged as a conceptual approach that offered a strong curricular foundation for students, enabling them to integrate disciplinary knowledge and reflection-in-action, which, as Noel Stowe argued, "prepare[s] graduates in applied practice and conceptual approaches appropriate to the types of questions asked of practitioners and to the settings of their practice."[2] Reflective practice, I contend, is public history's signature pedagogy. At Loyola University Chicago, students are introduced to this approach in History 480, Public History: Method and Theory, the first course put in place when Loyola's public history program opened in 1980. The ability of students to appreciate by the end of the semester the tie between disciplinary training and reflection-in-action—the two basic components of reflective practice—varies. Some students get the dynamic among disciplinary knowledge and its ways of thinking, skills, and dispositions and reflection-in-action by the end of the course, while others leave the course tied to reflection-in-action rather than reflective practice, only to internalize it by the end of their master's or doctoral program, demonstrating their understanding in their public history oral examination.

This chapter explores the integration of reflective practice into History 480, with an emphasis on the fall 2019 course. Additional insights are drawn from the significant reworking of two sessions in 2020 as well as from the reflections of students enrolled in the course from fall 2014 through fall 2019. Why reflective practice? Early public history educators believed in the necessity of a distinctive organizing structure that integrated practice, theory, and execution to guide both individual course design and training structure.

Finding a Signature Pedagogy

The formal inauguration of public history as an element of the graduate history landscape found program directors wrestling with the challenge of designing both the curriculum and individual courses. Those of us involved in the formative years of the 1980s grappled with how to balance historical training and understanding with application. We wanted not only to introduce students to the notion of transferable skills, as well as a range of venues where such skills could be applied, but also to train students as historians in order to integrate their education in historical thinking, content, and methodology with projects that took them beyond the more familiar confines of the graduate seminar and history classroom. We also searched for a language that best described as well as shaped this form of history education. For public history education to work, we believed, it needed to be something distinct, not just an add-on to existing forms of training in history or a selection of venue-driven vignettes.

The 1987 issue of *The Public Historian*, which focused on the public history educational landscape during these early years, represented an initial effort to address the question of how to structure curriculum and identify the most important elements of public history education.[3] While a good first foray into the shape of the curriculum as well as specific course design, it more importantly led to a focused search for an approach to public history education. As the volume took shape, it became clear that there needed to be a coherent design to courses and program structure, regardless of the way that public history had developed in specific campus settings. The training needed to be identifiable and formational.

In 2000, the National Council on Public History (NCPH) assigned the Curriculum and Training (C&T) Committee the task of developing a set of program guidelines based on the perception that the diversity of existing programs made public history training far too ambiguous. Using the list of programs in the most recent NCPH *Guide to Graduate Programs in Public History* as its base data field, the C&T Committee, of which I was chair, launched a study that included a formal survey instrument, conversations with program directors, and website analysis of the curricular structure of master's-level public history programs.

What we discovered was ultimately unsatisfying and problematic. While some consistency existed in terms of hours required for the degree, the programs displayed little uniformity about what was seen as appropriate for training in public history. Not even the most basic commonsense assumption—that internships represented an integral part of every public history student's experience—panned out. Finally, when we asked public history program directors what they saw as defining the field of public history and its training, we received lots of comments about training for applied venues and educating students for nonacademic environments, with only a few observations about a relationship between disciplinary training and applied activity. There was nothing to suggest, other than a collection of courses, that anything conceptually defined the education we were providing our students.[4] The survey revealed that training in public history was ad hoc in nature and that a shake-and-bake approach within any history curricular structure was just fine: take a few courses, season the experience with a collection of applied courses of varying design, and out of the mix a graduate will be able to "do" public history.[5]

Reflective Practice: Public History's Signature Pedagogy

The response to these findings led to the embrace of reflective practice as the approach to public history education, drawing on insights from larger conversations about the nature of knowledge and action as well as Donald Schön's discussion of reflective practice. Ernest Boyer and Ernest Lynton challenged existing approaches to knowledge production in the academy and argued for a broadening of what was considered scholarship.[6] Central to the pursuit of public history is the production of knowledge and scholarship in both traditional and nontraditional formats. Important in this context were Boyer's notions of the scholarship of application, of teaching, and of integration in addition to the scholarship of discovery. Of particular interest was Boyer's definition of application, a two-way street in which both knowledge and application pushed the boundaries of the other and expanded both types of scholarship.[7] The training of students in public history engages students in all four of Boyer's categories, and the work products and publications reflect the dynamic relationship between knowledge and application, regardless of the presentation format or location of the activities—that is, as class projects or in other types of audience-driven settings.

Donald Schön examined the nature of professional practice and the approaches taken by professionals engaged in work outside the academy. Like Lynton and Boyer, he was interested in the nature of scholarship and how it could be understood in a variety of settings. Schön argued that successful professional practice integrated *disciplinary training* (my italics) and work settings outside the confines of the academy and engaged in a process that combined "knowing in action" and "reflection-in-action."[8]

Noel Stowe integrated many of these insights in his 2006 article in *The Public Historian,* in which he argued that public historians "apply history based-thinking in a wide range of professional arenas."[9] In settings where the work occurs or the questions are asked outside a traditional academic research enterprise, public historians draw on their disciplinary thinking and skills—that is, they bring disciplinary learning (historical thinking, methods of historical research, theoretical approaches in history, ability to frame questions, understanding of historiography and content, ethical sensibilities) to the topics and locales at hand. Reflective practice, Stowe believed, should be the primary conceptual focus in public history curricula that include history courses, applied courses that interweave historiographical material, research skills, applied skills in project settings, and practice-based reflections (how to approach a project, how to solve problems, how to move beyond the discipline, how to frame questions, and so on).[10] It is not just about audience or venue; it is an approach to the integration of knowledge and action. He contended that public history curricula "must" be consciously designed from the get-go—overall and individual courses—to "prepare students for the approach to professional historical practice."[11]

Reflective practice represents public history's signature pedagogy, which distinguishes it from other curricular design and course structures in the field of history. Signature pedagogies, a term coined by Lee Shulman, represent "types of teaching that organize the fundamental ways in which future practitioners are educated for their new profession." In overall programmatic composition as well as in individual course design, students "are instructed in critical aspects of the fundamental dimensions of professional work—*to think, to perform, and to act with integrity.*"[12] Such pedagogies allow us to make manifest goals and outcomes as well as tell us much about the nature of disciplinary knowledge and the worldview of members of the various fields of knowledge and practice. Signature pedagogies not only identify the approach to teaching and course structure but also define the mission and overall scaffolding for programmatic design. Although Shulman focuses on professions such as law and medicine, the basic principles associated with signature pedagogies are applicable across the discipline and should inform the way we think about history curriculum and course design among the various degree options. We need to know why—and be able to articulate why—we structure our programs and courses as we do (that is, their mission), and understand how the parts make up the whole, how the courses develop the habits of mind and practical skills for the degree, and the outcomes we wish for our students. Signature pedagogies establish the conceptual structure for carrying out an educational endeavor.

Shulman argued that these pedagogies are more pronounced in professional education settings because training in the professions must meet both the demands of the academy and the practice or applied settings in which the graduates of professional education programs operate. In this context, professional education combines both education for understanding (content and theory) and preparation for "responsible practice in the service of others." It is the combination of theory, knowledge, and application that results in understanding and action in a range of different contexts that places the best public history education squarely within his definition of signature pedagogies and that should shape both the way we structure our programs and how we design our courses.[13] It is within the context of our pedagogical structure that we engage in formation, the transformation of novice students into aspiring professionals. During this process, students acquire a combination of knowledge, analytical tools, and practice that shapes their educational experience. It is an intentional process, and the students involved in it are defined by it.

Signature pedagogies possess three dimensions: surface structure, deep structure, and implicit structure. Surface structure involves the "operational acts of teaching and learning, of showing and demonstrating, of questioning and answering." Deep structure refers to the "set of assumptions about how best to impart a certain body of knowledge and know-how." Finally, implicit structure reflects a "moral dimension that comprises a set of beliefs about professional attitudes, values, and dispositions."[14] When these structures are all well developed in a curriculum, students leave a course or program understanding how to "work a situation—to understand its values, construct, context, cultural overtones, and relevant social, economic, and political facts."[15] In public history training, students emerge with the ability to use skills honed in the study of the content of history (historical thinking, knowledge of a time period, research, problem-solving, critical analysis) and preparation in applications (tours, exhibitions, finding aids, collection management, historic district/structures nominations). In doing so, students also gain an agility of mind to approach a range of challenges and appreciate the inherent ambiguity of the process of professional work. This result, of course, is not serendipitous but intentional—highly structured in design and implementation as well as in student formation.

Public history education, when viewed through the lens of reflective practice, mandates that it move beyond an ad hoc or mishmash nature to a pedagogy that offers it definition and programmatic scaffolding, one that possesses all of Shulman's three structures: surface, deep, and implicit. Regardless of whether it is a full-fledged program, a track, a minor field, or a single course, the public history education offered should be identified by specific "operational acts of teaching and learning, of showing and demonstrating, of questioning and answering," based on a "set of assumptions about how best to impart a body of knowledge and know-how" reflecting a "moral dimension that comprises a set of beliefs about professional attitudes, values, and dispositions."[16] It should be more than just history education with a twist but identifiable by its curriculum, just as history education is different from math education, and characterized by defining elements, just as with legal or medical education.[17]

History 480: Public History: Method and Theory—Fall 2019

How to put this into practice, of course, is the issue. At Loyola University Chicago, students first encounter reflective practice in the public history program's core course, History 480, Public History: Method and Theory. Since my arrival at Loyola, I have been uncomfortable with the name of this course, as I see theory coming before method, and the name reinforces some of the predispositions of students who think they have come to a course of study that is primarily about method. The current course description flips the title to help reshape their expectations, although some students will express regret that the course is not primarily about techniques: "This course explores the field of public history with special emphasis on the theoretical and methodological challenges faced when presenting history outside of a formal classroom environment. Also under consideration are the professional and ethical responsibilities of the historian both inside and outside of the university setting. Students will be able to understand the theoretical and methodological issues of importance to the field of public history, reflect upon ethical issues involved in the collection, curation, and presentation of history, and participate in applied projects drawing upon public history methodologies and presentation modes."[18]

Attention to reflective practice appears in the course outcomes associated with History 480. These include understanding the theoretical and methodological issues important in the field of public history; an introduction to a range of activities constituting the field of public history; sharpened investigatory, analytical, and expository skills essential for the study and practice of history; enhanced interpretive and proposal-writing skills; teamwork skills; attention to the variety of ethical challenges facing public historians; and an understanding of reflective practice. Over the course of the semester, students will not only read about and discuss reflective practice but also begin to see it play out in the two applied projects. What I have found, however, is that understanding, incorporating, and appreciating reflective practice is a process—one that many students appreciate near the end of their program, after they see it integrated across our other public history courses. At the conclusion of History 480, they typically get reflection-in-action but do not always see the ways in which their disciplinary understanding integrates into the process.

Students are drawn from four different programmatic tracks. For students in the master's in public history program, the dual program in public history and library and information science, and the doctoral program in American and public history, this is a required course in their major field. Some of these students may bring some applied experience into the program, and some have taken a public history course as an undergraduate. Students in the traditional MA and PhD programs can take public history as a minor field. While some students may bring prior experience, most feel that in today's world it is important to have this added exposure. Depth in the understanding of disciplinary knowledge varies as well, as some students enter with a bachelor's degree in hand and others with a master's degree.

Each of the public history courses in our program includes applied activities. In History 480, the focus is on teamwork development, writing for a general audience, and proposal writing. Writing for a general audience is essential in virtually every aspect of public history, as are teamwork and proposal writing (or grant writing). Over the course of the semester, students grow accustomed to the fact that teamwork is an important aspect of public history work. At the same time, they get experience in writing a proposal and developing a proto-tour project, which they then present to a partner organization's board of directors. Unless students bring outside experience to their graduate study, they have rarely worked in teams and are highly suspicious of them. Nonetheless, it is part and parcel of what they will do in the field. Presenting to a client also forces students not only to think about their audience for the proposed project but also to figure out how to pitch a project to a professional audience. It also sensitizes them to the fact that even good proposals and projects do not get supported.

For the team project, we often partner with the Rogers Park/West Ridge Historical Society, and this was the case in the fall of 2019. Loyola University Chicago is located in East Rogers Park, and students engage with the community during their Loyola experience. The historical society is a small primarily volunteer-run group that has been working to generate a larger presence in the neighborhood. Its mission is "to collect, preserve, and share the story of the diverse community of Chicago's far north side. Established by local residents who believed their part of Chicago was a place with much to celebrate, the Society today serves the community through its publications, neighborhood tours, Living History programs and other educational and outreach efforts."[19] In the society's description of its activities, it specifically references its relationship with Loyola: "In 2014, the Society forged a partnership with graduate students in the Public History program at Loyola University, offering opportunities for students to develop and execute public history programs in the 'real world' along with volunteers from the community."[20]

Over the years, some of our students have served on the society's board. Others have donated their time and energy to specific projects that have enabled the organization to think outside the box. For the class project, the student teams, which I set up in advance, respond to a request for proposals that focuses on a tour that could be offered by the society. Over the years, some of the tours have been implemented, while others have served as the germ of an idea that captured what a tour may have focused on but in a changed format—for example, a tour about food became a cookbook and a tour of religious sites became a community-wide open house of sites of worship throughout the neighborhood. Students often work on these projects after the course has ended.

The project is introduced during the sixth week of the course. By that time, the students are comfortable with one another, have analyzed a tour, and have discussed interpretation. To get students thinking about the nature of tours, students select a tour to review for their first assignment. This gets the students thinking about the characteristics of tours—structure, engagement, big idea, and so on. In this way, the students start the semester thinking about the structural elements of tours, how they work, their challenges, and issues of accessibility. Readings about the nature of tours and tour design as well as on the importance of the big idea are on reserve to provide additional context and background for the tour review and project. The experience primes students for their own tour project.

The students are given a request for proposals document: "The Rogers Park/West Ridge Historical Society (RP/WRHS) invites proposals for tours within the Rogers Park and/or West Ridge neighborhoods in Chicago."[21] The document includes a scope of work, the elements of the proposal, cover letter, proposal narrative with its required elements, the guidelines for the creation of the tour brochure, details about the presentation, and the breakdown of the teams.[22] In fall 2019, a senior public history PhD student assisted with this part of the course. She discussed the project with the class, connected them with the historical society, and, along with me, fielded questions. I introduced this element of the course in 2015 as a way for our doctoral students to experience serving as mentors. Each doctoral student selected has been through the tour proposal process.

Over the course of the semester, I structure in time at the end of selected sessions and reserve the class before the presentation as open time, so that the teams can meet without having to find a time that fits all their schedules, always a challenging aspect of the group project. We spend time during the introduction of the project discussing project management. Some students approach me early in the project to share information on topics and strategize about approaches to their topics or to doing group work. Students often meet with me or their doctoral student mentor over the course of the semester if they find themselves faced with thorny team issues and need to talk through the situation. The goal is for them to figure out how to address the issue. They are guided by a handout that describes different types of group behavior, from a marginal participant to a robust one. Students evaluate their own behavior and that of their group members at the end of the project. This allows me to discuss strengths and weaknesses relating to group work in the project evaluations and factor them into students' grade.

Student assessments of the process are mixed. Generally, they appreciate the opportunity—despite all the angst—of developing a project and engaging with stakeholders. It is a particularly good learning experience when they see the limitations of what they have produced. Reflecting on the presentation of a project to the board of directors, one student wrote that the board's questions "demonstrated how client expectations and restrictions can clash with public historians' original plans. If we had consulted with the board members, or one representative more frequently during the development process, we could have avoided some of these pitfalls." The postproject assessment allowed this student to understand why it was important to keep an organization's resources in mind during project development.[23] Some students, however, complain that certain tours or ideas capture the attention of the board while others do not. Also, some of them bridle at the questions the board asks, such as, "Can you give us a better sense of how a small volunteer society can find the resources to do this?" and "Can you be more specific about the audiences served and their interest level in this type of tour?" I must be very clear in the postmortem session that these are the types of questions that boards generally ask, and asking these questions doesn't mean that they don't appreciate the hard work that went into the proposal and planned tour. It is important that students learn that good projects might not be the right fit for a particular organization and that it is very important to think carefully about the capacity of an organization to put on certain types of programs. By the time students leave the program, they get this, but in the moment of the project wrap-up it is clear that some students question why they should pull out all the stops for a proposal because they may have heard from other students that the board hasn't selected all the projects for implementation.

The other major project is a blog assignment, which is introduced in the third session of the semester.[24] The blog focuses on a particular topic and is to be written for a general audience, ultimately leading to a blog publication. In fall 2019, we worked with Lori Osborne, director of the Frances Willard House Museum and Archives and director of the Evanston Women's History Project. She oversees the website Suffrage 2020 Illinois: The Fight for the Vote in Illinois. The project was designed to share information about the long-fought battle women in Illinois and elsewhere waged to become political citizens and use the voting box as one tool in the continuing struggle for equity and inclusion in American society. Illinois ratified the Nineteenth Amendment in 1919, the first state in the nation to do so. The project's goal, in addition to the student outcomes, was to increase public knowledge about the challenges faced by women in Illinois to win suffrage; to consider contemporary beliefs about justice, social change, and social engagement; and assess the legacy of the drive to secure full citizenship in the political arena. This project was the most successful element of the fall 2019 course. I put materials on reserve to give students the background necessary for context and insight, so they would feel grounded, and Lori Osborne provided a list of resources as well. And though students needed to focus on writing for a general audience as opposed to an academic one, their comfort level was higher with this project because it was individually driven. All the students' posts can be found at https://suffrage2020illinois.org/.

The readings for each weekly topic are a combination of classics and newer material. I use the course readings for the end-of-program oral exam, so I have made the reading list robust. However, I have tended to overdo this. The most persistent complaint in my class evaluations is reading overload—so many selections that it is impossible to talk about them all. As I have reviewed my syllabi, I have concluded the complaints are on target. I want to push the students, but they focus too much on coverage and fail to see the larger issues on the table. I also try to give them a sense of the field over time, and some of them balk at reading older items and mining older case studies, even though these studies highlight issues that will be on the table in many of their discussions. The selection of readings continues to demand a delicate balance between coverage and depth, useful older texts and more recent works on the topic at hand.

I structure the course so that students facilitate the various topics under consideration. Service as facilitators counts as part of their participation grade and ensures that all students participate in a substantive way over the course of the semester. Service in this capacity gives them agency and experience in framing questions and shaping issues. It also helps them gain mastery so that they leave the course with deeper knowledge of one aspect of the material to complement the knowledge gained over the course of the semester. They are able to move beyond saying what the authors had written and more easily talk about the material in their own words.[25] While they are hyperaware that they have gaps in their knowledge, they are well on their way to thinking more intently and creatively about the material. I believe this experience is an important part of a student's growth during the transition from undergraduate to graduate student.

Students, however, have mixed feelings about serving as facilitators. I used to employ the term "discussion leaders," but it became clear that they took it to mean teachers rather than facilitators. A larger number than

I generally expect think that because it is an introductory class, the professor should lecture. Perhaps this is understandable, as most of the students are transitioning from an undergraduate to a graduate course structure, but it also reflects a belief held by some of them that public history is only a technique. They expect the course to be a collection of methods described to them with essentially fill-in-the-blank schema for the projects. This mindset has become more noticeable over the past three or four years and most especially the last two years.

The students don't go into their facilitation session blind. I meet with the facilitators (usually two per session) the week before their session and send them a follow-up email that talks about facilitation and framing questions. If there is something I particularly want them to highlight, I let them know. Every once in a while, students will complain that they shouldn't have to lead a discussion on a topic they don't know very much about, but these students are in the minority, and even they learn that this is part of a graduate education—pushing them beyond the boundaries of prior knowledge. I always frame each session at the opening of the class, summarize at the end, and set the stage for the next session. In the past, I did this conversationally. Now I am much more direct, indicating the framing, summarizing, and stage setting as discrete elements of the class session.

The structure of the topics takes us from discussions about the past and the present; through the relationship among history, public history, and heritage; to interpretation, memory, social justice, controversy, and ethics. The goal is to layer students' exposure to information so that they see the connections between each week and the interconnections among the various issues under discussion. The earliest sessions focus on what folks think about history, shared authority, thinking historically, the history of the history profession, the history of public history, and heritage. Our discussion of interpretation, which follows this introductory section, serves as the platform for the rest of the semester.

The information proceeds in what I call a saw-toothed fashion, or what James Lang would see as interleaving. Lang discusses this in terms of examinations and learning that moves students from information to understanding. By selecting readings that reinforce principles discussed previously with those that move the discussion forward, I am able to see students building their knowledge and connecting information over the course of the semester. Most students, however, don't see it that way, as during the semester they see only the small picture and not the larger one I see. Some of the students feel the discussions and readings get a bit repetitious. It is a familiar refrain in some of the course evaluations. However, the method allows me to see that they are applying knowledge gained to new settings, which reinforces what they know and expands their horizons. Lang would express the process this way: the course creates a setting that "require[s] students to connect new material to older material or to revise their understanding of previous content in light of newly learned material."[26] The information they confront over the course of the semester ultimately lives beyond the confines of the class.

We begin the semester with the topic "Possessed by the Past/Negotiating the Present/Shaping the Future." The centerpiece of this session is Tony Horwitz's book *Confederates in the Attic*, which I ask the students to read over the summer.[27] Despite the age of this volume, it works well to set the stage for the class. For better or worse, current events, regardless of the year, direct attention to many of the themes in the book. We use it for our exploration of the public and the ways people approach the past, and as an excursion into the interplay between past and present. Discussion focuses on whose past was privileged, how the past gets remolded, the interplay of history and heritage, and the levels of comfort with challenging pasts. As we discuss the various encounters with the past explored by Horwitz, I introduce the notion that public historians constantly negotiate between the past and the present and do so in ways that are mindful of the future. I ask students to identify useful insights for public historians. Regardless of the class composition—little or no public history experience to a range of previous public history involvement—this session gets everyone talking and engaged with the material. Students will occasionally integrate information from this session into other discussions as the semester progresses, but it is less about the material covered than about insights into the interplay among past, present, and future.

The public's understanding of the past and engagement with it serves as the focus for the next session. We examine Roy Rosenzweig and David Thelen's *The Presence of the Past* and responses to that study; Michael Frisch and Benjamin Filene and the notion of shared authority; and selections from Nina Simon's *The Art of Relevance* and Ian Tyrell's *Historians in Public*.[28] How does the public connect with the past? How do different groups engage with the past? How do we connect or collaborate with others interested in the past? How have historians in the past attempted to engage with the public? What does it mean to share authority, and what are the limitations? These are generally the issues the students bring to the discussion. While some classes discuss the varieties of insights in the Rosenzweig-Thelen volume, some find the repetition and overexplanation unnecessary and focus on that rather than extracting useful observations from the study. The fall 2019 class did a combination of both approaches. Although they ultimately drew on some of the insights in the study, they felt compelled to bring up the issue of repetition in the study repeatedly during discussion. Other groups have engaged with the material differently. In some classes, the facilitators give the class a survey; use the results to frame the discussion; and tie it to discussion about the book, Simon's discussion of audience, and sharing authority. In the future, I may draw on selections from the Rosenzweig-Thelen volume and add the reports from the survey sponsored by the American Association for State and Local History, the NCPH, and the Organization of American Historians. The first report, *Communicating about History*, has recently been released.[29] The survey sample is small, which provides limitations, but it is more recent and could make for an interesting discussion of change and continuity and what the insights from the two studies combined mean for the work of public historians.

Since public history is always in conversation with history, the next session is titled "History and Its Disciplinary Structure." The goal of this session is to talk about how we understand history and how it has developed as a profession. I want the students not only to see the changing nature of the profession and the various ethical issues involved with the pursuit of history but also to see historians grappling with understanding history and how it works in the world. Over time, I have approached this session in a variety of ways. In fall 2019, I went with an approach I have used for a few years. In addition to Carl Becker's "Everyman His Own Historian," Gerda Lerner's "The Necessity of History and the Professional Historian," C. Vann Woodward's "On Believing What One Reads," and the first two chapters of Tyrell's *Historians in Public*, I had students read two chapters from Joyce Appleby, Lynn Hunt, and Margaret Jacob's *Telling the Truth about History* and two chapters from James M. Banner Jr.'s *Being a Historian*.[30] The fall 2019 class seemed disengaged from the Appleby, Hunt, and Jacobs and Banner material, so I decided to try a different approach in fall 2020, replacing those readings with Peter Charles Hoffer's *Past Imperfect*.[31] What I found in assigning Hoffer's book in 2020 was that students were seeing—for the first time, in many cases—the sweep of the profession and engaging with ethical issues in history. The introduction of Hoffer's book into the mix generated a better discussion than my previous selections and provided students with the context for seeing the changes in the way the profession approaches data and makes arguments, and helped contextualize some of what they were discussing in a different required course, Twentieth

Century Approaches to History. It also alerted them to the ways that much of the public thinks about history, owing to the fact that the consensus school still reaches deep into the public mindset as to what history is.

I generally use this session to talk about thinking historically and history as inquiry in order to move students beyond their own definitions of history. Thinking historically and history as inquiry are two of the important disciplinary dispositions that shape reflective practice, and I have decided to add a selection from Sam Wineburg's *Historical Thinking and Other Unnatural Acts* to help move this part of the discussion forward in the future.[32]

After this session on history, we move to a consideration of public history as a field: "Public History: Creating a Field."[33] What I hope to do in this session is give students a sense of the history of public history and some of its early challenges as well as introduce them to reflective practice. Students tend to approach this discussion in one of two ways. Some groups focus more on the history of public history and the response of the history profession, while others focus primarily on the notion of reflective practice and reflection-in-action. Sometimes students see reflective practice as Stowe describes it and see Schön's reflection-in-action as an element of it. Others appear more comfortable with reflection-in-action—which seems more tangible—and less able or willing to understand how disciplinary knowledge and dispositions work in reflective practice. The reflection-in-action approach dominated the understanding of students in fall 2019.

Reflection-in-action seems to students a method, and this perception becomes how some of them initially understand the notion of reflective practice. "Reflective practice," according to one student, "is a cycle of assessment, planning, action, and reflection. It is important to note what while reflection and assessment need to happen formally at the end of a project, it is essential that those two steps are also part of the process as a whole, and that the public historian, or their team, are constantly assessing the project and redirecting themselves when necessary."[34] "I define reflective practice," wrote another student, "as two forms of one exercise: reflection in action and post action reflection. The former should be done while you are in the midst of the project while the latter is done once the tasks are finished. If appropriately utilized, they can both be effective tools for public historians."[35] In both instances, the students separated historical knowledge and dispositions from the process of working a project.

The students aren't alone in thinking that reflection-in-action is the centerpiece of reflective practice and unmoored from disciplinary thinking. Stowe's notion of reflective practice integrates the discipline and the skills honed in disciplinary practice while engaging reflection-in-action. Cherstin M. Lyon, Elizabeth M. Nix, and Rebecca K. Shrum have an excellent discussion of reflection-in-action in *Introduction to Public History*.[36] Their discussion is practice driven and nicely describes reflection-in-action but does not suggest that the process of reflection-in-action is necessarily a piece of something larger. They do suggest that one might draw on "primary and secondary source research" as necessary during a project, but what they present as reflective practice is not reliant on historical understanding nor on Schön's own definition of reflective practice, which is based on disciplinary knowledge and its deployment in a range of practical settings.[37] Reflection-in-action is just one part of his understanding of the process. In a subsequent chapter, they focus on thinking historically. However, given the way they have the material organized, practice and thinking historically both happen but are separate, and they miss the opportunity to illustrate the integration of historical thinking and tie it dynamically to practice, which is reflective practice as it pertains to public history.

The next class focuses on heritage tourism.[38] I have tried over the last couple of years to integrate environmental issues into the discussion, with mixed results. Depending on the composition of the class and their backgrounds and interests, sustainability drops off the radar. Instead, they focus on definitions of heritage and how heritage plays out in various settings, with no attention to the environmental consequences of heritage tourism. I don't know if they question the relationship among environment, sustainability, and heritage or are simply uninterested in it, but it is like pulling teeth to get them to address it. This was the direction the class took in 2019.

The class enthusiastically discussed the pros and cons of heritage and the public's attachment to it, but as in other years, it was necessary to push them to approach the topic more analytically. To do this, I had to make sure that they attended to the notion of the tourist gaze, which is covered in one of the readings. They followed this injection with discussion about how public historians handle inauthenticity and explored whether it is worth correcting. In the 2020 class, they explored Diane Barthel-Baucher's question about whether heritage is a human right, and this approach generated a great deal of discussion and framed their understanding of heritage.[39] This variability is one of the reasons History 480 is interesting to teach. No two cohorts approach the material the same, and the nuances provide interesting insights into the way individual backgrounds and experiences shape student understanding of the material and the issues involved. Heritage surfaces in discussions held in subsequent weeks, and it is at that point that students begin to move less artificially into the analysis of heritage rather than continuing with the more descriptive type of discussion exhibited in the session on heritage tourism.

The "Interpretive Challenge" followed the discussion of heritage and, as is typical, was lively.[40] I think this is because those who are uncomfortable thinking theoretically see interpretation as tangible, despite the fact that it is theoretically driven. Interpretation is what public historians do, and it seems concrete. Freeman Tilden's *Interpreting Our Heritage* serves as a platform for the discussion, and although a handful of students over the last couple of years feel compelled to point out the age of Tilden's observations, others embrace the wisdom of his principles. Other topics of conversation center around issues of connectivity and difficult histories. Questions raised include these: How can interpretation be used to guide the audience through the process of learning about difficult history? What role does connectivity play in audience engagement? Shawn Halifax's essay asks them to think about plantations as sites of African American interpretation and encourages them to think about the nature of interpretation and who should serve as interpreters in sensitive settings. Other issues explored, though not always tied insightfully to the case studies assigned, included the way that interpretation can change over time at a site and the relationship between entertainment and education.

The next session, "Power and Production in History," asks students to consider silences and how they affect what we know and what we need to work against in our collection, preservation, and interpretation of the past. The centerpiece of the unit is Michel-Rolph Trouillot's *Silencing the Past*.[41] Each group of students approaches this unit differently, but the bottom line remains the same—even though some of the students feel compelled to point out that they don't know anything about Haitian history, which is, of course, besides the point, as they do not need to know it to understand what Trouillot is discussing. They leave this session with a deeper understanding of the constructed nature of the past and how interventions at any point in the process can affect what is known. Some classes extract what they see as the basic principles from Trouillot and focus on how elites manipulate what remains and what is known. Other groups focus on the archival elements of the readings, and this was the case in 2019, since the student facilitator had worked as an archivist prior to entering the public history doctoral program. The students discussed the nature of archival practice, its ethics, and the role that archives play—and, by extension, what happens digitally in terms of heritage representations and consumption. As in all classes regardless of the year, they brought the discussion back to considering the role of the public historian in these settings.

The next session focuses on memory and meaning.[42] Over the years, I have structured it in a variety of ways. Sometimes there is a book-length study, such as Andrew Denson's *Monuments to Absence*, supplemented by articles.[43] Other times I have assigned all the articles in the Horton and Horton volume, *Slavery and Public History*, along with a few articles that explore the notion of memory and the relationship between memory and history. In fall 2019, I assigned numerous articles from David B. Allison's edited volume *Controversial Monuments and Memorials*.[44] What I have found, regardless of the combination, is that some groups of students focus narrowly on case studies rather than look for patterns and use selected examples to illustrate their point. This approach dominated the fall 2019 class, and it was difficult to get them to articulate the larger issues. As a result, I have decided on another approach. In fall 2020, I assigned a small selection of articles that allowed the students to explore memory and public history and then had them look at two studies, Denson's *Monuments to Absence* and Ethan J. Kytle and Blain Roberts's *Denmark Vesey's Garden*.[45] Half the class read one book, and the other half read the other book. I led the discussion of memory and public history and then the two groups took the large issues raised in the general discussion and applied them to their particular case study. This approach worked well, and students did a better job of moving beyond the specific case studies to an integration of theory and how it works in specific instances.

The most unwieldy session is titled "People's History, Media History, and Public History."[46] There are linkages between these topics in terms of the folks involved in the projects I want the students to consider, so the structure is not as random as it might appear. James Green and Jeremy Brecher provide insight into the strand of public history known as people's history. Their early efforts to work with communities and their reflections on what worked and did not work highlight the timeless issues of this kind of work. Over the years, historians have engaged with different media. James Green and Nina Gilden Seavey, for example, deconstruct the film/television process, and Betsey Beasley and David P. Stein explore other ways to engage with public audiences. Tyrell discusses initiatives in the past, and students have the opportunity to assess the varied ways that historians have attempted to engage with publics over time. Linda Shopes, Mireya Loza, and Rose T. Diaz and Andrew B. Russell explore oral history and memory and its relationship to communities. Student facilitators often have the class view clips of recordings or films and use them to tease out issues of importance as well as strengths and weaknesses of the visual and aural world. Because this session is not as tightly interwoven, student facilitators can find it difficult; this is where the complaint "Since I bring no prior knowledge to this segment, how can I facilitate discussion of the readings?" often surfaces. Other students, however, appreciate the opportunity to dive into the media or think about community engagement and ask their classmates to try to define best practices.

"Historic Sites: History, Politics, and Understanding" is one of the liveliest sessions and can have unexpected consequences.[47] Social justice is part of the Jesuit mission, and many of our graduate students are attracted by that part of the university's mission. Thus, they are predisposed to find any discussion about conscience, public engagement, and meaning of interest. Conversation is animated and students tackle a range of issues, from the necessity to tell difficult stories to the limits of presentation to whether any museum or site should confront issues of conscience. The fall 2019 class was no different in this respect.

One of the most interesting of the sessions on this topic happened about four years ago. We had a very politically conservative student who questioned many aspects of the readings over the course of the semester, suggesting that they were too liberal or did not reflect the interests of the public. By chance, he was the facilitator for this session. Over the course of the discussion, he shared that, given his views, he could now better understand why certain groups felt that these issues needed to be confronted in public settings. It was one of those moments in class when you can actually see how engagement with the subject matter pushes the boundaries of understanding. While I am under no illusion that an entire worldview shifted, I do feel that the student left us more open to some issues than when he started the program.

Our final topic for consideration is titled "Historians, Ethics, Contestation, and Controversy."[48] This session offers students the opportunity to examine two ethical codes and short essays on ethics and practice, followed by an exploration of ethical issues, with a particular focus on the case studies written by David Crosson, Larry Tise, and Robert Weyenth. They often debate the relationship between codes and the sometimes murky world of practice. The other part of the class explores controversy, with Weyenth, Ernest Boyer, and Jack Davis holding center stage. The students typically deconstruct the articles and, now that their knowledge of many of the issues on the table has deepened over the course of the semester, think about other approaches that might work, the responsibility of historians, and the challenge of community expectations. The fall 2019 class, like many of the classes, spent a lot of time discussing the *Enola Gay* issue, but it did also explore issues related to collecting (Crosson) and the historian as provocateur (Weyenth). It was harder to get them to discuss ethical issues in the abstract.

The last assignment for the course is a three-page reflective essay that asks students to select one of the two major assignments—the team project or the blog—as their focus and to draw on their understanding of reflective practice and the way that it shapes the nature of public history practice. The essay has four parts: introduction (thesis and scope), discussion of reflective practice (definition and description of operation) and its relationship to public history practice, discussion of the relationship between either the tour proposal experience or the blog to the process of reflective practice (using examples to illustrate points), and conclusion. This assignment not only gives them the opportunity to think about reflective practice in light of their experience but also offers me insight into the nature of the learning that has taken place. As indicated earlier, many of these essays focus on reflection-in-action. For example, one student argued, "Essential to the successful practice of public history, reflection-in-action sets public historians apart from academic historians."[49]

Other essays, however, suggest that the students have begun to internalize the engagement of the discipline and reflection-in-action in their understanding of public history. According to one student, "In addition to acquiring a base knowledge of the historiography of the discipline and the necessary research skills, public historians must also develop the ability to construct a framework for historical analysis appropriate to each situation that will bring an ethically grounded result suited for the audience at hand and within the constraints of the organization, agency, or institution of employment."[50] Another student suggested that case studies and firsthand experience allowed the class to "to appreciate the crucial role reflective practice plays in real-world combinations of historical theory and method."[51] Professional practitioners, suggested another student, approached a project "by framing it as a discrete problem using . . . understandings that make up their discipline. . . . By continuously reflecting on their processes, practitioners can repeatedly reframe their problem, refine their approach, and create a successful result."[52]

Students leave this course with theoretical constructs and practical experience that prepare them for other applied courses in the program, as well as an introduction to the theories and methods that will help them flourish once they leave the program. Not all students see this by the time the class is over; rather, they focus on the small picture—too much reading, complaints about the shortcomings of some of their classmates as facilitators, no lectures. Still, when they sit for their oral exam at the end of the program, they demonstrate that they internalized more than they realized during History 480. I think this is always part of the challenge of an introductory course. I can see their progress during the semester as they talk more confidently about what they are reading and make connections they would not have been able to make at the beginning of the semester. They, however, need distance to see what they learned. What they all agree on when they leave the program is that reflective practice, rather than reflection-in-action, defined their educational experience.

Notes

1. Johnson, "Editor's Preface," 5.
2. Stowe, "Public History Curriculum," 39.
3. See Johnson and Stowe, "Field of Public History." Looking back at this volume with fresh eyes clearly revealed shortcomings as well as pointed to new directions. It also showcased the challenges many of us faced in figuring out how to teach public history courses. I would never teach an introductory course as I have constructed it in this volume in today's world, but it does stand as a point along the evolution of my own thinking as well as where we were in 1987. Like many other new program directors faced with designing the introductory course during this period, the structure was more smorgasbord than conceptual, ensuring that a variety of areas were covered rather than integrating select elements into a curricular whole. It was venue driven—museums, archives, consulting, business. There was a lot of material but nothing to define the approach to that material as something special or useful.
4. Mooney-Melvin, "Characteristics of Public History Programs."
5. An exploration of 2015 descriptions of public history programs included on the National Council of Public History website clearly makes this point. As of 2015, only limited change had occurred. https://ncph.org/program-guide/
6. See Lynton, *Making the Case*.
7. Boyer, *Scholarship Reconsidered*, 80–87.
8. Schön, *Educating the Professional Practitioner*, 22–23, 26–27. See also Schön, *Reflective Practitioner*, chap. 9.
9. Stowe, "Public History Curriculum," 45.
10. Stowe, "Public History Curriculum," 47.
11. Stowe, "Public History Curriculum," 40.
12. Shulman, "Signature Pedagogies in the Professions," 52. Italics in original.
13. Shulman, "Signature Pedagogies," 52–53.

14. Shulman, "Signature Pedagogies," 54–55.

15. Johnson and Stowe, "Field of Public History," 18.

16. Shulman, "Signature Pedagogies," 54–54.

17. Some of these ideas were presented in a slightly different format in "Reflective Practice: Public History's Signature Pedagogy," at the National Council on Public History annual conference, April 2013, and at the European University Institute, February 2015.

18. Course description, History 480 syllabus.

19. "Mission and History," Rogers Park/West Ridge Historical Society, https://rpwrhs.org/history/.

20. "Mission and History."

21. "Request for Proposals: Rogers Park/West Ridge Historical Society," Fall 2019.

22. Depending on the number of students in the class, there are three or four teams. In creating the teams, I consider public history experience; other experience that could prove useful to the project; and distribution of gender, race, and ethnicity. The goal is to create relatively level playing fields. An issue that arose for the first time in fall 2019 concerned the use of the word "teams." Some students believed that the use of the word introduced competition into the process. They complained that its use was destructive, and they resented being placed in competition with one another. While I see the use of the word "teams" as just part of the work landscape, I chose to use the word "groups" this year but explained why I did so to the fall 2020 students. This group of students didn't think it was an issue at all.

23. Ruth, reflective practice essay, 2015.

24. I used to have two group projects. I finally decided that two was one too many and adopted the blog for the second major assignment.

25. See Lang, *Small Teaching*, chap. 6, for a discussion of the power of self-explaining.

26. Lang, *Small Teaching*, 83. See also chap. 3.

27. Horwitz, *Confederates in the Attic*.

28. Simon, *The Art of Relevance*; Filene, "Letting Go?" 7–12; Frisch, *A Shared Authority*, introduction; Tyrell, *Historians in Public*, chaps. 3–4; Rosenzweig and Thelen, *Presence of the Past*.

29. Miller, L'Hôte, and Volmert, *Communicating about History*.

30. Appleby, Hunt, and Jacob, *Telling the Truth about History*, chaps. 2 and 6; Banner, *Being a Historian*, chaps. 1 and 2.

31. Hoffer, *Past Imperfect*; Becker, "Everyman His Own Historian"; Woodward, "On Believing What One Reads"; Winks, *Historian as Detective*; Lerner, "Necessity of History"; Tyrell, *Historians in Public*, prologue, chaps. 1–2.

32. Wineburg, *Historical Thinking and Other Unnatural Acts*, pt. 1.

33. Conard, "Pragmatic Roots of Public History Education"; Corbett and Miller, "Shared Inquiry into Shared Inquiry"; Stowe, "Public History Curriculum"; O'Donnell, "Pitfalls along the Path of Public History"; Schön, *Reflective Practitioner*, chap. 9; Gardner and LaPaglia, *Public History*, pt. 1; Scarpino and Vivian, *Career Paths in Public History*.

34. Beatrice, reflective practice essay, 2016.
35. Mabel, reflective practice essay, 2019.
36. Lyon, Nix, and Shrum, *Introduction to Public History*, 12–15.
37. Lyon, Nix, and Shrum, *Introduction to Public History*, 13.
38. Barthel-Baucher, *Cultural Heritage and the Challenge of Sustainability*, chaps. 2 and 7; Mooney-Melvin, "Harnessing the Romance of the Past," 35–48; Figal, "Between War and the Tropics; Kammen, *In the Past Lane*, chap. 9; Kelleher, "Images of the Past"; Lowenthal, *Possessed by the Past*, chap. 6; Glassberg, "The Changing Cape."
39. Barthel-Baucher, *Cultural Heritage and the Challenge of Sustainability*, 27.
40. Tilden, *Interpreting Our Heritage*, introduction and chap.1; Spock, "Practical Guide to Personal Connectivity," 11–12; Tramposch, "Mickey and the Muses"; Rose, "Interpreting Difficult Knowledge"; Melish, "Recovering (from) Slavery"; Halifax, "McLeod Plantation Historic Site"; Christopher, "House of the Seven Gables."
41. Trouillot, *Silencing the Past*; Wallace, "Visiting the Past"; Jimerson, "Ethical Concerns for Archivists"; Carter, "Of Things Said and Unsaid"; Cameron, "Politics of Heritage Authorship"; Allison, "From Columbus to Serra and Beyond."
42. Bodner, *Remaking America*, prologue and chap. 1; Vlach, "Last Great Taboo Subject"; Horton, "Slavery in American History"; Black, "The 150-Year War"; Tell, "Remembering Emmett Till in Money, Mississippi"; Hayashi, "Transfigured Patterns"; Glassberg, "Public History and the Study of Memory."
43. Denson, *Monuments to Absence*.
44. Allison, *Controversial Monuments and Memorials*.
45. Kytle and Roberts, *Denmark Vesey's Garden*.
46. Green, *Taking History to Heart*, prologue, chaps. 2, 4, and 7; Tyrell, *Historians in Practice*, chap.s 5 and 6; Loza, "From Ephemeral to Enduring"; Brecher, "Report on Doing History from Below"; Diaz and Russell, "Oral Historians"; Beasley and Stein, "Podcasting History"; Shopes, "Oral History and Community Involvement"; Seavy, "Film and Media Producers; Tyrell, *Historians in Practice*, chaps. 5 and 6.
47. Ševčenko and Russell-Ciardi, "Sites of Conscience"; Ševčenko, "Sites of Conscience"; Kaufman "Historic Places"; Rose, "Three Building Blocks"; Lee, "Stories We Collect"; Goulding, "Tule Lake"; Landrieu, "Speech on the Removal of Confederate Statues in New Orleans."
48. Weyenth, "History He Wrote"; Tise, "Jacques Cousteau"; Boyer, "Whose History Is It Anyway?"; Davis, "Struggle for Public History"; Crosson, "Museums and Social Responsibility"; Conard, "Roundtable"; American Historical Association, "Statement on Standards of Professional Conduct," 2019, www.historians.org/jobs-and-professional-development/statements-standards-and-guidelines-of-the-discipline/statement-on-standards-of-professional-conduct; "NCPH Code of Ethics and Professional Conduct," 2007, https://ncph.org/about/governance-committees/code-of-ethics-and-professional-conduct/.
49. Nancy, reflective practice essay, 2014.
50. Chloe, reflective practice essay, 2013.
51. Lily, reflective practice essay, 2017.
52. Peter, reflective practice essay, 2012.

2 The Great Syllabus Swap

LINDSEY PASSENGER WIECK
REBECCA S. WINGO

We (Wieck and Wingo) have been friends for about a decade now. We first met through mutual friends at a Western History Association conference, or at least we think so. However it happened, our friendship stuck, and we stayed friends during the nonconference season. We supported each other as we dissertated and later as we both entered the job market, even while we competed for the same jobs. We cheered each other on, sharing job materials, tips, and strategies, all of which subverted the cutthroat nature of the academic job market.

We were two of the lucky ones. Wieck joined the faculty at St. Mary's University in San Antonio, Texas, in 2017. She currently directs the undergraduate public history track and the master's program in public history. As of 2018, Wingo also directs the public history graduate and undergraduate programs at the University of Cincinnati. We share a job title, but when we first started, we also shared a common concern: neither of us were formally trained in public history. How could we hit the ground running in our new jobs and maintain the stamina needed to improve and revamp our courses as quickly as possible?

Building on an ethic of care and support from our time together on the job market, we established the Great Syllabus Swap. The premise is simple: we swap the syllabus for our Introduction to Public History course with the understanding that the other will improve the readings and assignments before returning it. With this swap, we essentially double the speed with which we can improve our syllabi and, by proxy, our students' experience. We're basically the backwoods backpackers of academia: packing out the other person's rubbish to leave the syllabus better than we found it.

Our classes aren't identical because our universities aren't identical. Wieck's courses tend to be smaller than Wingo's (though neither exceed forty). Wieck's students tend to be history majors, while Wingo gets the dabblers (and works her tail off to recruit them to the dark side). Wieck's students are predominantly Latinx, while Wingo's are predominantly white. Both have to navigate their students' hectic work schedules, but Wieck has found she needs to make sure that some residential students can complete their work entirely on campus, while Wingo has had to make her assignments suitable for off-campus students too.

Despite all the differences in our classroom composition, we share many teaching practices. We have a similar teaching philosophy, emphasizing hands-on, collaborative practice and skills-based training. We believe current events can help students understand that history shapes our present and is always relevant. As two white middle-class women, we work hard to create a rich learning environment by actively decentering white and male voices and generating a classroom in which all students feel seen and heard. We both challenge our students to investigate who writes history and to ensure that they help produce historical narratives that are more inclusive of diverse voices.

Because the conventional is boring, we've framed this chapter as a dialogue about the Great Syllabus Swap. We discuss how the swap emerged, the benefits for us as professors as well as our students, our favorite assignments, and our advice for selecting your own swap-mate. While we focus on our undergraduate intro course, we have extended the practice to our graduate public history and digital history courses as well.

Like most great sagas and odysseys, the Great Syllabus Swap is not merely about a syllabus exchange. Along the way, our heroines confront several common experiences within academia: impostor syndrome, anxieties about teaching a course for the first time, the value of peer review, and the ongoing standoff between formal and experiential training. In some ways, the Great Syllabus Swap is a larger-than-life story about a very small support group, but it's also a model for scholarly collaboration, classroom partnerships, and community engagement. We hope that the following discussion helps others think about establishing their own practice of syllabus exchange for public history and beyond.

Authors' Note: *The following transcript is a conversation about our syllabus swap and Introduction to Public History course methodology. For the purposes of this chapter, we have liberally edited the transcript for ease of reading, to eliminate our annoying verbal tics, to create full sentences, and to make ourselves generally sound smarter. You're welcome. We've also made several additions to the transcript to improve clarity and context, and to add general (occasionally snarky) commentary. These are typically denoted by brackets.*

You can decide which are clarifying and which are snarky. We hope you enjoy all the goofy awkwardness that follows.

The Syllabus Swap

Like every good tale, there is an origin story. This telling of the Great Syllabus Swap includes some plot twists, including infidelity, impostor syndrome, and the Alamo. Never fear, unlike the Battle of the Alamo, this story does have a fairy-tale ending.

> *Rebecca S. Wingo*: I thought we could start by outlining how this syllabus exchange got started. It actually predates our own collaboration—like, you [Lindsey] were cheating on me before there was a me. Do you know what I mean? [*Laughter*] Do you want to explain how the syllabus exchange started for you?
>
> *Lindsey Passenger Wieck*: Sure. I was hired as an assistant professor at St. Mary's University in a department that had a growing undergraduate public history program. In my first semester on campus, I taught an Introduction to Public History class for undergraduates, and I supervised an undergraduate public history internship. Also, that year, I moved across the country with two kids, including a newborn. I also was starting a public history master's program at my university. I had a lot going on.
>
> *Wingo*: So . . . no pressure.
>
> *Wieck*: No pressure at all. [Just kidding, there was so much pressure.] I was familiar with different public history methods because I had dabbled in digital history and oral history, but I had never really been formally trained as a public historian. I was also countering a lot of impostor syndrome and felt overwhelmed to do this from scratch. I was really lucky to have a colleague, Leisl Carr Childers [now at Colorado State University], who taught public history for several years and shared her syllabus with me. I used her materials as a starting point. I was lucky to have someone I trusted who was so generous in sharing her materials. But my impostor syndrome was magnified even more by teaching in the home city of the Alamo. And I knew nothing about the Alamo.

Wingo: Is that because you didn't remember the Alamo?[1]

Wieck: Oh, I remembered the Alamo. Just nothing about why it was important. [*Laughter*] I've learned a lot about the Alamo over the past several years, and now I can talk your ear off about it. But I worked to build in some of Leisl's readings, structures, and reflections on local history as best I could. I got by, but I hated that first syllabus. My students were really happy with the class, but I just didn't love how it all fell together. [I struggled to find readings that really popped for my students and to create projects that were meaningful for them. The assignments I had weren't scaffolded toward our bigger projects. As I identified who my students were, I was able to identify these issues and to start building curriculum around them.]

And this is where Rebecca Wingo comes into the story. Rebecca, how did you become involved?

Wingo: I started my job the year after you did, so I got to benefit from all the challenges that you overcame. In a very similar way, I had dabbled in various aspects of public history, but hadn't been formally trained. I spent hours googling other people's syllabi, finding assignments online, looking at books, reading the books. It almost felt like I was taking comprehensive exams right before I took the job, and I was overwhelmed. And so I asked you for help.

It was an absolute testament to our friendship that I was able to be vulnerable with you and put my impostor syndrome on full display. Looking at your syllabus really grounded me. You and I have a lot of shared pedagogical goals, so reading your syllabus quieted a lot of the other noise that I was hearing on the internet.

Wieck: I got the syllabus back from Rebecca after the first semester she taught it—our third combined time around—and it was much improved. It fixed a lot of the problems and added some new and excellent assignments. It solved so many of the issues that I struggled with the first time.

The first time around, I found a lot of readings that I thought would work great because the internet said they would work great, but they just didn't resonate with my students. I was in love with how Rebecca made the syllabus magical with her edits, in a way that I don't think I would have come up with after just one syllabus or one semester of revision. [In particular, she integrated engaging readings that led students directly to some aha moments and developed new assignments that scaffolded student skills throughout the semester.] It was really exciting to see it transform. Then I was able to fix some things that didn't work as well as Rebecca planned either.

Wingo: What I really appreciate about this process is that it opened the opportunity for us to do this with other syllabi as well. We've exchanged some digital history syllabi, some graduate level syllabi, lots of project ideas and how to scale them to different classrooms. Even our internship programs now have a lot of components that mirror each other. There's a lot of strength in this practice.

Wieck: By making ourselves vulnerable and giving each other feedback, we've also strengthened all aspects of our teaching and research and professional lives.

In this section we talked a lot about how we were "informally" trained in public history, which ultimately fed our impostor syndrome beasts. And yet we both had the grounding, knowledge, projects, and skills to be hired as directors of public history programs. So what constitutes academic credentials in this field?

Public history is a big umbrella that incorporates many subfields, which practitioners spend lifetimes mastering. Academic public historians are often asked to be jacks-of-all-trades, knowing just enough about each subfield to pique our students' curiosity and open career paths. While neither of us received formal training in public history, we gravitate toward this type of public-facing, community-based work. We gained valuable experiences by experimenting with public and digital history work—hosting History Harvests, digitizing archives, doing oral histories, making maps and visualizations—and, later, by exploring and articulating best practices as we teach others.

Opportunities for informal learning also exist through a variety of professional organizations, like the American Association for State and Local History and the National Council on Public History. While academic knowledge typically centers book knowledge, it's important to recognize that public his-

tory expertise is grounded in community knowledge, experience, repetition and revision, and many other spaces. Public history is not only a product but also a process, one that requires listening, learning, humility, and grace. Ironically, it was only in letting go of the typical academic's chokehold on expertise that we have counteracted much of our impostor syndrome.

We learned these things together. The Great Syllabus Swap was built on an established friendship and trust. In the process, we've streamlined course production and deepened our respect for each other. See? Happily ever after.

The Professor Perks

There are some real, tangible perks to the Great Syllabus Swap. When Wingo first taught the course, her initial thought was, "Wow, Lindsey just saved me so much time." While that's certainly true, the practice of the syllabus exchange also creates a culture of peer-reviewed syllabi, diversifies the course readings, and demonstrates new ways of tackling big topics—all while giving you that crucial extra time to binge-watch the latest shows . . . er, we mean to grade stuff.

> *Wingo*: Let's talk about how this actually benefits us as professors. You mentioned the peer review of our syllabi—that doesn't happen very often. It's not part of a standard academic practice. I think it needs to happen more often because it exponentially improves the quality of the syllabi for us and for our students.
>
> *Wieck*: Another benefit is that it helps keep our readings current. Since we started doing this, very few of the original readings on the syllabus are still there. Instead, we've built up a body of really exciting diversified readings, and we've chosen things that the other wouldn't necessarily have considered. [In fact, we struggled to create a shortened syllabus to include with this piece *because* of how often we update our readings. Even more dramatically, Wieck's syllabus has radically transformed during COVID times to focus on rapid response collecting.] Do you have an example of how you've added something that you might not have found otherwise?
>
> *Wingo*: Totally. I love a reading that you included from the *Texas Observer*. It's by Daniel Blue Tyx and it's called "Signs and Blunders: The Fight to Commemorate a Massacre by the Texas Rangers."[2]

I'm in Cincinnati, so the chances of me ever coming across an article from the *Texas Observer* are very slim. The article is about how in 1918, Texas Rangers roused all the Mexican and Mexican American boys and men in a small town in western Texas called Porvenir, marched them to a cliff, and killed them all. A few days later, the Rangers returned and burned the village to the ground.

The story itself is gripping, but the article mostly talks about the commemoration of this event one hundred years later. It got my students to consider who owns history in a context outside their own. They were able to be critical of the commemoration in Texas in a way that they couldn't be critical about local events. The article dissects issues of politics and race and memory and commemoration. It not only diversified my syllabus but also showed my students that racial questions are more than just Black and white, as they tend to be in my city.

I paired the article with an NPR report about the sign that marks the lynching of Emmett Till.[3] Locals keep destroying the historic marker, riddling it with bullets. A few years ago, some white college students even posed next to it with guns. The article reinforces that commemoration is about more than history, and it set my students up to talk about Confederate monuments.

The other thing I like about both pieces is that they have audio, and they can reach different kinds of learners.

Wieck: Yeah, at St. Mary's about 70 percent of our students identify as Latinx. I've worked really hard to try to find examples, readings, and case studies that refer to South Texas and borderlands history. The Tyx article is one of them. Rebecca's readings also opened avenues that I overlooked in my local focus. Two of those are Ashley Farmer's "Archiving While Black" and a piece by Mark Auslander about Ashley's Sack, both of which are wonderful.[4] [The first considers the experiences of Black visitors to archives and asks questions about inclusion in public history spaces. The second traces the history of Ashley's Sack, an item on loan to the Smithsonian National Museum of African American History and Culture, to consider the agency of enslaved peoples and Black Americans throughout U.S. history, and how that history is told. Both of these readings help my students consider issues of inclusion and accessibility in the field.]

One of my favorite class days of Rebecca's that I adopted was a series of readings that asked students to consider Confederate monuments. I'd previously shied away from this topic. It's something I felt uncomfortable teaching because I didn't know enough about it. Rebecca's class outline gave me a good way to engage with this. Students read five items, including [former New Orleans mayor] Mitch Landrieu's address on removing Confederate statues in his city, an American Historical Association statement on Confederate monuments, and Karen Finney's reflection on bringing down Robert E. Lee statues.[5]

For this day, students also found articles that talked about the controversy of Confederate memorials. Since each student brought an article to class, it put us all on a more even ground. We each had our own entrance point for talking about this sticky topic, and it gave everyone their own area of expertise to share. This is a great example of how passing the syllabus back and forth opened the opportunity to talk about something that I had otherwise been avoiding.

Wingo: One of the other perks for us, I think, is that we can continue to refine our assignments. Can you think of an assignment that improved as we passed it back and forth?

Wieck: Hold on, I'm going to cough. [*Coughs*]

Wingo: [*Fake coughs loudly*] Solidarity.

Wieck: [*Laughs*] It's infectious. So in my first semester teaching this undergraduate Intro to Public History class, I wanted students to learn how to use WordPress—both as a platform and as a place to reflect on class topics. I had them write nine or ten blog posts, at least a couple hundred words each. It was so much for them to do and so much for me to keep up with. It didn't achieve what I wanted it to achieve. I still think it's really important to use WordPress, since it's one of the most commonly used content management systems (CMSs) online, but I needed to find a way to focus this assignment and have it be less labor for the students. I shared those thoughts with Rebecca when I passed the syllabus to her the first time, and I left that as a problem for her to solve . . . miraculously.

Wingo: And then I did! It was fantastic!

Wieck: Woo-hoo!

Wingo: I do remember thinking, That's a lot of blogs—both for me to grade and for my students to write. So I came up with an idea. I wanted to instill the idea that more words aren't necessarily better and that less words are more, especially for public history. I created something called Public History in the Wild. We're going to talk about that particular assignment in more detail later on, but basically the students still learned how to use WordPress while also learning how to write bite-sized chunks of text that mirror short exhibit labels more than blogs.

  I let them include some personal reflection as well. The first time they ever write these short posts (they have a one-hundred-word limit), they hate it. They hate it so much. They're like, "Why can't we just have a few more words?" But that's not the point. By the end, they get very good at it. Ultimately, I was able to manipulate Lindsey's blogging assignment into something less onerous that also enforced some of the tenets of public history communication.

Wieck: My next time around teaching the class, I found this assignment to be such an amazing improvement. It's much easier to read hundred-word blog posts. I had students write four of them over the semester, and I gave them a chance to write a fifth one for extra credit. It's shorter, and it also helps ground students' experience in different kinds of public history concepts, like label writing and reading the landscape. Rebecca even had instructions for accessibility, like adding in alternative text for images and things like that. Students still got that CMS experience but in a much more contained way—and in a much more effective way. It also fit well into my class because we started to move toward a focus on place-based storytelling. This activity gave students practice in reading the landscape.

  This is yet another example of how passing the syllabus back and forth helps us refine and improve our assignments and other pedagogical components at a faster rate than we could do on our own.

Wingo: I completely agree. We basically double the speed at which we get a better syllabus. There are still ways that we can improve. Lindsey and I talk about this pretty openly, like "OK, this time, let's try to find more international readings about public history" or "This time, let's take out at least three white men and replace them with women and scholars of color." We are intentional about the ways in which we improve the syllabus.

Wieck: This provides us with ways that we can improve the syllabus on each of its fundamental levels. We can look at the readings on a single day. We can look at how topics are organized. (We've done that a lot.) We can make these changes not just at the individual class level but also at the course level, and with the big picture in mind.

The moral of the story is that two sets of eyes are better than one. Each exchange of the syllabus yields a range of improvements, from individual readings and assignments to more holistic course adjustments. It is also a more efficient use of our time. As professors and directors of our programs, the demands on our time come from our community partners, departments, institutions, and students. Creating efficiency is an enormous benefit.

The Pupil Perks

The Great Syllabus Swap began as an entirely self-serving endeavor that helped us both tread water in our new jobs. As the practice unfolded and we got more comfortable in our roles, we began focusing on centering the student experience. After all, students are our biggest critics. They help us keep the readings current, relevant, and fun. Our assignments become more refined and our expectations clearer as we try out new projects and methods with our classes.

Wingo: We would be totally remiss if we did not point out the ways in which the syllabus exchange is beneficial for our students. The big way for me is that it weeds out all of the unpopular readings. The first time I got the course from Lindsey, she left notes that said things like "Students did not like this article. Replace next time." I took those notes and found replacement readings. When I passed it back to her, that was already complete.

One of the things that I love doing in my class is turning the readings and their popularity into a game. I have my students play something I like to call Boo-Meh-Yay. Three-quarters of the way through the class, I just read the titles of the articles and chapters aloud. Then the students verbally vote "boo," "meh," or "yay." If the students say "Oh, I don't really remember that one, so I don't think that I have an opinion," then I know that the reading didn't stick and needs to be replaced. They really get into it and start screaming out "Boo!" or "Yay!"

Wieck: [*Laughter*]

Wingo: It's a way to make the students feel involved in making the course better for the students that follow. And then what ends up happening too is my students recommend this class to their friends because they feel heavily invested in how it turned out.

Wieck: Yeah, and both of us now have moved to creating the syllabus in an HTML web format. I know I make some of those annotations directly into the HTML. In the most recent time I passed it back to Rebecca, she was able to see things hidden in the HTML comments about "students hated this reading" or "I hated this reading" or things like that. To that end, we've refined the process of passing on our students' perspectives about the things that we teach in this class.

One of the other ways that this syllabus exchange has been great for our students is that as Rebecca and I refine the assignments, we're able to cater them more to our students' needs. Whereas Rebecca tries to make sure that all of the assignments can be completed off campus, I want to make sure that assignments can be completed on campus *or* off campus. We can take these ideas that we share and make sure that they are relevant and accessible to our different student bodies.

Wingo: We keep updating the readings too. You know, maybe there are only three to five articles that the students really don't like, but having a living and breathing syllabus, and keeping it current, makes history more relevant to the students in general. That whole process also improves departmental recruitment and retention.

Wieck: So, in conclusion, this process is really great for us and our students.

At the end of the day, the students may even benefit more from our exchange than we do, since the syllabus reflects their choices and preferences.

Our Admirable Assignments

One of the best parts of the Great Syllabus Swap is seeing the creative assignments the other comes up with—and then being able to borrow liberally from their assignment design and rubrics. For example, Wieck even includes assignment infographics in her classes. The visual layout helps different learners understand the assignments and visualize where they need to be in the coursework during any given week. Wingo loved this idea so much that she did the same.

Watching each other work and teach is really inspirational. It's also really goofy. Please read on for more information about public history and toilet stalls.

Wingo: Do you have a favorite assignment?

Wieck: I do. My first semester teaching this class, the research project I came up with for students worked, but it wasn't great. My second time around, I drew a lot from Rebecca's expertise doing History Harvests and collecting oral histories from the community.
[A History Harvest is a community-based digital archive designed to prioritize object-based stories from communities otherwise underrepresented in traditional archives.][6] Again, I wanted to make sure that the coursework was accessible on campus to my students. So we had a History Harvest on campus, where we invited campus community members, brothers, priests, faculty members, and some other students to come to our local Marianist archives.[7]

Our students each had their own table and a set of questions. They each researched a particular campus landmark. One student was researching the bell tower, another student was researching the sculpture garden, and so on. The students crafted questions and the visitors rotated from table to table, shared what they knew, and told stories about different places. We started to collect these amazing stories about the campus spaces around us.

Let me give you an example. On campus, we have a retirement community for the older Marianists in the United States, and so we have a cemetery here for Marianists who have passed away. This one brother who came to the History Harvest was involved with the maintenance of the cemetery. He's the one who digs each grave. He told us a story, I think it was from 1985, which was two big snowstorms ago. It snowed so much that night that he could not dig the grave he needed to dig. He also told us about where they sourced gravestones and provided the student researching the cemetery with a lot of information to work with.

This proved to be an incredible opportunity to start a larger project, to collect oral histories about campus spaces, and to do this place-based storytelling that's starting to take root on our campus. I'm really grateful to Rebecca for all of her guidance and mentorship through this process.

Do you have a favorite assignment?

Wingo: I do, and it's the Public History in the Wild project that was born out of your original blogging assignment. Let me describe it in more detail. Basically, the premise is that students have to look at their environments through a historical lens. They have to wander around and notice that there's history everywhere—in the building on the corner, in the historic restaurant down the street, in the statues that we have on campus, in the names of the buildings that we have on campus.

Students have to look around and then investigate. For instance, why *is* this building called McMicken Hall? Well, it's named after Charles McMicken, one of the university's original donors, who was also a slaveholder. Then, they have to turn on their critical lens. Like, why *are* we commemorating a former slaveholder? For the course blog, students not only practice writing for a public audience but also practice writing concisely in preparation for writing exhibit and label text later in the semester. They learn to read their environments like a public historian. It also familiarizes them with their local history.

And they learn a WordPress platform. For virtually any job they do in the future, they're going to need to understand how to run the back end of a website, promote things on social media, or understand the basics of information architecture (tagging, subjects, and categories). They learn that they can use platforms like WordPress for different functions—building a blog or website or populating an archive. I think it's a really powerful assignment.

Since Lindsey and I are both digital historians, it lets us infuse some digital history components, or introduce them at least, via projects like History Harvest and Public History in the Wild.

Wieck: What worked well for me about the Public History in the Wild assignment was that it scaffolded really nicely into my final project. Students were doing the assignment, where they were investigating the landscape around them. I facilitated a day for a field trip on campus where I invited a geologist and a poet to give us a walking tour of St. Mary's. It was fascinating because the poet would read us a poem about a sculpture and then the geologist would get down on the ground on his hands and knees and point to the types of rock that were used to construct the thing. They talked about a sculpture, they talked about a chapel, they talked about a fountain, and they talked about a big bell that was hanging. It was a cool way of reading and learning the landscape.

So we took this energy and skill set and ran with it. Because public history involves so many different methods of output but a semester is only so long, we decided to use the body of research they created from their oral histories and the archives to create three different outputs. First, they created posters that we used to build a small exhibit. Then, they did a walking tour as their final exam.

But the part that we're most proud of, I think, was that they built an Omeka site to showcase all of this called Rattlers Remember (http://rattlersremember.stmupublichistory.org/). This class did all the work to make the logo, to figure out what the site would look like, to invite people to the History Harvest, and to publicize this work to the community. They gained a lot of different expertise through this project and explored all sorts of digital skills while working with one body of research.

Wingo: The Public History in the Wild assignment scaffolded into my final project this semester too. I did a project inspired by Thomas Cauvin at the University of Luxembourg. He posted on Twitter and asked something like, "My students are doing public history exhibits inside of bathrooms. What should the project be called?" And I replied, "Obviously In-Stall History, and I'm going to do that now. Thank you."

My students ended up adapting our exact same blog from Public History in the Wild. They worked within the same categories and tags that they had already established and were familiar with. Then they created these long blog posts based on archival research that they had conducted in our university archives. Finally they designed a one-page poster advertising their blog post, and it had a little QR code in the corner. I had them go out and plaster the campus with posters inside bathroom stalls, because that is where you literally have a captive audience.

They had so much fun with it. We put a blog counter on the posts so they could see how many people viewed their blogs. Some of them got over 200 hits within the first week, which is a miracle considering Facilities Management was going around behind us ripping off our posters. In no other class did students have a final project that had a reach like that. They were excited that people were consuming the work that they had put so much energy into over the course of the semester. And it all came from that same scaffold for Public History in the Wild. It was really, really fun.

The majority of our assignments can be assembled, disassembled, and reassembled into something new, kind of like Legos. We can take the building blocks of each other's assignments and scaffold them into something new. Students recognize and are familiar with some of the pieces, which makes them more confident in the assignments.

During the Boo-Meh-Yay exercise in the fall of 2019—in what felt like a real-life movie experience—Wingo's Public History in the Wild assignment got a slow clap that evolved into a standing ovation. Sure, the students were being silly, but we prefer to think that they genuinely appreciated seeing their world differently and applying the skills they gained in their final In-Stall History project.

Without the Great Syllabus Swap, it would have taken many more years to refine these assignments into something worthy of a slow clap.

Three Terrific Takeaways

Well, it's actually six terrific takeaways, since we each came up with three; but Wingo insists on alliteration (the compromises we make to keep the peace), and so here we are with our segment on "Three Terrific Takeaways."

Wieck: What do you think are the three biggest takeaways you want students to have when they leave your course?

Wingo: I want students to have the ability to read their environments through a historical lens. History is everywhere.

I also want them to see that history is relevant to virtually all current events. They should be able to take things that they read about in the news or see in their cities or towns and be able to understand the historic roots of the events.

And also, because nothing is ever done in isolation in public history (or literally any other job outside the academy), I want my students to be able to collaborate. We foster that in the classroom, and we foster it again through the group projects at the end of the semester.

What about you?

Wieck: Well, I, too, like all three of those takeaways, so I'm glad you said them so that I can have three totally different takeaways.

Wingo: It's almost like we planned it that way.

Wieck: It's suspicious.

Wingo: [Laughs]

Wieck: First, a wise colleague and friend, Shannon Murray, once shared the motto of her public history practice as Shut Up and Listen, which is something my students and I returned to a lot. I want my students to understand that who tells history matters. It's important that we listen to people around us, hear their stories, and make sure that we're not in an echo chamber of history. It's not just about telling our perspectives.

As a related piece of that, my second takeaway is that I want students to understand that history is made up of multiple perspectives. It's important that we look for those perspectives and reflect them in the public history work that we do.

I think so often students come out of their high school history classes, and even some of their college history classes, believing that history is a fact that you can memorize and that it's this neutral thing. We talk a lot about how it's not neutral and about who creates history.

I think all three of mine sort of interweave together in thinking about listening and who makes history and what perspectives to look for.

It's easy to lose sight of one part of the mission when you are focusing on improving another—the forest for the trees and all that. Having the balance of the other person's perspective through the syllabus exchange ensures that we're getting as close to accomplishing our goals as possible.

Picking a Partner

When it comes to choosing a fellow syllabus swapper, there are three important criteria: a shared pedagogical approach, respect, and trust. We speak in this section about "trusting" each other, but we don't really define what that means. For us, trust means that we believe the other has vetted a new source or reading, has searched for topics that will generate productive classroom conversation, or, in the case of a specific community or group, has included voices representative of that community or group. Paired with respect, trust also means that we take each other's constructive critique at face value, as something that is meant to improve our shared scholarship.

> *Wingo*: If you were to give any advice to fellow faculty members about this syllabus exchange, what would it be?

> *Wieck*: I talk to other people pretty frequently about feedback on my syllabi, or about my classroom learning experiences or my assignments. I have great colleagues who provide me with feedback about this all the time. Twitter is fabulous for this, and also other social media.

[*Wingo interrupting here: This is something I admire greatly about Lindsey's approach. She's constantly sharing her advice, assignments, and syllabi on social media. She developed quite a following of academics and practitioners who participate in generative conversations around pedagogy. We all benefit from her generosity.*]

I think what Rebecca and I are doing with this exchange is a little bit different, since it's a sustained partnership. We are actually passing the full syllabus back and forth and coediting it. I think finding somebody whom you trust, whom you respect, and who has similar pedagogy as you—but also, somebody who sometimes has different ideas from you, too—is valuable.

Be conscious of who you're choosing. I'm not sure we chose each other consciously. I think we just kind of fell into it by matter of circumstance, but I'm so glad that we did, because this has been an amazing partnership.

The other thing I think you have to be prepared for is constructive criticism. It's easy to feel hurt feelings if somebody provides critique on something that you're doing. So, for example, when I gave Rebecca my HTML, she told me what a slob I was. Then she dissected my sloppy HTML. [*Laughter*] But I'm really happy that she went through and cleaned up my HTML because when I take that syllabus back this fall, hopefully it will have shiny, clean code for me to work with.

Wingo: No. I just actually wrote back in your errors for the version that I will send to you. [*Laughter*] I think we always have to be ready for critique, and that's also why you should choose somebody that you do trust and respect. I know, when it comes from Lindsey, that it also comes with a gigantic hug if I need it. I don't let my feelings get too hurt because I know that she's just making me better.

Wieck: It's also important to find somebody that you have fun with because we can get the serious work done, but we can tell jokes alongside it. I think that makes it ultimately a favorable experience and one that you look back at and you say, "Well, that was a lot of fun," not "That was a torturous experience."

Wingo: Right.

Wieck: Most of the time.

Wingo: And all of this does remind me that I need to send that syllabus back to you. So . . . [*laughter*] I'll do that.

[*Wieck here: She still hasn't sent it back . . .*]
[*Wingo here: I did. Eventually.*]

Adaptive Assignment Architecture

One of the strengths of the Great Syllabus Swap is that two brains combined can overcome obstacles as they arise. There is a lot of flexibility in our syllabus, from substituting new readings to building entirely new assignments. Wieck is scheduled to teach the syllabus next, but the COVID-19 pandemic affected not just what we teach but how we teach it. We held this conversation when Wieck's fall 2020 semester hung in limbo. We wondered: Would class be in-person or not? Is it even ethical to hold class as usual? How can we plan for the fall with so many unanswered questions?

Before we recorded our conversation to provide you with this delightful transcript, Wieck expressed her anxieties to Wingo about the coming semester. What kind of project could her students do collaboratively if they had to be apart? How would they reach the public in an era of social and physical distancing? How could they serve the community when gatherings were unsafe? The following conversation demonstrates the flexibility of our syllabus and the creative power of our teamwork.

Wieck: We have now each taught this class two times each, I think, right?

Wingo: Yes.

Wieck: Starting this fall will be my third round teaching it, and the fifth time all around. I might be teaching it online thanks to COVID-19. We had finally created this wonderful, beautiful, perfect smooth-running model of a class, and now I might have to overturn it and create something brand new.

But even if I have to turn this into an online class [***Author's Note:** And I did end up teaching it online. #Fall2020 #CovidCampus*], I'm glad to have my syllabus partner in tow. Already today, we started brainstorming what this might look like. I really wanted to try the In-Stall History project with my students, but since there maybe aren't public bathrooms in their life anymore, Rebecca had the idea that they could use streetlight posts and call it Illuminate History. Presuming they have streetlights around them, this has potential.

Wingo: Well, I'm really excited to see what happens with that and, of course, to steal some of your ideas next year.

Wieck: That's the best part. This is a partnered-theft relationship.

Wingo: [*Laughs*] Partners in crime?

Wieck: Yeah. Collab-banter-ating.

Wingo: [*Laughs*] Oh, I think I'm going to stop the recording now.

Dear Reader, it was probably a good thing we stopped recording.

Our Concluding Comments

The language we create within the academy around teaching separates it from scholarship. Professors are rewarded based on three categories: research, teaching, and service. But we all know the truth: developing a syllabus is scholarship. The choices we make about the methods, readings, and topics that we teach are part of a scholarly practice. Just as coauthoring an article or a book befuddles historians who are used to researching in silos, coauthoring a syllabus befuddles those who are used to teaching in silos. The Great Syllabus Swap puts our syllabi through a more rigorous peer review than one can imagine—a challenging, fun, and meticulous peer review.

There is a lot of smaller labor we didn't mention in our conversation that goes along with the syllabus exchange. When one of us scans a chapter from a book that the other might need, we send it. When one of us wants to test a new assignment, the other edits it. When one of us needs advice about a student, we call. We promote each other's work. We promote the work of the scholars we select.

We are two of the luckiest goofballs on the planet for finding each other. Our pedagogy has vastly improved as we learn and relearn how to teach better. It's deepened our friendship, too. Now we talk about kids and mammograms and Wingo's horrendous love life, and also racial and social injustice and our fears over the future. And pedagogy, of course. You cannot rely fully on luck to find your co-swapper, but you can build a syllabus swap into your practice. Perhaps even a great syllabus swap. We highly recommend it.

Notes

1. If this joke went over your head, dear reader, we can do nothing for you. Just keep reading.
2. Daniel Blue Tyx, "Signs and Blunders."
3. Elliott, "'Why Don't Y'all Let That Die?'"
4. Farmer, "Archiving While Black"; Auslander, "Slavery's Traces."
5. Landrieu, "Speech on the Removal of Confederate Monuments in New Orleans"; American Historical Association, "Statement on Confederate Monuments," www.historians.org/news-and-advocacy/aha-advocacy/aha-statement-on-confederate-monuments; Finney, "I'm Black." (Karen Finney is Black and also the great-great-great-great niece of Confederate general Robert E. Lee.)
6. For a case study on History Harvests, see Anderson and Wingo, "Harvesting History, Remembering Rondo"; Wingo and Sullivan, "Remembering Rondo."
7. St. Mary's University is a Marianist institution. The Marianists are a worldwide family of Catholic brothers, priests, sisters, and committed laypeople, and their Characteristics of Marianist Education shape the university's mission. In this project, we took advantage of the National Archives of the Marianist Province of the United States located on campus, as well as the many Marianist brothers and priests with a vast knowledge of the history and lore about our campus.

3 The Big Picture Goals of Public History

EVAN FAULKENBURY

I tried to remain calm, but on the inside, I seethed. Class had just started, and I asked my students, as I always do at the start of each session, if they had any announcements, questions, or concerns about anything before we dove into the day's subject. One student in the back raised his hand. This student (let's call him Tim) began complaining that the group project seemed unfair and amounted to unpaid labor. I felt blood rushing to my face, but I kept my voice calm and asked Tim to explain what he meant. A bit more nervous now as the room's energy shifted, Tim suggested that the research wasn't exactly too hard but that our partner organizations were profiting off student effort, and to him, that didn't feel right. I kept my face passive, but I felt annoyed. "Insubordination! Mutiny!" I inwardly shouted to myself. I noticed other students shifting in their seats, but I wasn't sure if they agreed with Tim or just felt awkward about a student challenging a professor in class. I did the only thing I felt I could at the moment: I asked the rest of the class what they thought.

No one backed up Tim, although I imagine some may have kept quiet not because they didn't agree but because they didn't want to feel embarrassed. A few students did speak up in support of the project, in particular a shy student I'll call Cynthia. She said our project was cool because other people beyond the class will be able to use it and because it actually benefits the community. Cynthia's comment ended the discussion, and I breathed a bit easier. But after our class ended, I couldn't stop thinking about Tim and what he'd brought up. I came to admire Tim for being brave enough to say what was on his mind in front of the class, and I felt ashamed at feeling so defensive. I started thinking about his comment more deeply: What exactly was the point of the project?

At the same time I taught this class, I read a book by Norman Eng called *Teaching College*. Two points of his stuck out to me. First, most students don't really care about my class. "Ouch!" I first thought, but I began thinking on that point. Sure, students likely enjoyed parts of my public history class, but on the whole, the majority think about my class practically, and for good reason. They want to earn the credits they need to graduate. In hindsight, students may look back fondly on my course as one that shaped them, but in the moment, they're just trying to get through. And second, since students often think this way, it's important to stress Big Picture Goals. Each student has these in mind, if ill-defined. Whether they dream of becoming a high school teacher, a museum curator, a doctor, a librarian, or of having any career that requires a college degree, their higher education classes— in any subject—should hone skills and knowledge that can take them where they want to go.

Tim's question and the discussion that followed helped me focus the remainder of my public history class on students' Big Picture Goals. Based on Eng's book, I used the term "Big Picture Goals" to get students to think deeply about their career ambitions. In class, no matter the topic of the day, I had students make connections between public history and their personal Big Picture Goals. Using this phrase repeatedly during class helped students realize the elasticity of public history—they began to perceive how creating a museum exhibit, drafting a social media plan for a historic site, or planning a documentary film sharpened skills that could be adapted and highlighted when they pursued different jobs and opportunities after finishing their undergraduate degree. A class on public history, I discovered, does this almost intrinsically, but professors have to be the ones to help students not miss the forest for the trees. Tim and others in the class struggled to see the big picture, and that fell on me. Why should students study public history and work on a group project that involves the wider community? To me, it's because public history compels students to actually *do* history out in the real world, honing those skills that are useful to their Big Picture Goals.

The story of my fall 2019 semester HIS 280: Introduction to Public History course began well before the first day of class. Since arriving at SUNY Cortland in the fall 2016 semester, I have taught this course every semester. Right before I arrived, my department made the class a requirement for all history majors. As far as I can tell, it's unique for a history department to make public history mandatory for undergraduates, putting it on par with historical methods and a capstone research seminar. Requiring public history has pushed our students to think of history beyond classrooms and more as a type of community service, which also sharpens their skill set of research, writing, and communication for future job prospects.[1] Because of this requirement, I teach one section of this course each semester, usually with an enrollment between thirty and thirty-five students. For public history, that's a big class, and the size has dictated how I structure lessons and projects. Often, students take this course before or at the same time as their historical methods class. As a result, many students are at the sophomore or junior level learning public history alongside (or even before) the traditional methods class, where they begin to figure out historiography, research, writing, and what it means to be a historian. Public history shapes their education from the start.

In semesters past, I had my public history class work with local museums and archives, and for the fall 2019 semester, I wanted to experiment with Clio. For anyone with a smartphone or internet connection, Clio can steer people toward historic sites and museums. Developed by Dr. David Trowbridge at Marshall University, Clio allows users to explore history all around them using GPS to connect with real places, and those with an account can create new entries. On August 8, a few weeks before the semester began, I met with three community stakeholders to coordinate the project: Tabitha Scoville from the Cortland County Historical Society (CCHS); Meghan Lawton from Experience Cortland, our county's visitor's bureau; and Eric Mulvihill, Cortland County's historian and clerk of the county legislature. The CCHS had already experimented with Clio, and Tabitha was interested in a project focusing on Cortland County's historic roadside markers. As in many states, historic markers fill the landscape around New York, and in Cortland County, over one hundred blue signs are scattered across small towns and rural roads. While community leaders continue to add new ones every so often, most historic markers in Cortland County have stood for decades, and in 1989, the CCHS even published a booklet about fifty such markers. But each marker has only a few lines of text, and while many indicate important stories, they are too often neglected. The four of us decided that our class project would have students research all fifty markers from the 1989 booklet and create entries for each one on Clio.

Overly ambitious? Probably so, and as I'll explore later on, problems multiplied toward the end of the semester. But in theory, this public history project made sense. It would involve multiple stakeholders from the community, prompt students to research in the CCHS archives, enable students to hone their digital skills, and allow students to work on a project that Experience Cortland could market toward tourists and locals. Students would create a project that had lasting benefits to our larger community, and in doing so, they would gain useful skills. I wasn't yet thinking about Big

Picture Goals, but I believed that students would gain practical knowledge from this project. The CCHS, Experience Cortland, and our county's historian committed to the project, and we left the meeting excited for the possibilities but also anticipating that challenges would arise.

With a project in mind, I sat down to draft my course syllabus. I like everything neatly laid out and planned, but I've learned to create some flexibility in my syllabus because a class never ends up as I originally envisioned. I've experimented with different schedules, and I've settled on a survey of a variety of public history topics. This semester, we covered museums, ghost tours, graphic history, preservation, living history, monuments, historic sites, photography, archives, oral history, podcasts, film, digital history, and careers for history majors. Since this is an undergraduate class, I tried to showcase how public history is a lens through which anyone can learn about, appreciate, and even love history. At the same time, I emphasized ethical dilemmas and problematic forms of public history, such as former slave plantations that ignore racial violence and glorify a nostalgic white past. And I included diverse voices in my syllabus, so that students can appreciate the growing inclusivity of the field.

In my syllabus, I attempted to explain what exactly public history means. As anyone who has taught public history knows, this is no simple task. Our discipline has batted around definitions and explanations for decades, and while that ongoing conversation is important, my undergrads don't really care. As they're just learning about the subject, the last thing I want to do is scare them off with too much theory and abstraction. So, rather than define public history, I came up with five pillars of public history, and I put these into my course description: (1) outside classroom walls and reaching a universal audience; (2) collaborative, meaning that public history involves working with other people and community partners; (3) includes the interpretation of primary and secondary sources; (4) relevant to current events and our everyday lives; and (5) public history is all about memory, shaping how we as individuals and as communities remember the past.

With my syllabus built, Blackboard turned on, and roster in hand, on August 27 I walked from my office to an adjacent building, climbed three flights of stairs, and met my class of thirty-five students for the first time. I always have butterflies in my stomach on the first day of class, and they never go away. Even after months with the same group of students, as soon as I begin getting ready to walk over, my stomach gets queasy. Performing as a teacher never comes easy for me, but once I arrive and class starts, my brain goes into some kind of automatic drive, and I begin to relax.

On this first day of class, I arrived early to check my roster, walk around the room, and say hello to students. Once the clock hit 11:40 A.M., I started class with the Question of the Day. I do this at the start of every class, and it works well to jump-start everyone's brains and to track attendance. The question usually involves the reading due that day, or in this case, it tried to strike a current-events chord: "In your opinion, do you think Confederate monuments should stay as they are, be destroyed, or something else? Why?" The weirded-out looks on their faces at such an unexpected question were priceless to behold. After allowing a few minutes for them to write short responses on paper, I asked for volunteers to read what they wrote. Several spoke up with very different ideas from each other. Good! Our start of the semester accomplished what I wanted: to get them thinking about public history and its relevance to our current world. We spent the rest of this first day exploring how public history serves as a vehicle for understanding why history matters, discussing how Confederate monuments relate, and looking over the syllabus.

After class ended, I retreated to my office to prepare for my other courses (this semester, I also taught a course in African American history before 1865, and I facilitated the undergraduate public history internship course). The butterflies wore off, and I thought the opening class session went about as well as could be expected. I was nervous, but so were they, and together, we grasped the main idea of the class: public history is all around us, it's complicated, and it's interesting.

First impressions really do stick. My first impression of Tim was that he was engaged and focused. I could also tell that Cynthia was shy. One other person stood out to me on that first day, an older nontraditional student I'll call Natalie. She sat in the front row and intensely focused on me the entire class. She raised her hand at almost every question I asked, and she participated in a way that comes from maturity. Later in the semester, I would learn that Natalie had returned to college despite living a county away and being an involved grandparent. I do my best not to have favorites, but when you have someone like Natalie sitting in the front row and expressing a love for the subject, it can be tough not to.

On our second day of class, I met with Natalie, Cynthia, Tim, and thirty-two other students once more to pick up where we left off. For this period, I hit rewind, and before we went any more in depth about public history, I wanted to discuss what exactly we mean by "history." I asked the class how they would define history, and several raised their hand and talked about a broad understanding of the past. I gave everyone who responded a positive remark, and then I told them two things that history is not. First, I explained, history is not about memorizing facts, dates, and names. I like to emphasize this point, because for many, this is an opposite approach to how many of them learned in high school. And second, I said, history is not the past. I let my statement hang in the air for several seconds and looked around at their quizzical faces. I told them that history is all about interpreting sources, and that history isn't just about learning what happened but why.

We continued our discussion about the nature of history, and then I moved back into the realm of public history and the five pillars by discussing a case study about the Jack the Ripper Museum in London. In the May 2017 issue of the journal *The Public Historian*, Claire Hayward published a fascinating review essay about this new museum.[2] In short, stakeholders misled the community that a new museum about women's history would open in London's East End, but that museum turned out to be one that clumsily dramatized violence against women. We walked through the museum on-screen, and I led them in a discussion about the pros and cons of this museum. The class noted many more cons than pros, and we talked about how the museum did not meet the five pillars but how a community-based, grassroots response had grown up in opposition: the East End Women's Museum. I love talking about messy and controversial topics, and I brought my class into the wild world of public history, hoping that this lesson would stick in their minds as we moved ahead.

The following week, class revolved around one of my favorite topics—graphic history. Since I first started teaching this class in 2016, I've cut or changed nearly everything, except this week. We read *Battle Lines* by Jonathan Fetter-Vorm and Ari Kelman, an absorbing book that most students find interesting, and we discussed the art, imagery, color, facial expressions, and sources in class.[3] On Tuesday, we focused on chapters one through seven, and on Thursday, chapters eight through fifteen. These sessions zoomed by as we went in depth on each chapter. I opened class with the tried-and-true method of Think-Pair-Share. Students first wrote down what their favorite chapter was and why, then paired up with another student to discuss, then shared with the entire class. One of the main reasons I like devoting the entire second week of the semester to graphic history and *Battle Lines* is because the book is deceptively complex. Animation and comics have an undeserved reputation for simplicity, but they communicate emotion and abstract ideas in a way no other form can. Students found the book interesting, not altogether realizing right away that it pushed them to reimagine the importance of the Civil War through a form of public history.

After we finished *Battle Lines*, students began their first assignment for the course—a reflection essay, consisting of both a first and a final draft. I asked students to first turn in a three-page essay in which they analyzed one of the chapters in *Battle Lines*, then after I evaluated their first draft and gave them written feedback, they had a chance to edit and expand their essay for the final draft. I asked them to reflect on their chapter and also to explain whether or not graphic history is a useful form of public history. This assignment works well as a soft initiation into deeper critical thinking about public history that will be useful throughout the semester. For my part, when I graded, I spent much more time on their first drafts than on their final drafts. For the first drafts, I did some line editing and wrote them a longer comment at the end of the essay. I started with a compliment or two, then focused on how they could improve for the final draft. I always try to keep my language warm and positive, even for students who did not do well. Almost universally, given the opportunity, students improve with their final draft, improve their overall grade outlook for the course, and think deeper about the usefulness of public history.

The next section of our course focused on museums and historic sites. We started with the basics: What exactly is a museum? Why do museums matter? How are museums public history? I introduced them to the idea of free-choice learning and how exhibits affect visitors by going through virtual tours of the National Museum of African American History and Culture, the Museum of the American Revolution, and the National Civil War Museum. Students split up and did a Think-Pair-Share about memorable museum experiences they've had, and we talked about why the public generally trusts museums.

I should pause here and clarify that my teaching so far had been far from perfect. Several of my class discussions fell flat, and I failed several times to help students see the bigger picture and think through how public history related to their Big Picture Goals. One day, students were supposed to read an essay by historian James Oliver Horton before coming to class, and I wanted to discuss it with them.[4] I asked them to share their thoughts about the essay, and I heard crickets. The same happened a few days later when we discussed a common read about how Fort Sumter has interpreted the Civil War through the years. Once again, very little engagement took place in our discussion. I left both classes feeling frustrated, not only with myself for not structuring better class sessions but also with the students for not reading the material before class or being unwilling to speak up. Even though I know the fault lies with me, I sometimes can't help but blame students for not trying harder. It's wrong, I know, but it's a struggle I continue to confront.

After their *Battle Lines* essay, the students' next project focused on a small research paper about a historic site or monument. We read selections from James Loewen's *Lies Across America*, and students conducted research on whether or not a particular site has changed its interpretation of history since 1999.[5] Some of the students' more popular choices were the Abraham Lincoln Birthplace National Historical Park in Kentucky, Fort Pillow State Historic Park in Tennessee, and Stone Mountain Park in Georgia. In class, I taught them about research, citations, and how to search for trustworthy sources, all skills they will continue to hone throughout the history major. Once again, I had them turn in a first draft that I heavily marked and commented on, then they had the opportunity to rewrite for a larger percentage of their total grade. Overall, I was pleased with their progress between the first and final drafts. Throughout the first six weeks of the course, they had made significant progress piecing together what public history entailed and how public history shapes our present.

After six weeks, it came time to begin our group project. I like delaying the group project to around midway through the semester so that the first half can be dedicated to in-class instruction, reading, writing, and figuring out the finer points of public history. On October 8, Meghan Lawton and Eric Mulvihill joined our class to talk with students about the value their project would have for the community for years to come. For the Question of the Day to open class, I asked students to write down positive and negative qualities in group members when working on a collaborative project. Students then shared with the class their thoughts on positive qualities—carrying equal weight, being responsive, acting maturely—as well as negative qualities—not taking the project seriously, letting others do all the work, not communicating well. Letting students come up with this list themselves and sharing it aloud served as an accountability tool, a type of verbal contract I hoped would keep everyone on track.

After discussing what makes for a positive group experience, we started talking specifics about the public history project. Our collective goal was to make fifty of Cortland County's old, rusting historic markers newly visible through Clio. Meghan and Eric talked to the class about the purpose of the project. Eric explained how many of these roadside signs had become run-down over the decades, and most had only a few lines of text, so it was difficult for most people to grasp the significance of the history they mark. Meghan talked about how Experience Cortland planned to market this Clio project as a fun activity for tourists to do when they visit Cortland. I shared with everyone how this project would require us to do public history, meet the five pillars, get to know our community better, and overcome a challenge. But at this point, I hadn't yet read Norman Eng's book, nor had Tim questioned the purpose of this project. As much as I'd like to think I explained the project's purpose on that day, looking back, I didn't demonstrate how it would factor into their Big Picture Goals.

During the rest of the class period, I divided the class into groups and gave more specific instructions. I split the students into ten groups, with each one responsible for locating, researching, and creating Clio entries for five markers. I told the groups that they would need to find their markers and take photographs for their Clio entries. I tried to make that part sound fun—like a scavenger hunt! I showed them Clio, demonstrated how to log on and edit, and passed out a detailed set of instructions. First drafts of their five Clio entries would be due in November, and after I edited them and met individually with groups to give advice on improvement, final drafts would be due in December by exam time. We closed class by saying that the following Thursday, the class would meet at the Cortland County Historical Society, where we would be introduced to the archives and shown how to research information pertaining to our markers.

This was an important class day—perhaps the most crucial in the entire semester. Looking back, however, I would probably give myself a C for this session. We talked about the importance of this project for the community, but since most of the class came from outside Cortland County, I should have done more to help students care about local history. And I should have explained more clearly how this project would help develop important skills for their future. I also failed to appreciate the burden we placed on student groups to drive their own cars, pay for gas, and locate historical markers from around the county. Without addressing that head-on, I believe I sowed some indifference, and maybe even some antipathy, into the project during this class period.

A week later, our class met at the Cortland County Historical Society. The CCHS is only about a ten-minute walk from campus, and even when the weather turns snowy, most students can get there without too much trouble. Tabitha Scoville directs the CCHS, and she and I welcomed the class, showed them around the research room, and directed them to where they would likely find information related to their markers. Some groups had markers regarding well-known people, such as the birthplace of Alton B. Parker, the Democratic candidate who lost to Theodore Roosevelt in the 1904 presidential election. Others had more obscure markers, such as those about early European American settlers in the county. Tabitha pulled dozens of research files on prominent families and settlements, as well as a number of printed books with information about county history. We pointed out all these resources to the students, letting them know they had to conduct research at the CCHS to build their Clio entries on primary and secondary sources.

Until students came together within their groups and actually went out on the road to find their markers, I believe this project seemed vague and strange to them. I saw many apprehensive faces at the CCHS, as well as during the previous class, when we introduced the project. Group projects can be scary, I told them, but they are essential for practicing public history. Over the next few weeks, I started hearing from students in the moments before and after class about how they took an afternoon, ventured out together, discovered their markers in sometimes obscure settings, and photographed them from all angles. For many, this turned out to be the most fun part of the assignment and the beginning of bonding with their group mates. Several groups seemed to gel, even giving up their usual seats to sit with one another during class. Seeing how well they started to do once they actually got started made me think about how I can jump-start projects in the future to shorten that awkward, frightful stage at the beginning, perhaps by conducting mini group projects earlier in the semester.

As groups took time outside class to begin exploring their markers and conducting research at the CCHS, our class sessions continued to cover different avenues of public history. On October 24, our class focused on oral history. I was extra nervous about this class because the chair of my department was sitting in to write a teaching observation report. I broke the ice at the start of class by having students pair up and conduct mini oral history interviews with each other for about ten minutes about where they grew up. I used this activity to explain the uses of oral history as a powerful form of public history. I discussed with them the slave narratives conducted by the Works Progress Administration, Studs Terkel's interviews about the Great Depression, and oral histories conducted by the United States Holocaust Memorial Museum with survivors.

This class on oral history was the first one after I finished Norman Eng's book, and I began thinking about this class in terms of students' Big Picture Goals. After discussing these emotional oral history collections and playing several examples, I asked the class what oral histories like these have to do with their Big Picture Goals. Several students spoke up, most revolving around their desire to become social studies teachers. One student, I'll call him Nate, became almost emotional as he described how his favorite history teacher in high school had relied on oral history to teach. Those lessons motivated Nate to want to become a teacher. "Yes!" I thought, as I saw Eng's ideas come to life in my class. Seeing students make connections between public history and their own ideal career paths boosted my own teaching morale that day. For the final fifteen minutes of class, I had students break into their Clio groups and do a thought experiment. Instead of Clio, I asked them, how would they create an oral history–based podcast episode about their five markers? Their ideas ranged from the silly to the profound, and sharing them aloud enabled students to visualize different ways to make oral history (and public history) applicable to their future selves.

The following class concentrated on documentary films as public history. We surveyed a handful of my favorites, including *I Am Not Your Negro*, *O.J.: Made in America*, and Ken Burns's *The Dust Bowl*. I showed some clips, and we discussed what made film an effective form of public history. One of the vital takeaways I wanted them to grasp was how documentaries connect the past to the present. Even if they don't explicitly state how, films like these make an implicit argument for why knowing history matters. Like the previous class, I asked what films like these have to do with their Big Picture Goals. Several offered ideas, and we even talked about film and media as a career path for history majors. Similarly to the last class, I had the Clio groups join together for a thought experiment and brainstorm how they would create a short documentary film about their five markers. Doing these activities helped group members become more familiar with one another and pushed them to think about the project through multiple public history formats.

At this point in the semester, a few weeks had passed since introducing the group project. Most groups had found and photographed their markers and begun researching at the CCHS. At the start of a class period in early November, when I had planned to dive into the controversies surrounding the *Enola Gay*, the Smithsonian, and the "history wars" of the 1990s, Tim raised his hand and questioned the purpose of the group project—the story at the start of this chapter. I don't want to be repetitive here, but this serves as a reminder that even though I had thought at this point that I had been thorough, the larger purposes of public history and this project had not been made clear enough. His comments woke me up, and in the weeks that followed, I made a bigger effort to connect the dots for students and focus on Big Picture Goals.

As students prepared the first drafts of their Clio entries, we took a week off from our normal classes and went on a field trip to the Harriet Tubman Home in Auburn, New York. I had been preparing for this trip for weeks, booking a tour and a bus for the afternoon of November 8. The previous year, I had successfully attached an $11.00 course fee to HIS 280 to pay for bus travel and museum admission for one or two field trips per semester. The total trip would add up to about four hours, including the round-trip bus ride and two-hour tour of the historic site. Most students were able to come, and I wrote excused-absence forms for a few who had to miss other classes to go on this trip. We met at the bus stop, piled on, and drove over country roads and along Owasco Lake to Auburn, the small community where Harriet Tubman built a life for herself following the Civil War.

The privately held Harriet Tubman Home has preserved the land and buildings for decades, and had recently entered into an agreement with the National Park Service to become a federally protected historic site. The land comprises Harriet Tubman's brick home, a large farmhouse she converted into a home for the elderly, an office, and a museum. We parked across the street and walked through the property to the museum. Paul Carter, one of the best tour guides I've ever met, welcomed the class into the museum. Students milled about the museum for about fifteen minutes, exploring multiple exhibits and panels about the long life of Harriet Tubman. Paul then gathered the class together and launched into his prepared tour. Paul's passion for Harriet Tubman's memory shone through, and students sat riveted for about thirty minutes as Paul guided the class through her biography. He interacted with the class, asked questions, and demonstrated her importance to American history. Students later told me one of the most memorable parts of Paul's tour happened when he passed around a small two-pound cast-iron weight. A white enslaver had hit Tubman with a similar weight (he had been aiming at another enslaved person), and this injury caused Tubman to suffer seizures throughout her life.

Next, Paul guided us across the property to explore Tubman's home for elderly and infirm African Americans. We walked throughout the home and thought about Tubman's role in caring for so many people throughout her lifetime. We also walked around her brick home, but we could not go inside, as it was undergoing renovations. We explored the property, trying to envision what life had been like on these grounds over one hundred years earlier. On this trip, the class experienced public history firsthand. No longer were we stuck in a classroom learning these concepts from afar. Students began figuring out what it means to do public history, thinking about why preserving historical spaces matter, and even considering if such career choices could be available to them.

For the field trip, I had considered making students do an assignment of some kind, but I decided against it. Perhaps doing so would've made students pay greater attention to the particulars of the site, and it could've kickstarted a deeper discussion about our trip when we met together again as a class. But one of my ideals for this class is simply to make public history fun. Since many of these students are just entering into the upper tier of the history major, I don't want to scare them off. As they take other crucial classes about historical methods and content-heavy courses, I want my public history class to remind them that history is everywhere, it's entertaining, it's adventurous, it's economically beneficial, and it's a career possibility. Creating an assignment for a field trip seemed to me like it would drain the excitement.

By our next class period on November 14, first drafts of all Clio entries were due. To do well on these first drafts, students needed to include multiple sources from their research at the CCHS, include photographs of their markers, accurately place a GPS pin onto their markers' locations, write a short overview of their markers, and include about 500 words about the larger history and context that the markers represent. Most significantly, however, what I wanted was effort. I wanted to see groups working together, digging deep into research at the CCHS, and putting as much detail into their Clio entries as possible. Out of ten groups, three first drafts exceeded my expectations, four were average, and three demonstrated a lack of effort and coordination among students.

For these first drafts, I went through all fifty very closely, line editing and giving advice throughout each entry. I emphasized again and again that the stakes for this kind of project are higher because Experience Cortland would be advertising the project to the community. Not only did the information need to be backed up with evidence, but the writing, grammar, and spelling had to be professional. The images needed to be clear, the hyperlinks needed to work, and the layout required precision. I bled all over these entries with my red pen, but as these were only first drafts, I graded more benevolently than I would for the final drafts.

The following week, instead of our regular class, I met with every group for about fifteen minutes to go over each of their five Clio rough drafts. Not surprisingly, one of the best groups was the one that included Natalie. Along with her three group mates, Natalie's five markers were the products of hard work. For example, one focused on the history of John Albright, a New

Yorker who fought with the Continental army during the American Revolution. The blue roadside marker was placed in 1940, and all it says is "John Albright—Revolutionary Soldier, built this house in 1827 for his daughter, Mrs. Nancy Griffeth." The information it presents is a far cry from the wider history of the Albright family. Natalie and her group mates dedicated a lot of time to research at the CCHS, and they narrated a story well over 500 words that contextualized Albright's life and importance to Cortland history. The British captured Albright multiple times, he survived the winter at Valley Forge, and he fought in the battle at Yorktown. After the war, he acquired land in what became Cortland County and helped build a community that exists to this day. The first draft contained some stylistic errors, and I suggested what parts they should revise and lengthen, but overall, this was a solid first draft.

The group that included Tim submitted first drafts that were good, not great. One of their five markers was about a school built in the small town of Preble in 1801. The marker reads "First School Built in Preble 1801, Ruth Thorp, First Teacher, Served the Towns of Tully and Homer." I imagine few would find this information very interesting, and so this group did have a tough task to deepen and broaden our understanding of why this history is important. They researched at the CCHS but had trouble finding much information about the school, community, or Ruth Thorp. Their first draft included some useful information, but it lacked depth, clarity, and a discussion about why this history matters. During our fifteen-minute conversation, I praised them for what they had accomplished so far and tried to gently urge them to put more effort into researching the community and Ruth Thorp at the CCHS.

Meeting with the three groups whose first drafts were poor was, in a word, awkward. I hate situations like this, in which I have to be blunt yet strive for understanding and encouragement. Two groups hadn't finished all five of their markers, and one group had become antagonistic toward one another because of perceptions that not everyone was doing their part. Fun for me to sort out! I asked questions, listened, and offered advice for how they could still do well on this project. I stressed that I was looking for effort, but that I wasn't really seeing any yet. Judging from their body language, they seemed to all understand what I was saying but were having trouble visualizing exactly what I wanted. I told them that they had to spend time together researching at the CCHS, and that they needed to work together to write and structure their Clio entries. One challenge I kept hearing was that their schedules didn't align and they were only communicating by text or Google Docs. That issue seemed to compound the problem because they weren't interacting with one another in meaningful ways, and they weren't collaborating to build standout entries. I gave these groups extensions to turn in all their entries, and I let them know I wanted to be kept in the loop as they figured out how to finish their first drafts.

Looking back after these meetings, I realized that I should've been more focused on how this project could affect their Big Picture Goals. I had started discussing these goals more broadly in our full class sessions, but I had the idea (after the meetings had all ended) to ask each student what their Big Picture Goals were and to imagine how the Clio project could potentially help achieve them. This could have grounded our fifteen-minute meetings in a way that boosted their morale, rather than me simply praising them for some parts of their entries and telling them what they needed to fix for their final drafts. Ultimately, no one in this class will graduate and become a professional Clio entry maker. So the burden falls on me to demonstrate how and why this project sharpens skills that will benefit their future.

The week after Thanksgiving break, I concentrated our two class sessions on discussing their future as a graduate with a history degree. I had prepared an in-depth class session for that Tuesday, but a snowstorm prevented half the class from showing up. I didn't want students to miss this information, so on the fly I had the class form a circle with their desks. Instead of a regular class, I decided to have a conversation. I asked them questions about why they had chosen to study history in college, what their career goals were, what kinds of knowledge and skills they had learned this semester, and how public history can play a role as they decide what to do with their lives. Maybe it's just that time of year, but many students became sentimental. They talked about their love of history, how they want to be teachers, who inspired them, and other personal stories. Instead of me preaching at them about the value and skills of public history, they articulated many themselves. I think the best moment came when one student (I'll call her Becky) shared openly about her doubts about going down the history major path. Rather than try to convince her, I told Becky to choose what she loves to do, to not overthink it, and to talk with her family. I hope this exchange helped other students see that professors have their best interests at heart, whether they stay in the major and boost our enrollments or not.

On Thursday, our last normal class day, I got back on track and shared resources with the class about how to make their history degree work for them. We discussed a useful article about applying for jobs with a history degree; looked at the American Historical Association's *Careers for*

History Majors guide; and talked about ways to gain experience through internships, entry-level jobs, and graduate school.[6] (The previous year, I had created a two-page guide for our department called "Why Study History?," for which the faculty came up with twenty reasons. On the back page, we listed over a dozen websites that advertised jobs, along with tips on how to search for and apply to history-related jobs.[7]) I then split the class into their Clio groups, and I handed each one a different entry-level job advertisement I found that morning on the National Council on Public History's job postings web page. I asked the groups to figure out how they could apply for that job, banking on the experience they had gained in our class. For example, one job was for a social media specialist at the Smithsonian, another was with visitor services at the Manzanar National Historic Site, and another was for an assistant site manager at a former slave plantation in North Carolina. After groups brainstormed among themselves for about five minutes, each group shared with the class. I wanted to emphasize exactly how they could capitalize on their history majors using actual examples and end class on a positive note.

With the last week of class over, all we had left was for groups to polish their Clio entries and present on their five markers during our final exam period. Let me back up here and explain how I wanted our Clio projects to end at the semester's conclusion. I envisioned fifty ready-to-go Clio entries that could go live right after the semester concluded and that Experience Cortland could immediately begin using as a marketing tool. A quick spoiler: that's not what happened. The Clio entries were, as a whole, too disjointed. Some ended up polished and well-constructed, some were OK, and many weren't necessarily bad but weren't up to the standards of a professional advertising campaign. In short, the semester would conclude without the Clio project finalized. I really didn't like that. I like finished projects, and I hate leaving loose threads. One part of teaching public history that I'm still trying to learn is to be more at peace with the process, to become less of a perfectionist, and to remind myself that students are learning, even with less-than-stellar final projects.

Throughout the final two weeks of the semester, I met many times with groups to discuss their Clio entries. I counseled them on how to find additional sources, how to locate a few missing markers, how to make their entries stand out, and how to rewrite for a public audience. I also had to intervene in two groups that weren't working well together. I had them come to my office hours, and we openly discussed the problems they were having. Issues usually revolved around lack of communication, and each group left (I think) more willing to work with their partners. I also kept in touch with the CCHS staff, since they were the ones hosting students conducting the research. Even though I kept reminding students that they had to make sure that their five Clio entries were professional in appearance (correct syntax, no blurry images, working hyperlinks), since their names would be attached and the public would use them, I'm not sure how much that sank in versus how much they just wanted to finish and wrap up the semester.

During exam week, students turned in their completed entries, and instead of giving a final test, I had each group give a short presentation to the class about their five markers. About halfway through, I realized I had made another big mistake. The room had low energy, the presentations were boring, and the students didn't seem well prepared. And with ten groups all sharing one after the other, their talks soon became repetitive. Instead of making them do boring presentations, I should've organized some kind of open-air showcase where students and our community partners could've walked around, chatted, and played with the Clio entries at their leisure. Instead, I made our final time together as a class about as dull as possible. After everyone finished, I trudged back to my office. I felt as if I had really blown it. The Clio entries overall were decent, but they would need significant editing before Experience Cortland could use them, and I hadn't ended the class on a high note about the value and fun of public history. I had also failed to make this final presentation relate to their Big Picture Goals.

Over the next few days, I reviewed all the Clio entries, assigned final grades, and began wrapping up the fall 2019 semester. I thought that overall, the first 90 percent of the class went well, we enjoyed ourselves, and I accomplished the goals I had for the class. But I hadn't planned out the end of the class and the Clio project very well, and as a result, the class ended with a thud. We had an anticlimactic ending, and I feared that I didn't leave them with a positive note about the semester, the project, or public history itself. Even as I write this, I'm left feeling a little bit down about how the semester ended.

Maybe I'm being a bit too harsh on myself. In between when students submitted their first drafts and final drafts of their group projects, I had them turn in a final reflection paper about what they learned in the course and what skills they'd take away. In her paper, Natalie wrote, "The historical markers research was probably the most rewarding assignment a historian major could be assigned. Researching the significance of the historical sites [and] learning that data on my own made it more rewarding. . . . I felt like Sherlock Natalie; it was learning, but it was fun." And Tim, whose comments about the project had rattled me earlier in the semester, also found positive elements in the project and the course itself. "This class is one that expanded my understanding of history," Tim wrote, "not just in content, but in principle. History isn't just a book and classroom; it is so much more. It is all around us. . . . This is a class that I will take the knowledge I gained and apply certain aspects of it to my career as a future teacher/historian."

Even if I didn't always articulate them well, their Big Picture Goals gained some clarity through a semester of learning and doing public history.

Notes

1. For more on why my department requires all history majors to take a public history class, see Faulkenbury, "Practicing History."
2. Hayward, "Waxworks and Wordless Women."
3. Fetter-Vorm and Kelman, *Battle Lines*.
4. Horton, "Slavery in American History."
5. Loewen, *Lies Across America*.
6. American Historical Association, *Careers for History Majors*.
7. SUNY Cortland Department of History, "Why Study History?"

4 Upbuilding an Inclusive Future

A Semester of Reciprocal Learning

TORREN GATSON

On the first day of class, I gazed around the seminar classroom and asked myself one simple question: Is it possible to teach inclusivity to students who have no previous experience in the matter? I imagined that the semester's experience would lead—or perhaps enhance—their moral and ethical understandings of the dire need within public history for inclusivity. Whether successful or not, my goal remained steadfast in teaching museum and historic site interpretation. That course presented an opportunity to guide my graduate students through a journey of understanding, which would hopefully arrive at a better appreciation by the end of our semester. This chapter makes a critical intersection in the pedagogy of public history by demonstrating how public historians and educators alike approach seemingly difficult topics of diversity and equity in order to promote hospitable learning environments and all-encompassing mindsets around studying, interpreting, and displaying inclusive histories.

It is apparent that while public history serves as a bridge that links historical thought with public interpretation, at times the profession has fallen short in creating a more inclusive community. Unfortunately, numerous unforeseen barriers revolving around issues of equity and inclusivity have stifled success both within the classroom and while working with students and community partners. While students pursue work with underrepresented minority communities now more than ever, there remain gaping holes concerning radical inclusivity, ensuring equity, and limiting implicit bias within public history. I define *equity* as the appropriate deliverance of fairness and justice. Likewise, in order to grasp the concept of equity, one must first understand *inequity*, which is the situations and systemic principles that deny fairness and justice with historical narratives or historical enterprises.

My account serves two purposes. First, I will present the often overshadowed vignette of an individual who identifies as an African American and my view of teaching public history. Second, I will display the methods and methodology I use to prepare budding public historians by sharpening their perception of race and culture within public history.

By the end of the course, my students will be able to think deeper, ask more thought-provoking questions, and create impactful public products that reflect equity and inclusivity in the realm of public history. In my opinion, true knowledge comes from walking with a person during their journey for understanding. To that end, I documented my weekly experience through a graduate seminar for an entire semester. This glimpse at classroom dialogue, readings, assignments, and the healthy exchange of ideas paints a vivid picture of my journey toward upbuilding an inclusive future. I must admit I was unsure if historic interpretation charted a course for shifting dialogues on inclusivity and equity within the realm of museums and the field. To that end, I wanted to know whether teaching inclusivity through museums and historic site interpretation can provide copious opportunities to educate and prepare students for an ever-changing visitor.

The goal of an analysis such as this is to highlight vignettes of classroom experiences, shortcomings, and the ultimate successes in helping students carve out their professional identity while steeped in an understanding of the power and impact of diversity and equity. This review of my semester serves as an imprinted testament to that endeavor.

I am an assistant professor of public history who personally identifies as an African American. Professionally, I identify as a publicly engaged scholar, a professional who captures the African American experience in America outside the classroom through cultural or historical landscapes. Understanding the influence public history has in its ability to conjure historical memory, foster discussion over what many label as "difficult histories," and educate the public through interactive experiences, I was eager as a new faculty member on the tenure line to mold my own graduate course from a somewhat limited course selection. Shooting for the stars, I envisioned creating a class that would thrust students into intense dialogue on race, inclusion, equity, and equality through the lens of various historic sites and museums. I realized that this was perhaps most doable in a course centered on interpretation. I elected to teach a course named Museum and Historic Site Interpretation. The desired objective for student outcomes was to demonstrate the importance of being active participants in inclusion and creating culturally responsive pedagogy while examining the field. While primarily composed of master's and doctoral students who identify as white, there were a few students of color enrolled. One challenge in preparing courses for new graduate students is the varying levels of critical thought and analytical skills. This is on top of finding new and innovative ways to engage. So when building the structure of the course syllabus, I strove to include works that, in diverse ways, discuss inclusivity and the prevalent lack thereof to give students a sharp perspective of the field. I wanted to design a course that blended the readings and understandings of the field with a community-engaged project. Working with "live" partners is perhaps the lifeblood of the profession and the fuel that propels the field.

When it came time to select the reading list for this course, I took a long time compiling what I envisioned to be a snapshot of the necessary books to frame an understanding of interpretation and its place within the realm of historic sites. Like many of my colleagues, the reading list and assignments hinge on the level of students in the course. Introducing graduate students to public history through a course like this was exciting. I aimed to provide students a visual of the slow transformation of the field through scholarship and practice. In that, I envisioned emphasizing the silencing and complete eradication of people of color and the lack of inclusivity, including compliance for people with disabilities.

The readings for this course ranged from Freeman J. Tilden's timeless classic *Interpreting Our Heritage* to Frank Vagnone and Deborah Ryan's provocative *Anarchist's Guide to Historic House Museums*, plus several others works from scholars including W. Fitzhugh Brundage, Amy Lonetree, and Michel-Rolph Trouillot. From my brief yet extensive experience in teaching, in order to reach students and to prepare them for the professional world, the readings and course interactions must be directly relevant to their life experiences. The ideas of correlation and relevancy play a critical role when discussing race, class, and gender.

By the first day of class, I was nervous and eager to formally meet the students (in a classroom setting) and to begin reviewing the syllabus. Due to its growing size, my academic institution determines days and times of courses. This semester my course was every Monday evening for three hours. There has long been a belief among some instructors that teaching gets easier with practice. I have a contrasting view. I do believe that teaching is a passion, and nothing invigorates me more than seeing budding professionals grasp theoretical and practical applications of public history as I once did. But teaching is also a labor of love, which I have to manage and tweak in order to ensure that I am adequately and appropriately serving students. Furthermore, there are not many professionals who receive an entirely different client base every four months for whom they must overhaul their entire management system (syllabus) to accommodate. For those reasons, I believe that teachers become masters of their craft, and through that advancement comes a command over teaching, but it never gets easier.

First Class Meeting

At our first class meeting, my goal was to get a feel for everyone's level of public history knowledge and what area of the field they were hoping to enter after graduation. It is important to know where students come from and where they believe they are going in order to engage with them. In this seminar-style course, each student was responsible for a different week's readings, as well as leading the discussion. All the students appeared to know the protocol for traditional seminar instruction. After discussing the academic side of the syllabus, I shifted our focus to the collaborative project connected to the course. This semester I was fortunate to partner with a local historic site in Greensboro, North Carolina, which was searching for guidance on interpreting the site and better engaging with the diverse population of Greensboro. That site was the Historic Magnolia House (HMH). The HMH was a prominent hotel featured in *The Negro Motorist Green Book* that played a vital role in the Greensboro civil rights movement. Students would be building an exhibit highlighting the site's history, its marginalized beginnings, and its role as an African American safe haven in the city of Greensboro. Students immediately perked up after hearing about their project, as if they were now being released from the purgatory that is traditional seminar-style discussion into a more elevated practical application.

Interestingly enough, my two doctoral students in the course were especially excited, as the doctoral program at the University of North Carolina at Greensboro has a traditional degree in American history. This course would provide those two students, along with their colleagues, a chance to work with a partner not associated with the university. After assigning students their readings and doing some syllabus housekeeping, I ended class early in order for students to secure the readings and begin diving into the literature. But before ending class, I gave one overarching instruction for the semester: to find within every reading the people(s) or central public discussion *left out* of the research. With that idea in mind, I wanted them to theorize why these people(s) or ideas were left out, and how, if applicable, these readings could have been more inclusive. I then quickly scanned the room looking for glossy eyes or smirks of eager students ready to dissect each reading to find the missing narratives. It was immediately clear that this class was torn in their ability or willingness to engage with inclusivity: these topics made some visibly uncomfortable.

Second Class Meeting

I designed the second class meeting to give students, many of whom were from varying schools across the country, an example of what I expected during their presentations and class discussion. I accomplished this by leading a class discussion on Freeman J. Tilden's *Interpreting Our Heritage*. I am a firm believer in modeling the behavior or tenor of any occasion, so I delivered to students a PowerPoint presentation and prepared questions to lead an in-depth discussion of the book. In *Interpreting Our Heritage*, Tilden proposes the "six principles of interpretation," and I began with prompting the students to create a seventh and outline how this would help the field at large.[1] This assignment accomplished two goals. It allowed students to envision how they could personally facilitate the advancement of the field, and it unveiled how students would incorporate the aspects of inclusivity I spoke about on the first day of class.

To my surprise, one student jumped at the chance to critique the book for completely ignoring African Americans within the context of state parks and historic sites. Their seventh principle was to promote culturally responsive pedagogy, which to them meant identifying and nurturing cultural strengths to highlight overshadowed historical advancements of groups of color. Hearing their seventh principle was encouraging because it crystallized that this crop of graduate students was capable of recognizing the interwoven fabric of systemic oppression through suppressing people of color within the realm of public history. Yet I also realized from the class discussion that ensued that the students were split on their views of culturally responsive pedagogy as either absolute or nonexistent in the field. This meant that my semester would include an uphill battle to show some students why inclusivity affects all, while also highlighting the decent job that nominal institutions are doing concerning inclusivity instead of highlighting their institutional errors, preventing students from throwing out the baby with the bathwater. Discussions of inclusivity can, at times, be a slippery slope. While I believe that students must be able to discern inequity in interpretation, perhaps I was unsuccessful if those same students could not appreciate the efforts struggling museums or historic sites take while striving to build more inclusive narratives.

Third Class Meeting

By the third class meeting, my students were entrenched in the readings while searching for instances of exclusion and opportunities for further development of healthy practices of diversity. To my astonishment, it did not take long. The week's reading, *Creating Colonial Williamsburg* by Anders Greenspan, presented a depiction of the more covert example of exclusionary practices.[2] Many of the students, both in their reviews and during class discussion, scrutinized the author's assessment of "historical accuracy." One student wrote, "I take issue with Greenspan's equivalence between historical accuracy and truth in representation and interpretation and 'indoctrination.' The two are not the same, and some might argue that Colonial Williamsburg's Americanist interpretation and mission of its first forty or so years was closer to indoctrination than current programs." I was literally in shock! As a practicing public historian, it's hard not to hold Colonial Williamsburg in high esteem as one of the forefathers of creating a historical experience. Yet for that student, Colonial Williamsburg's faint attempt to attract visitors fell on deaf ears because of the lack of truth and transparency within its interpretation. One of the underlying lessons from this reading and that particular week was how hard organizations work and struggle to remain relevant in society while promoting a story that encompasses a growing civic body.

While stressing to students how critical it is to put historical accuracy first and then create a narrative supported by the most wide-reaching comprehensive analysis of the sources available, I could tell that for some, the subtle yet restrictive narrative that Williamsburg pushes somehow outweighed the righteousness of truth telling. As scholars have noted, Colonial Williamsburg had an African/African American population upwards of 40 percent during the colonial era.[3] Yet today, Williamsburg produces a narrative highlighting less than 10 percent. As students further examined in Greenspan's argument, over the years Colonial Williamsburg has made attempts to remain relevant as the social and political climate in the United States shifted. Within those attempts came expansion of educational programs and the growth of the historic area itself to include infrastructure required to support a growing tourist population. Among every cohort of students, there are usually one or two pessimists. Luckily, when uncovering fault and error in how we approach providing balanced and comprehensive histories, pessimists often find error more quickly than others. Such was the case during our discussion.

Class Exhibit

After concluding our third discussion, it was time to delve into the student's course exhibit. The HMH had been left in decay for much of the 1990s, and after a battle among the former and current owners, longtime Greensboro resident Samuel Pass purchased the property in hopes of returning it to its former splendor. Mr. Pass's daughter, Natalie Pass-Miller, became the interim director of the site and one of our community liaisons for the exhibit. I split students into two groups. One was responsible for the project's mission, and the other for the project's vision. Both groups brainstormed in their breakout sessions about the critical points necessary to create mission and vision statements. The group responsible for the mission statement wanted to focus on illuminating the untold stories of the site while enticing the community to engage with this rich history. The group drafting the vision statement foresaw this exhibit as the beginning of a longer conversation between the community and a historical treasure through which the community could invest in long-term civic and cultural engagement. One goal in these breakout sessions was for students to grasp how the exhibit would both enhance the community's understanding of the significance of the Magnolia House and push students to find ways of fostering ideas of shared authority, becoming active participants with community history. I incorporated wall-size sticky pads for students to collectively share ideas.

This project was as much a new endeavor for me as it was for the students. As a new faculty member in a new city, I understood that community engagement is important for securing lasting partnerships. Coupled with that was the reality that the HMH, like much of East Greensboro where it resides, has been historically left on the margins of historical upkeep. This created an interesting pairing for the students. Unlike other classes, we were going to ensure that this exhibit not only created lasting interest in the site but would become a beacon of education for the importance and practice of cultural responsiveness. Throughout the semester, various breakout sessions created opportunities to correlate the readings and discussions with our exhibit.

Fourth Class Meeting

We began our fourth class discussing the many dimensions of memory and excerpts from W. Fitzhugh Brundage's book *Where These Memories Grow*.

The discussion quickly swirled into conversations of Confederate monuments and lasting imprints on cultural landscapes. A typically quiet student, who displayed her fiery position on race and memory in reflection essays, stated that it is important to recognize who is left out of the conversation of Confederate monuments in the South. She believed that it was possible to concurrently have a genuine and difficult conversation about the Confederacy, slavery, and their interlocking ties to white supremacy without coddling those who subscribed to the "lost cause" of the Civil War. I thought it was a monumental assertion in class dialogue, and I anticipated a lengthy debate. Yet scanning the room, I saw a few head nods and attentive stares. I tried to prolong the conversation so that others might join in; however, bombarded with the feeling that many of the students did not feel as if they had a pass to speak on such issues, I decided to change course. I shifted the conversation to discuss a trending phrase, "white privilege," reminding students that privilege is not a two-way street and that silence has become an effective tool against true change. Fundamentally, it is obvious that all people have privilege depending on the situation. However, white privilege refers to the often-proscribed societal advantage that directly benefits only people who identify as white.

The work that we as historians, especially public historians, should be doing is dispelling myths perpetuated since Reconstruction and the beginning of memorial societies in order to begin implementing culturally responsive pedagogy. There is no better place to start than in the museum or historic site. So I asked the class how—through interpretation, through community engagement, or through annual giving to museums that tell inclusive narratives? Silence. I realized then that the politically correct tenor of the current student knows which words to say and what conversations to engage in on a superficial level, but ask them to draw the map and then chart the course to inclusivity, and they are lost.

Essentially, collective memory fails when it does not truly embody collective narratives and thus leads to conflict by excluding the stories and perspectives of many within the society. For instance, the MHM, while operating as the Magnolia Hotel and a site in *The Negro Motorist Green Book*, serviced hundreds of patrons both famous and ordinary. Daily operation took a dedicated staff of cooks, waiters, bellhops, and family members. Now, if we told the story of the house but left out the story of the logistical support, would we be telling an inclusive story or a celebratory narrative of the highlights of the hotel? Likewise, through ordinary stories or difficult narratives, we unravel the real story—and while it is not always beautiful, it is truthful and therefore more engaging for an American audience thirsting for a bottom-up narrative.

That day's lecture was significant in that it conveyed how healthy yet uncomfortable dialogues push historic sites and museums to change. Some of my students had direct experience working in museums and historic sites. One student remarked that complexities caused by museums' and historic sites' inability to communicate, or rather their reluctance to do so, create division. To combat historically oppressive legacies, we must engage in difficult yet truthful conversations at historic sites and museums to eradicate historically propagated whitewashed narratives of history that often silence perspectives of color. With this understanding, whenever possible I push my students to clarify their word choice and, in so doing, articulate their perspective of tough dialogue. I asked this student what the word *complexity* meant to her, to which she replied, "Difficult histories." I then replied, "Meaning?" and we finally reached our target when she yelled out, "Stories of people of color, systemic racism, gender bias, issues like that, professor!" Her flowing words poured out of her like running water. Public historians must show how heritage totems came to be collective memories contributing to regional identities. Examples are prevalent on the American landscape. Of course Confederate monuments, but also other cultural and social landmarks, historic sites, and even objects have the ability to impute collective memory. I let her words sink in with the class and then I replied, "Thank you." These students have to acknowledge issues and remove analogies or sympathetic phrasing. Many of these students were awaiting license to begin tearing down injustice, as if they believed either their current rank of education or their lack of experience gave them a less meaningful perception or made them ill-prepared to speak against the removal of oppressive and offensive histories.

After this class, I spent a considerable amount of time in my car reflecting on the day's discourse. Like many, I'm sure, I wondered if there was a firmer form of pedagogy. I thought perhaps diversity and inclusivity training, but quickly reaffirmed that for graduate students in our current society, uncomfortable dialogue and consistent gentle nudging were the best solution, as many of our students were clearly at different levels of engagement, acceptance, and action regarding Confederate monuments or historical sites that removed any mention of people of color. But I also found great promise in the class exhibit. It appeared that while students were not always able to directly voice their thoughts, when breaking out and working on the class exhibit, I frequently overheard them referring to readings and proclaiming how their exhibit would not make those same careless mistakes.

Fifth Class Meeting

Since the class was reading Michel-Rolph Trouillot's *Silencing the Past*, I entered class determined to plant roots surrounding best practices and inclusive pedagogy. Since the early 1990s, museum professionals and public historians alike have assessed the lack of equity among museums and the communities they serve. The American Alliance of Museums, for example, published reports urging museums and historic sites to "reevaluate their service to communities.[4] Essentially the argument was that equity was a reciprocal action that required direct facilitation from museums in order to gain the trust of visitors and ensure their return. While this premise is perhaps true, I wanted to instill in my students the fundamental principle that equity was more an issue of ownership than a conversation of excuses from museum professionals. To me, this meant that museums needed to reinforce their role in society, and after showing this vested interest, only then could a genuine conversation occur concerning the number of visitors or their experience at the museum or historic site.

We have arrived socially and culturally to a time when museums must prove their authenticity concerning inclusivity and equity. I posed a question to the students about how Trouillot's work touched this subject from a historical interpretation perspective. One of my doctoral students, who spent a considerable amount of time teaching gender politics, offered an interesting viewpoint. She first mentioned how much she really appreciated the readings and then delved into how she viewed the correlation among her previous studies, my comments, and the week's readings. She then asserted that although she approached equity primarily through the lens of women's and gender studies scholars such as Michel Foucault and Judith Butler, she appreciated Trouillot's use of historical evidence to show how power dynamics change over time, affecting our collective understanding of history. She then pronounced that she believed that public historians must be diligent in rectifying these confined narratives, which often favor Western ideologies. Her word choice was spot-on, and I then unpacked the term *rectify*.

I urged the class to consider the reality that to be responsive to changing communities, the museum field must focus on what it means for institutions to serve ever-changing communities led by the values of cultural responsiveness, cultural sensitivity, and cultural fluency. It was fascinating to see the students processing the reality that future employment could hinge on their ability to not only relate to other cultures but appreciate and cater directly to their needs in order to cultivate sustainability. Nearly halfway through the semester, we began to wrap our heads around the realities of the challenges and issues within museums and historic sites with regard to interpretation. Now the true work began as I carved out ideas of how to create change. This was a teachable moment for the class, because for much of society until recently, equity, equality, and change have been theoretical conversations. Yet in light of numerous recent events, including social and politically motivated upheaval directly affecting people of color, museums and historic sites are taking action. But alas, the questions of when and how remain. Museum professionals have a duty to remain equipped and willing to engage in both planned and unplanned inclusive conversations. The most positive way to cultivate such a conversation would be to maintain an antibias mindset. These kinds of conversations are central to the construction of historical thought taking place inside museums and will affect how museum professionals view equity and access across communities.

Young twenty-first-century professionals, newly minted from the academy, are not waiting for visitors to help guide them in interpersonal conversations. In essence, adults need to become comfortable being uncomfortable, a theory that I unpacked for my students. I informed them of Peggy McIntosh, a scholar of race theory and white privilege. McIntosh, who identifies as a white woman, argues that fear of being labeled a racist and fear of losing self-esteem, rooted in a deep anxiety of how the world envisions their actions, plagues white individuals. From this moment, the class and I began our journey toward teasing out direct action and, in essence, how professionals can eradicate those fears, biases, and prejudices to foster better understanding and present a stronger historical narrative. The class concluded that direct action meant meeting community members "where they are." In order to do so, the class began envisioning creating events to unearth culturally relevant history.

Sixth Class Meeting

Public historians share the blame in silencing narratives. Conversations of authority and power dynamics in the field often allude to this conclusion. Yet I was pushing the class toward a solution—or at least pragmatic implementation of strategies to enhance awareness of such issues. Students were responsible for weekly reviews and critiques of the readings. Within a history program, the museum studies track offers a vehicle for the students to empty their feelings and ideals about the readings, our discussions, and their place in the context of it all. While many of the reviews are just that, reviews of the literature, I received a few during the course that connected the readings to our class discussion and project, and contextualized race, place, and space with regard to inclusivity. My favorite example came from an astute student who wrote, "As public historians, it is our responsibility not only to acknowledge and interpret previously silenced history, but to address why and how histories are silenced. At no stage of development is history neutral. It is an active process of narrative inclusion and omission. Actors with power are in play every step of the way, be they the historical actors themselves, the archivists, or the historians themselves."

Reading the student's words was affirmation for me that the readings had sunk in and that the student was able not only to correlate the issues to our class discussions but to consider how to organize around ensuring that those issues will not reappear in future work. Steering young professionals toward understanding is the goal of most student outcomes. Reading this student's review and perspective amplified my goal of the course, which was to engage with students in discourse centered on providing and ensuring equity at historic sites and museums.

The reading for the week was *Decolonizing Museums* by Amy Lonetree. The message I wanted students to reflect on is that colonization is ongoing, and therefore public historians must be attentive to their perceived authority over another group's history. Although Lonetree refers to Indigenous groups, public historians focusing on any groups of color should foster authentic dialogue with the community they seek to serve. This dialogue will take different forms. One potential form of dialogue that gives the community direct authority over its material history is community archive programs. This is a practice in which the community is asked to bring its material history, whether photographs, documents, or keepsakes, and allow the museum to retain copies or images to aid in comprehensive storytelling.

Following class discussion in an HMH breakout session, I brought in a representative from the university library to discuss the inner workings of collecting archival material from community members. His message crystallized the understanding that this information, this history, this materiality, in some cases belonged to the community. And it is our job to serve. His appearance in class energized students, because soon they would be engaging with community partners and members. Watching the students engage with the guest speaker truly educated me on just how impactful it is for students to engage with the public and not solely rely on theoretical ideas or logistical planning and course readings. Similarly, these experiences reinforce just how difficult and fragile molding practitioners, not pure academics, can be. When the representative from the library left, I informed the class that we would host community archives day at the HMH. I then split the students into groups and released them to begin planning. Group work, at times, is more than a collaborative exercise; it is an excellent illustration of student bias or lack of shared authority over historical projects. At times, group work gets complicated by the difference in students' prior experience and educational prowess. Those varying levels, coupled with being forced to merge those different ideas and points of understanding to create one project, can cause frustration. Before students executed the community archives day, I planned for a week's discussion on the visitor experience.

Seventh Class Meeting

In many ways, the discussion on reimagining new expectations of historic sites and museums and their visitor experiences proved most fruitful in terms of student interaction; all students, including myself, have at some point been a visitor to a historic site. The experience provides students with direct, tangible evidence of how to attract visitors to the site, involve them in the creation of historical interpretation, and retain visitor interest in returning to the site. To support such a layered conversation, students read Frank Vagnone and Deborah Ryan's *Anarchist's Guide to Historic House Museums*, Nina Simon's *The Participatory Museum*, and John Falk's *Identity and the Museum Visitor Experience*.

Students could hardly wait to share their reflections on the *Anarchist's Guide* because in so many ways the work resonated with the need to undo the stifling interpretation of traditional museums and historic sites to engage with an ever-changing, diverse selection of visitors. I was astonished that where before I needed to prompt students with questions concerning how we overlay aspects of diversity or inclusivity, students now wasted no time finding the correlation in the readings. One student remarked how refreshing it was to see authors clearly and provocatively call for a complete overhaul of interpretation. The student cited a poignant reference from the *Anarchist's Guide* that argued for engaging guests in a changing dialogue, thus fostering opportunities for both the site and the visitor to cultivate historical interpretation together. The best examples of this are the anarchist tags, which allow visitors to curate their ideal experience and force museum professionals to adapt to their community. Historically, as Vagnone and Ryan noted, we tend to convey history as something that happened to someone else, thus stripping the very important aspect of association through lived experience.

One of the students of color brilliantly responded to the book, noting that this piece of scholarship will be most beneficial to her in her future career as a public historian. She further contended that the book was impactful because it supported her long-standing supposition that there is no need to lie or produce enfeebled or inaccurate interpretation when there exists plenty of ambiguity in history. Moreover, the connection among that ambiguity often leads to the very root of our frustration: a lack of incorporation of inclusive and diverse narratives.

Hearing her words, I felt as though if the semester ended at that moment, I'd have succeeded because at least one student grasped the reality and need for change in the area of interpretation. In hindsight, I wonder if it is even possible to discuss these topics of the field in light of current social movements without seriously focusing on current scholarship that analyzes cultural interactions. Those interactions must move beyond diversity training and incorporate a host of interdisciplinary literature to foster deeper conversations and, more importantly, begin strategic planning to implement change—for example, readings such as Mary-Frances Winters's *Inclusive Conversations*, in which Winters provides practical applications to engage in inclusive conversations. In essence, this work invites conversation rather than attacking viewpoints.

Even after shifting focus to Nina Simon's *The Participatory Museum*, our conversations continued to swarm around how to create more inviting space for visitors. I appreciated the level of attentiveness that both of the doctoral students displayed in the class. For both, public history in practice was a new dimension to their scholarship. Nonetheless, I suspect they were attracted to aspects of the visitor experience because of its direct correlation to the successes or failures, in theory, of the interpretive exhibits created and facilitated by curators. While discussing *The Participatory Museum*, one of the doctoral students emphatically argued that to create an active and effective participatory museum, collaboration among public historians and the museum's visitors and community is crucial. This meant that the authority and privilege typically given to the museum's curators must be blurred and shared with the site's visitors and community.

Simon believes that public historians must promote this shift in privilege by actively engaging with the community both in person and online. This means building trust with the community by holding more outreach activities, encouraging visitors to vocalize their criticisms, and conducting more oral histories.[5] In her seventh and eighth chapters, Simon laid out a number of ways to construct co-created exhibits. I told students to pay particular attention to her suggestion about designing a challenge to begin the collaboration. This same doctoral student then said that she believed by blurring the structured hierarchies dividing curators from a museum's community and designing a challenge to spark the collaboration, museums can successfully develop co-created narratives and exhibits. Her command of the reading and passion for understanding pressed a firm notion in my mind that she was destined to teach. Interestingly enough, this particular discussion affirmed for me the understanding that learning is reciprocal. I could see her colleagues agreeing not only with her words but, more importantly, with her passion for connecting historical entities with the visitors they serve.

Putting Plans to Action

The students planned and executed the community archives day with nearly flawless precision. It was fascinating to watch students engage with community members by capturing oral histories and images that frame the HMH's importance to the city of Greensboro. They performed well under pressure, as the site was also hosting a public event, which gave the students a strong pool of potential people to engage. But I was most satisfied with the students' acute appreciation of the full scope of the exhibit, which they later designed, and its potential impact on the city of Greensboro. During classroom discussion, the students decided that they wanted to have the community archives day in multiple locations concurrently. Their goal was not to ostracize anyone unable to travel to that part of the city, while also casting a larger net in hopes of more opportunities for engagement with the larger community. One group of students set up shop at the Magnolia House, while another group set up at a local library not far from the Magnolia House.

After the community archives day, we dedicated our next few classes to debriefing and preparing for the creation of the exhibition script. I decided to split the class into small groups to allow everyone an opportunity to create a portion of the exhibit. The HMH is a rich African American story, but a large portion of our semester discussion fit squarely into the site's narrative and, more importantly, how we share that narrative. Unlike other sites in Greensboro, the HMH had not succeeded in preserving its rich history, and there was little documentation in terms of photography. The lack of organization made research and framing the big picture difficult. But the readings prepared the students to help the HMH control its narrative through a firm belief in affirming the HMH's authority over its own history.

In order to properly execute framing the site, the class created impactful and inclusive mission and vision statements. Students wanted to connect with people and expand on the vast perspectives local residents held about the site, while also encouraging dialogue around the site's cultural and historical legacy to the community. Initiating such a mission statement meant an integration of inclusion of all voices, viewpoints, and members of the city and state. This was significant because my concise tutelage on mission and vision statements conveyed to students the importance of words and that meanings evolve. Students took this information and crafted several versions of mission and vision statements, reserving the right to critique either if the project changed. Now, beyond the terminology, some had a difficult time putting theory to practice. I attempted to reaffirm that each opinion indicated investment and therefore ownership over the project. However, I contend that watching the students come together and respectfully discuss how to manage including various perspectives without neglecting or belittling any one viewpoint was a tremendous accomplishment, supporting my belief that teaching public history centered on community-engaged work from the standpoint of inclusivity and equity shapes everyday habits and promotes awareness. Prior to this semester, I was hesitant to proclaim that historic interpretation charts a course for transforming discourse on inclusivity. This course has shown me, however, that the future of teaching inclusivity through museum and historic site interpretation provides ample opportunities to upbuild students and prepare them to shape their respective future institutions.

Reflective Practice

At the onset of this semester, I was enthusiastic about leading a course that merged responsive practice with scholarly readings in planning for and executing a class-led exhibit. Truthfully, I was unaware of exactly where that journey would lead us. I believe that what students got most from this course was a keen awareness of issues of authority and culturally responsive pedagogy, as well as an awareness of white privilege and tearing down barriers within museums, which allows for professionals to begin dismantling colonized spaces toward a more inclusive narrative. Until now, I never put such a high value on simple "awareness." The reality is that as an educator and, specifically, a public historian, I can only instill values and best practices in the field. Those students must be the torch bearers of those principles and values throughout their professional careers. It is impossible to have a thought-provoking Pollyannaish conversation about history and expect to create change. But I am confident that those students, some of which are familiar with inclusivity and equity, can now have a deeper conversation within the confines of the field. Their ability to cultivate deeper conversation is pivotal, as the readings and our discussions put forth numerous examples of how equity, equality, and white privilege often act as a weight holding a vessel seeking to soar.

The shortcomings, and there were surely many, illuminate for me a need to find avenues to better explore the interdisciplinary nature of a course such as this. But it is worth noting that this exhibit continued through the following semester. Ultimately, in the true spirit of reflective practice, I probably learned more about how to target student learning and relevant course material than perhaps some students learned from the course.

Overall, this course had a tremendous impact on the students' engagement from a few areas. From the standpoint of class discussion and group interaction, students noted in their course evaluations that they saw class discussions as a great opportunity to learn about the experiences of their peers not just in the context of museums and historic sites but as they relate to aspects of inclusivity. It was energizing to know that students felt supported and understood the importance of their role in the field as budding public historians. A student noted in an evaluation that my persistent confidence in their abilities to think critically and engage in difficult conversations strengthened their self-confidence as they prepared to enter the job market. In some cases, I simply thought I was educating my students on the course materials and the changing landscape of the field. I was informed through their evaluations of the impact these teachings had on crafting their character. At the onset of this course I pondered if teaching inclusivity to students was possible. Interestingly enough, I found my answer to that question through my students' reflections. This semester taught me that public history is a perfect space in which to engage in both theoretical and practical applications of knowledge and culture. This is the perfect marriage of my skills and passion because ultimately, public history is my vocation and my avocation.

Notes

1. Tilden, *Interpreting Our Heritage*, 10.
2. Greenspan, *Creating Colonial Williamsburg*.
3. Trifone, "Half the History."
4. Hirzy, *Excellence and Equity*.
5. Simon, *The Participatory Museum*.

5 Digital Restorative Justice in the Public History Classroom
Data Literacy and Archival Literacy in Mapping Violence

JIM McGRATH

This chapter reflects on Mapping Violence, a spring 2020 ethnic studies undergraduate course at Brown University that I co-taught with Monica Muñoz Martinez and teaching assistant Edwin Rodriguez. While at Brown, I taught several digital public humanities courses during a five-year stint as a postdoctoral research associate at the John Nicholas Brown Center for Public Humanities and Cultural Heritage. Reflections on any of these courses may have proven generative for instructors looking to learn more about the work of public history in the classroom, but Mapping Violence seems like a particularly compelling case study for several reasons. First, it is a course designed for undergraduates, an opportunity to see how the value of our specific work and the more general value of our methodologies and outputs resonated beyond the purview of practitioners, peers, and graduate students already invested in and committed to the work of public history. Second, the public history work in Mapping Violence is active, is ongoing, and already extends beyond the classroom. So when we discuss project stakeholders, collaborators, and audiences with our students, we are referring to real people who are seeing and making use of the work students complete as part of course assignments. And finally, the mission at the core of Mapping Violence is one that likely resonates with contemporary educators in the humanities: How do we teach and reckon with long histories of state-sanctioned racial violence in the United States with students and with publics beyond the classroom?

The Mapping Violence course is centered on a digital public humanities initiative of the same name. Begun by Martinez in 2014, it "recovers lost and obscured cases of racial violence in Texas from 1900 to 1930, a period of now largely forgotten bloodshed."[1] Key components of this recovery effort involved archival research to learn more about documented incidents as well as violence that was obscured, explained away, or intentionally left out of administrative records (death certificates and police reports, among others) and news coverage; the creation of a database of incidents from that research; and the development of forms of data visualization and digital curation to make these histories visible and compelling to audiences. While Martinez shared and contextualized some of these historical narratives in a 2018 scholarly monograph, *The Injustice Never Leaves You: Anti-Mexican Violence in Texas*, she and her collaborators view a public-facing website about this subject matter as a more widely accessible and iterative space to document and discuss the severity of this period in United States history.

I joined Mapping Violence in the fall of 2015, helping Martinez with the project's development and management. Specifically, I quickly became involved in the establishment of its team workflows and with its approaches to data creation, visualization, and digital curation. Data literacy and archival literacy have been important components of this work—for Martinez (this project is her first large-scale digital initiative), for myself (this project is the first time I have contributed to a digital restorative justice initiative), for our undergraduate and graduate student collaborators (many of whom are new to digital scholarship, archival research, and public history), and for the project's imagined audiences, which include historians invested in data storytelling; descendants of the victims of racial violence; and the growing number of regional, national, and international communities interested in recovering these kinds of stories as part of the larger narrative of United States history.

Over the course of the project's life span, we have primarily focused on the creation of a database documenting incidents of racial violence. These efforts have relied on primary source records in physical and digital archives, secondary readings that contextualize and interrogate primary source documents that often provide misinformation or incomplete records, and field work by Martinez and other colleagues in Texas to gather oral histories, among other resources. Evaluating and synthesizing this information has required significant time and labor. Even with thorough assessments, there are still lingering questions and missing details in historical records. Given our project's commitments to creating public-facing narratives and resources, we want our information to be accurate, properly contextualized, and legible to nonacademic audiences. As we emphasized the importance of these project elements to students in courses like Mapping Violence, we tried to show them that good public history work is not defined by the speed or the ease with which content is published and widely disseminated but by care and thoughtful consideration of subject matter and its impact on our storytelling choices.

We believe that a data-oriented approach will help the project and its audiences document the scope and severity of these acts of violence and enable us to interrogate trends and patterns in this activity. For example, we can track Texas Rangers who were relocated after incidents of violence, identify the role that judges and law enforcement agents played in implicitly or explicitly condoning acts of terrorism, and recognize patterns in media coverage that reveal tolerance if not complicity in the creation of cycles of racial violence. But it can be particularly challenging to take a data-oriented approach when encountering the specific dimensions of historical uncertainty and competing narratives surrounding these particular incidents. For example, factual discrepancies across newspapers cannot always be resolved, and legal documents may be influenced by desires to shift blame away from the Rangers or white mob violence. So we have taken our time developing and refining these approaches before sharing our database and our efforts to curate and contextualize that data more publicly. And we aspire to be transparent about the decisions informing our particular approaches to data and source materials so that contemporary and future audiences understand the motivations and methodologies informing our public history work. These are pedagogical investments shaping how Mapping Violence collaborators introduce the project within and beyond the classroom.

Working with students on records of trauma in the classroom is difficult. It is vital that historians and their students reckon with what Martinez calls "a past that bleeds into the present, a suppression that continues to shape our future."[2] Similarly, we must reflect on how these pasts and our relationships to them influence our pedagogical approaches in the present. Humanities instructors who work with data and archives in any context should think carefully about how their readings, lessons, and assignments acknowledge the colonial and violent legacies of data collection and the creation of archives. These histories bleed into contemporary forms of cultural labor and knowledge production via the materials we use in our classes as well as the classrooms themselves and institutions. I will describe some of the ways we acknowledged the implications of taking up digital restorative justice work at Brown University in hopes that it encourages fellow instructors interested in similar approaches.

I began writing this chapter in the fall of 2020. In recent years in the United States, Americans have seen countless images of state-sanctioned racial violence, including the creation of institutional records and responses designed to distort what we're witnessing, victim gaslighting, the silencing of dissent, and the emergence of counternarratives documenting the realities of suppression and disenfranchisement. In response, many instructors in higher education have been developing syllabi, reading lists, lesson plans, and projects that engage with historical records of racial violence, or seeking out data sets of social media and other born-digital materials that have been disseminating the scenes unfolding in our streets. Instructors new to this work should seek out peers, colleagues, and resources created by practitioners who have already been working with similar data and archival materials in classroom settings or in other pedagogical contexts. I hope that my own reflections prove useful in this regard when thinking about approaches to data literacy, archival literacy, and digital restorative justice.

Preparing for the Course: Hybrid Practitioners in the Public History Classroom

In a 2019 *American Quarterly* essay on Mapping Violence, Martinez notes that Tara McPherson's description of the "hybrid practitioner" strongly influences her approach to teaching and collaborating with students on the project, given her shared belief with McPherson in the value of "artist-theorists, programming humanists, activist-scholars; theoretical archivists, critical race coders."[3] In working with the students enrolled in the Mapping Violence course, we thought carefully about the pedagogical methods that make the development of hybrid practitioners possible: describing models of digital restorative justice; developing course modules that invite students to think critically about the uses of data and archival materials; and encouraging collaborative, iterative, and self-reflective approaches to research and data creation. As public history work increasingly involves digital tools and publication platforms in our contemporary moment, we believe that the hybrid practitioner model has great potential for the field at large.

The dream of the hybrid practitioner model is that it cultivates individuals who are well-versed in uses of technology and increasingly aware of the cultural and ethical implications of specific use cases and perceptions of digital tools, platforms, and contexts. But in the labor conditions of higher education, a desire for self-styled hybrid practitioners can also be quickly distorted by the realities of where and how we collaborate in higher education. For example, we were fortunate to run the Mapping Violence course with two co-teachers and a teaching assistant, conditions that are not common in college courses due to preferences for individual instructors and the availability of funding for such arrangements, among other factors.

Having three course leads with different areas of specialization that intersected with the Mapping Violence project provided students with different perspectives on the relationship between specialized areas of study and public history work. Martinez has extensive knowledge of early twentieth-century histories of Texas and Mexico. She has also done public history work with collaborators in Texas: advocating for historical markers that commemorate victims of state-sanctioned racial violence and acknowledge the state's complicity in these actions, collecting stories from descendants of survivors, and participating in roundtable discussions and public programming (among other areas). I brought expertise in digital public history with an emphasis on the creation and uses of data and the development of digital initiatives for nonacademic audiences. Rodriguez provided insights on visual culture and the challenges of building trust with local communities in public history, perspectives informed by previous work at the Smithsonian's National Museum of American History and an ongoing project on rural El Salvador and migration to the United States.

Public history work is highly collaborative, given the prevalence of projects, programming, pedagogy, and other efforts involving multiple stakeholders. As more teachers are bringing public history methodologies and forms of collaboration into classroom contexts and spaces, we should be reflecting on how courses could be reimagined to productively mirror the working environments we value in project settings elsewhere. Instructors, particularly tenured faculty or department chairs who care about public history, should consider advocating to normalize co-teaching with peers in departments. Bringing in and compensating practitioners from other institutional contexts on or off campus should also be a consideration. For example, students enrolled in a course invested in archival and data literacy contexts for public history would greatly benefit from learning best practices from archivists, librarians, or community partners already working to document and disseminate their histories and lived experiences. Our pedagogical approach centers on hybrid practitioners as well as the value of collaboration. We want to help students grow more comfortable with forms of hybridity that blend humanistic, creative, and technical expertise, in part because they will be better equipped to speak to and work with a wider range of peers in professional contexts in the future, regardless of whether that work is taken up in the field of public history or elsewhere.

There are limitations to the hybrid practitioner model when it is abstracted beyond specific contexts. For example, while I have worked since 2015 on Mapping Violence and am familiar with the historical and archival dimensions of this work, as a white instructor who specializes in contemporary approaches to digital public humanities, I would not feel comfortable developing and teaching a course like Mapping Violence on my own for an ethnic studies concentration without a colleague like Martinez, who specializes in the historical subject matter, despite my status as a hybrid practitioner with relevant project experience. The development of hybrid practitioners should acknowledge tendencies to center, privilege, and support white students and scholars and work to resist and reimagine the systemic inequities prevalent in higher education. These contexts can (and should) be made visible and discussed with students in individual courses, but they also require departments and colleges interested in public history and digital public history to increase commitments to hire, compensate, and institutionally support and value BIPOC faculty and practitioners working in and around public history.

Investments in hybrid practitioners informed our approach to our syllabus, course topics, readings, and major assignments. We created a course reading list that was interdisciplinary and informed by our various experiences and backgrounds: it included essays and excerpts from ethnic studies and digital humanities scholarly sources as well as material from journalist, activist, and public advocacy contexts. We created lesson plans, assignments, and learning environments that asked students to apply these readings to particular research and storytelling contexts. Much of this work was highly collaborative and iterative, as students took on the work of archival research, data creation, and efforts to revise narratives in ways that centered the lives and experiences of victims rather than perpetrators of state-sanctioned violence. We also had to acknowledge the constraints of doing this work in a single semester, and the fact that we were asking students to take up a lot of labor for our course while also balancing other class work and professional and personal obligations. We wanted students to read primary and secondary sources, conduct archival research, create data from records that were both difficult to read (given the violence and the absence of justice often found there) and incomplete, and synthesize and analyze this research in public-facing forms of digital curation.

One might argue that this workload would be a lot to ask of graduate students in a single semester, let alone undergraduates. But the success of our summer 2016 collaboration with undergraduate researchers was a key factor informing our belief that Mapping Violence would work well as an undergraduate course. In her *American Quarterly* essay, Martinez notes how she spent the first few weeks of summer work "leading seminar discussions of key texts in Latinx border studies, histories of violence, and feminist archival research methods."[4] We paired these sessions with "workshops on analyzing primary sources, archival research methods, writing for public audiences, writing concisely, and the ethics of narrating histories of violence."[5] After introducing the theoretical and historical motivations of the project and making the approaches to archival research and data creation transparent, Martinez then assigned particular incidents of racial violence to students. The student team had access to a shared work space where they could compare approaches to research, storytelling, and data creation; Martinez, myself, and graduate student project team members were available resources in and around this space, accessible in person or via email. Students also had meeting sessions in which they could discuss challenges and raise questions, and the project's web application provided a mechanism whereby Martinez could share written feedback as students drafted and submitted content for review. While students had project roles with particular titles like "developer" and "researcher," Martinez notes how the developers "used critical race theory and feminist research methods to inform their programming" and the researchers took up the work of "creating design documents, wireframing, and managing data."[6]

Working on Mapping Violence in these conditions was a rewarding experience for students and for project leads like Martinez and myself. As we developed the Mapping Violence course, we considered how to transform these intensive collaborative research and writing experiences to our pedagogical approaches taken up over a semester block of time. Our cohort of summer 2016 collaborators included computer science undergraduates, whereas our spring 2020 course was limited to American studies and ethnic studies concentrators (due to degree requirements and available semester offerings). Martinez had successfully applied for Brown University internal funding to pay students for their labor in the summer, while students in the spring were enrolled for course credit. The summer project team met for hours daily, whereas students in the spring met once a week for a seminar. It was challenging to think through how a fifteen-week course centered on the project might resonate with and benefit students. And the impact of the global pandemic brought new difficulties as we debated how to proceed with the course in the wake of this traumatic disruption to everyday life.

Developing a Public History Lab Model

As Martinez, Rodriguez, and I refined our syllabus and course trajectories, we thought a lot about how to borrow from what worked particularly well in our 2016 work with undergraduates and what would be challenging to bring into our specific semester contexts. Our spring 2020 Mapping Violence course met once a week on Wednesday afternoons for two-and-a-half-hour class sessions. While we planned to adopt the summer collaboration's strategy of introducing students to the project's core arguments, historical contexts, and methodologies before asking them to take up individual research, we also knew that we would have to work within the constraints of the more glacial semester pace to keep momentum and maintain communication on student progress. And we had to acknowledge that students would be balancing our course obligations with their other classes, whereas our summer undergraduates were solely working on our project in terms of their academic obligations.

So in addition to our assigned weekly meetings, we decided that the Mapping Violence course would make use of a weekly "research lab," at which we would give students additional context and instruction on some of the project's research and data creation workflows. Over the course of the semester, we introduced students to online databases, to the conventions of particular primary sources (newspaper records, birth certificates, death certificates, census records), to the Mapping Violence metadata schema (the principles governing how we created and organized our project's data), and to its approach of composing victim-centered narratives and chronologies of racial violence. Major coursework involved the creation of metadata and narrative for three case study reports: incidents of racial violence identified from previous project work. Students researched and drafted these materials for peer review and instructor feedback.

Unlike science courses, humanities courses at Brown are not traditionally offered with lab components. We had planned to incorporate experiential learning and project-based coursework in Mapping Violence from the outset, but the more that we looked at the potential value of particular course readings and opportunities for discussion, the more we realized that students would have to find time outside our scheduled sessions to take up the work of archival research, data creation, and digital curation. The lab did pose some logistical challenges in terms of student availability outside set semester schedules. For example, we could not formally require students to attend these additional sessions because we were not able to get the course formally assigned as one with lab components, so we had to make resources and context shared in these meetings available to individuals who could not or chose not to attend. But introducing a regularly scheduled lab session, where interested students could take up their work on major course assignments while receiving additional training and feedback from me, Martinez, and Rodriguez, seemed like a way for us to offer further support and feedback.

After discussing and agreeing that a lab model seemed like an important course component, we had to consider how to introduce the project workflow in these sessions over the semester and how to complement and coordinate our weekly course readings and topics accordingly. We decided to introduce the lab sessions in the third week of the semester, in part so we would have time in class to introduce Mapping Violence and in part so we would not overwhelm students at the immediate outset of the class. We also developed some approaches to lab contexts that would distinguish these sessions from our regular class meetings. We wanted to make it clear to students that these were opportunities to take up research and writing while learning from peers, so it was important for us to center this work as opposed to instructor lecturing. Even when we were introducing students to a research database or to approaches to data entry, we tried to keep the more didactic elements of these course contexts brief. And we created documentation that circulated to the class at large so that students who opted out of the lab sessions or were otherwise unable to attend could still access relevant information on their own time.

Balancing class and lab sessions while maintaining course momentum became a major challenge, especially after the arrival of the pandemic led us to cancel lab sessions altogether for the final weeks of the semester. But as I hope to demonstrate in the reflections that follow, the use of both distinct spaces (the class and the lab) was overall a positive experience for both instructors and students, and I will likely revisit the public history lab model in future undergraduate courses. If you have worked on public history projects in academic or nonacademic contexts, you may have a sense of how the available time to actually take up various forms of project work can be consumed by planning and check-in meetings. Undergraduates have busy semester schedules, and they are still in the process of learning time-management skills and best practices themselves. The language of the lab helped us introduce this space as an opportunity to collaborate on the completion of course tasks. Other instructors in public history might gravitate toward other language and models, like taking an open-office-hours approach or writing accountability sessions, depending on the expected coursework. We found the public history lab model generative in decentering instructors and our lecturing tendencies while encouraging and expanding opportunities for collaboration and dialogue among students.

Introducing Mapping Violence and Legacies of State-Sanctioned Racial Violence

The Mapping Violence class met for the first time on Wednesday, January 22, 2020. Brown University students generally spend the first few weeks of the semester "shopping," which means that class rosters generally do not solidify and stabilize for a few weeks as they make their final course decisions. Our roster was a bit more stable than that of other classes due to our prerequisites and to the fact that several graduating seniors needed to complete the course as part of their degree requirements. We also had a waiting list in case students decided to drop the course. Given our course ambitions and our comparable lack of concern with student retention (a challenge that can face new courses that are highly specialized and require students to take up different kinds of work), we were comfortable spending our first class with a detailed overview of the Mapping Violence project, its history, and the ways its work would be taken up and inform the semester.

The course description for Mapping Violence emphasizes its interdisciplinary dimensions and the ways that the class deviated from other course contexts at Brown: "Mapping Violence is a research project that aims to expose interconnected histories of violence, the legacies of colonization, slavery, and genocide that intersect in Texas in the early twentieth century. Although often segregated in academic studies, these histories coalesced geographically and temporally. Students in this course will learn interdisciplinary methods combining ethnic studies, history, public humanities and the digital humanities to rethink the limits of archival research, historical narrative, and methods for presenting findings to public audiences. This research-intensive seminar will allow students to develop historical research skills and to contribute original research to the Mapping Violence project."[7]

We included these reference points here to make it explicit that the class would be pulling from a range of professional and academic contexts. For example, the interdisciplinary leanings of the class were one reason why I was a co-instructor in an ethnic studies classroom, given the project's digital contexts and the course's investments in data literacy and archival literacy. A graduate seminar may have dedicated more time in its initial course meetings to describing and situating our work within the strains of history, ethnic studies, public humanities, and digital humanities, or it may have begun with a critique of the academic forms of knowledge production and departmental siloing that can make collaborative and iterative work feel so out of place in higher-education classrooms. Instead, we wanted to begin by outlining the stakes of the project, its methodologies, its accomplishments, and the way this course was a productive extension of our work in other academic spaces. Transparency is an important component of our pedagogical leanings; we wanted to introduce our course objectives and our pedagogical approaches clearly and directly to students.

Martinez and I have discussed Mapping Violence in a few different contexts, and when introducing the project, we are often making a case for its necessity, its methodologies, its investments in data, its status as a digital public history project, and its ideas about audience. The description of Mapping Violence we provided students on the first day of classes was primarily drawn from a fall 2019 presentation on the project at Radical Cartography Now, a conference hosted by the John Nicholas Brown Center for Public Humanities and Cultural Heritage that focused on "Digital, Artistic, and Social Justice Approaches to Mapping." While Mapping Violence had been in development for several years at Brown, this conference was one of the more visible spaces on campus where we described our ongoing work and its value. The presentation's approach worked well when brought into the context of a class of undergraduates who were mostly unfamiliar with the project.

Martinez frequently emphasizes the Mapping Violence project's investment in "lives, not metadata," a provocation that highlights our concerns about the ways data has often been used to distort, defamiliarize, and even erase the people and lived experiences it documents and represents.[8] Critiques of existing data systems are at the core of Mapping Violence. We are interested in what is present, absent, and distorted in death certificates, census data, court transcripts and testimonies, commission reports, and other state-sanctioned forms of accounting for the government's view of the present and recent past. We are also critical of news media accounts and the ways those accounts can be remediated as data or granted legitimacy through their reception, recirculation, and status as archival records of historical moments. We also want these critiques and concerns to resonate more directly and immediately with academic and nonacademic audiences; thus, Martinez's coinage of "lives, not metadata," is also a reflection of our public history leanings and experiences.

Compared to other digital public history initiatives, Mapping Violence operates at a much slower pace, due in large part to our interests in (and concerns about) what happens when the stories of victims of racial violence are remediated as points of data. Often, the archival materials our project has reviewed contain more information about the agents of violence than their victims. The living were able to state their cases in news coverage and court transcripts, and legal decisions carry an authority in the historical record that can be louder and more forceful than the unjust conditions of trials and investigations. So when discussing Mapping Violence in spaces like the Radical Cartography Now conference and the undergraduate classroom, we want to stress the project's investments in restorative justice and the ways these commitments shape our approaches to the creation and use of data.

One way that we highlight the stakes of restorative justice and the need for public history initiatives (digital and otherwise) to take up this work is by documenting the legacies of state-sanctioned racial violence in our contemporary moment. We also wanted to stress in our course the ways that contemporary violence is part of a longer historical narrative in the United States, justifying the centrality of earlier incidents, and what we can learn about the twenty-first century from researching these earlier actions, their reception, and their legacies. And we wanted to provide students with opportunities to connect the past to our ongoing present.

In our second week of the semester, we were fortunate to have students hear from Michelle García, a journalist, essayist, and documentary filmmaker who has done extensive work on the border between the United States and Mexico. García and Martinez had previously spoken together on a July 2018 episode of *The Brian Lehrer Show* (broadcast on WNYC and streamed online) on the use of cages and the criminalization of migrants (including children), visible in the inhumane carceral policies taken up by the Trump administration and Immigration and Customs Enforcement: "100 years ago any Mexican was assumed to be a bandit or a revolutionary," Martinez observed on the program, connecting this long history to the "culture of impunity" prevalent in contemporary U.S. culture.[9] Two years later, Martinez helped bring García to Brown University to give a lecture titled "Beyond Borders: Life in the Middle Space," in which she discussed "the challenges of reporting from a region while avoiding reinforcing a border gaze" and her efforts to reject and reimagine a perspective informed by a century of policing, fearmongering, racism, and nationalist propaganda.[10] García graciously agreed to come to our class to talk more about her ongoing work, the importance of considering historical contexts, and their continued impact on contemporary debates and policies.

Public history courses often make use of guest lecturers. I find them to be particularly essential to graduate courses, so that students who are new to the field have opportunities to learn how practitioners operate in careers to which they might aspire. We imagined that students would have questions about García's path to work in documentary films, journalism, and public writing. But it was also valuable and important for students to see how theories and histories studied in the classroom had tangible impacts and resonances beyond academic spaces and contexts. García has written for a wide range of audiences in the *Washington Post*, the *New York Times*, the *Baffler*, and many other publications. We specifically asked students to read her three-part series on the border for The *Baffler*, in which she situated images and ideas of the border within "the American Imagination," defined and described acts of "border theater," and analyzed the uses of the border in Beto O'Rourke's campaign for the 2020 Democratic presidential nomination.[11] We wanted students to see models for how the topics and issues raised in our course were connected to contemporary culture and discussed in specific public-facing contexts and to consider how phrases like "border theater" made patterns and trends of behavior more legible and compelling to particular audiences.

Digital Pedagogy and Teaching the Unquantifiable

Data visualizations, infographics, and other forms of data-oriented storytelling have been important components of restorative justice work long before the twenty-first century, and earlier efforts can provide important context and insights on contemporary work. Many of these earlier forms of storytelling resonate with contemporary approaches to public history, given their rhetorical strategies, desired audiences, and social impact. For example, *Thirty Years of Lynching in the United States, 1889–1918* was a pamphlet published by the NAACP in April 1919. The first pages of the publication give readers a sense of the pervasiveness of lynching in the country by mapping these incidents: the country's southern states immediately stand out as the epicenters of the research conducted by the NAACP. The core of the pamphlet is "The Story of One Hundred Lynchings," a chronological account of incidents reported by the press and investigated by the organization designed "to give concreteness and to make vivid the facts of lynching in the United States."[12] The publication's appendix includes visualizations and other forms of analysis, providing alternative and at times more granular perspectives on the violence described in the document's central text.

We discussed *Thirty Years of Lynching in the United States* with students in our third week of the semester as part of a class unit on "Methods for Recovering Histories of Racial Violence," which also covered the work of Ida B. Wells-Barnett in *The Red Record* and the Equal Justice Initiative's 2017 report *Lynching in America: Confronting the Legacy of Racial Terror.* In addition to situating Mapping Violence within longer histories of restorative justice work, it was important for us to introduce project models that made what we felt was effective use of data in efforts to document the pervasiveness of racial violence. Even if these projects did not explicitly describe or situate themselves as public history efforts, these efforts imagined and spoke to particular audiences and ideas of publics.

We discussed the limits of these data-oriented approaches with students as well. For example, while the NAACP's map of the United States visualized the pervasiveness of lynching across the country, its decision to align its data points with states rather than cities or more specific regions raised questions about the presentation of data and the arguments fueled by these visualization choices. The challenges of visualizing incidents over time in this context led to conversations about what is gained and lost by decisions to focus on particular aspects of data at the expense of others. But I would stress that we did not argue that digital restorative justice initiatives are preferable to print-centric or multimodal approaches. These earlier projects and their creators clearly made choices about sharing their findings in multiple forms and anticipating the interests and needs of specific audiences, investments that web-based and interactive visualizations do not always foreground. It is telling, for instance, that the Equal Justice Initiative chose a more traditional print publication model for this particular 2017 publication, despite its uses of more contemporary forms of data visualization in other initiatives. So while we stressed to students that digital contexts will likely be a component of most if not all twenty-first century public history initiatives, we also discussed the value of using a range of media types and formats to meet audiences where they are.

We also used these early projects to introduce students to the research methodologies of restorative justice work: gathering and cross-referencing newspaper reports and legal documents, creating data records that bring individual incidents into dialogue with a developing collection of information, and telling stories with that data. "When I present our cause to a minister, editor, lecturer, or representative of any moral agency," Wells notes in *The Red Record*, "the first demand is for facts and figures."[13] Wells names key members of her audience here and does not think of "the public" in an abstract or idealized way. Wells and her peers in the NAACP also go to great lengths to circulate verified data; for example, *Thirty Years of Lynching* introduces its "authenticated" findings as "given credence by a recognized newspaper or confirmed by a responsible investigator."[14] But its authors acknowledge the limits of this approach and the reality that "more persons have been lynched than those whose names are given" in their accounts.[15]

In "Venus in Two Acts," Saidiya Hartman calls the archive of slavery "a death sentence, a tomb, a display of the violated body," descriptions that also resonate with Mapping Violence's encounters with records documenting victims of state-sanctioned racial violence.[16] "The dream," Hartman notes, "is to liberate them from the obscene descriptions that first introduced them to us." But Hartman also believes that her "own writing is unable to exceed the limits of the sayable dictated by the archive."[17] It was important for us to introduce Hartman's perspectives on "the limits of writing history through the act of narration" in a course that asked students to take up the work of restorative justice.[18] The questions and concerns Hartman raises are also concerns that audiences for public history projects may share, but we also wanted students to know that the concerns raised in "Venus in Two Acts" were also on our mind as we took up project work.

We also shared writing informed by Hartman's work in the context of data-oriented approaches. For example, Jessica Marie Johnson describes ideas of data and "the rise of the independent and objective statistical fact as an explanatory ideal party to the devastating thingification of black women, children, and men."[19] But like Hartman, who finds a "productive tension" in taking up this work while understanding its limits and making them transparent, Johnson asks digital humanities practitioners interested in the potential of data storytelling to "infuse their work with a methodology and praxis that centers the descendants of the enslaved, grapples with the uncomfortable, messy, and unquantifiable, and in doing so, refuses disposability."[20] Some public history projects have been (rightly) criticized for sanitizing troubling events, people, experiences, and moments. And in the

United States, we have seen an uptick in hand-wringing over history that emphasizes racial violence, settler colonialism, and white supremacy (we see these tendencies quite visibly in the reception history of *The 1619 Project*, for example). By introducing the work of Hartman, Johnson, and others to our students, Martinez, Rodriguez, and I want students to reflect on these elements of discomfort in Mapping Violence and other public history initiatives.

These concerns and recommendations resonate with the investments Mapping Violence makes in centering the lives and perspectives of victims of racial violence, their families, and their descendants. The early weeks of the course were at times dominated by the voices of Martinez, Rodriguez, and me as we introduced the Mapping Violence project and situated it within longer histories of restorative justice projects. Hartman's work, which we discussed in the fourth week of class, provided us with an opportunity to take a step back and discuss the stakes of the project and its impact from the perspective of the researcher and her encounters with archival materials. Many of our students were already familiar with "Venus in Two Acts" from other ethnic studies course reading lists, but they noted in discussion board posts that the piece took on new relevance and immediacy in the context of a course asking them to conduct archival research and narrate (through data and digital curation). Hartman and Johnson describe the affective dimensions of archival research and data creation, the impact of encountering traumatic records, the feeling that responses to these descriptions of past atrocities will feel limited in the present. While it was important for us to share exemplary models of data-oriented restorative justice work in the classroom, it was equally essential that we provide students with this context, as well as space to discuss the effects this work has on researchers and scholars.

It was also important for us to review and assess the work that Brown University had taken up to examine its own archival records and the ways the institution benefited from racial violence. We followed our discussion of Hartman's work with a review of *Slavery and Justice*, a 2006 report by the Brown University Steering Committee on Slavery and Justice that described "the University's historical relationship to slavery and the transatlantic slave trade."[21] The report was the product of several years of research, public programming, and collaborative writing, occasioned by and delivered in contexts quite different from the work Hartman had taken up and reflected on. But both texts had archival records of slavery and the legacies of their recorded actions and impact at their center. Read through the lens of Hartman, Brown's report, despite its reputation in some circles as an important reckoning with a violent past, felt insufficient and limiting.

The Brown report made recommendations for direct actions to be taken in pursuit of justice: the public dissemination of its historical findings and the creation of both physical memorials and a center to study legacies of slavery and injustice, among others. But the voices of the victims of slavery were often drowned out by the more extensive records of the Brown family; the remarks of nineteenth-century white college students reflecting on abolition; and the committee's own investments in situating these specific events within larger considerations of crimes against humanity, reparations, and truth commissions. "Let us begin with a clock," the report states, before describing a family artifact once owned by Esek Hopkins, commander of a slave ship named *Sally* owned by Nicholas Brown and three of his brothers. The rhetorical move seems intent on making invisible traces of the university's ties to slavery more apparent, but students found it striking that the report devoted more time and space to the clock and to Hopkins in its opening than to the deaths of over one hundred enslaved Africans on the *Sally*'s 1764 journey.[22]

Slavery and Justice is an important example of highly visible public history work with a clear impact on its immediate audience (the Brown University community and the institution's commitments to justice-oriented actions) and wider publics (communities at other higher education institutions began to seek comparable actions by their administrators and university leadership, with some colleges adopting similar approaches in the wake of the report's publication), but our interest in critiquing this initiative as well as acknowledging its value helped students prepare for the challenges they would take up in their own archival research.

Doing Digital Public History: Archival Research, Data Creation, and Digital Curation

Before our lab sessions began, we assigned students a case study from our project records to begin researching. These case studies documented initial records on incidents of interest to the Mapping Violence project and included citations where team members working before the spring 2020 semester had first come across these names and attendant narratives. One advantage of bringing an established digital public history initiative into the class was that project workflows, research materials, and methodologies had already been established and refined before the semester began.

We frequently reminded students that the kind of archival research, data creation, and digital curation they would be taking up would more often be the kind of work that graduate students (or established scholars interested in archival materials) might focus on. We did not want students to be disillusioned by the challenges of archival research, particularly in the project context in which we asked them to participate. Digital restorative justice initiatives feel necessary in part because official records have been distorted and require interpretation and additional context. We did not shy away from archival silences, contested narratives, and the emotional impact of reviewing records of lives violently disrupted and ended. But we also had our own project experiences to draw on in order to help students reflect on the challenges they would face in their research.

We began our lab sessions with an overview of how to search newspaper databases and secondary sources. Rodriguez gave a brief demonstration of where to access relevant materials, offered insights on revising and refining search terms (with a reminder that searching in these database contexts differed from more familiar interfaces and methods found on Google or social media networks), and provided advice on how to document research notes. This latter component was important because we knew how frustrating some initial searches on these case studies would likely be to students. We wanted to encourage methods of self-reflection and documentation that did not arrive too quickly at certainty. And we wanted students to get in the habit of saving archival records that seemed to have some immediate value, and to save these records in a manner that would make them legible and accessible to them over the semester. We prioritized having them add documents to Google Drive so that they could be easily accessed in cloud storage, encouraged them to save full pages or multiple pages of stories and documents (in lieu of screenshots of only the most pertinent details), and taught them to name files along certain conventions so that they could easily register and retrieve those materials.

Some students would quickly find that an initial account of an incident of violence might be called into question by later newspaper coverage. We wanted to remind students that their initial information on a particular case was not always the most authoritative, and that part of the research process was questioning the veracity of historical records despite general perceptions of their authority and validity. We reminded them of the frequency with which certain newspapers in our own contemporary moment published developing stories, and the ease with which an initial fact stated in a secondary record might be called into question. There are many different approaches instructors have taken on modules and assignments related to media literacy, and I have introduced undergraduates to the long history of "fake news" and primary-source reading strategies in other course contexts. The stakes of the research differed in this course because students were aware of the public-facing motivations. I have seen students grow frustrated by the questions primary sources complicated or failed to precisely answer when asked to generate more traditional course outputs like research papers. But in the context of this public history project, students seemed more motivated to search for new wrinkles and additional context, aware of what archival materials might illuminate and what might be unanswerable.

After discussing secondary sources like academic publications and newspapers that described violent incidents, we introduced students to databases of birth and death certificates. Though some of these archival materials may have a more compelling claim on a particular kind of authority and validity, we reminded students of the cultural and social conditions that generated and informed these records. Given contemporary concerns about a failure to hold agents of state-sanctioned violence accountable and the role that official documentation can play in creating barriers to restorative justice, students did not need much convincing with regard to these important contextual matters. If they found discrepancies between a coroner's death certificate and the circumstances surrounding a victim's fate documented in newspaper accounts, oral histories, or other records, they learned to document these discrepancies rather than dismiss contradictions or competing narratives. While examining birth and death certificates, students became curious about why and how they ended up in some of the databases we directed them to. In addition to helping them track down records and traces of victims, we discussed the motivations and methodologies favored by genealogical initiatives and services like FamilySearch. Further research into the latter revealed its use of prison labor in the creation and revision of genealogical metadata records, a context that we shared with students when coming across it in media coverage.[23]

Academic interest in genealogy and online databases used for genealogy can vary depending on research area and methodology, but wider publics have increasingly grown interested in these resources thanks to products like 23andMe and the PBS program *Finding Your Roots*. Journalists seem to be more proactive and curious about the ways genealogy projects and products are funded and what their motivations might be. We wanted to share this latter context with students as we began investigating genealogical resources further and reflecting on the implications of using FamilySearch as a resource in project research and class workflows, while exploring other databases and recommendations by organizations like Reclaim the Records. Some genealogical products or narratives can make these investigations into the past seem easier or more straightforward, especially if audiences and amateur researchers are met with visualizations of data and results more than primary records and contexts calling their verifiability into question. At times, public history work in the classroom can reveal how historical research is often very labor intensive, time-consuming, or even inconclusive or incomplete.

When students had gathered records, discussed their content with us in lab sessions, and felt as though they had reached a point of exhaustion in the research process, we turned to the work of creating data and drafting narratives that described incidents. In terms of data, we had students focus on the names of involved individuals (when available) and distinguish between victims of violence and aggressors. They recorded information regarding witnesses, judicial figures, and other people in researcher notes, which often materialized in case study narratives. Mapping Violence, as evidenced by its name, is invested in spatial histories, so we asked students to provide data on locations of incidents, geospatial metadata, and justification for their decisions.

This work of documenting spatial dimensions, which may seem relatively easy to obtain in contemporary contexts and accounts, was particularly challenging work, given that maps and names of particular regions had changed over time and that there were often discrepancies about how an incident was initially covered in newspaper accounts. For example, records from larger newspapers or national coverage may obscure, ignore, or provide incorrect information on hyperlocal contexts. Discussing these matters was often a productive kind of defamiliarization of our own present moment. Despite the ubiquity of Google Maps and the apparent ease with which we assign certainty to knowledge of physical space and regions (cross-referenced by internet searches), we discussed the fact that Google's cartographic imaginary was authoritative but not unquestionable, and that knowledge of local regions and places could still be incorrect in our twenty-first-century moment. Because students were encountering varieties of spatial representation in their research and were growing increasingly aware of how maps mediate our relationship to space and change over time, we hoped that these kinds of concerns and critiques about representations of space and place would resonate more immediately in this active learning context.

One of the most challenging dimensions of case study work was the creation of short narratives contextualizing the data. Given the kinds of audiences Mapping Violence is interested in, we knew that we did not want to simply publish a data set or a visualization of spatial data without providing context on the people represented in this data. But it can be hard to adhere to "lives, not metadata," despite the best of intentions, as our students often found. We had students write several drafts of case studies and offered feedback on their narrative strategies, and we also provided models from project work that preceded the course.

For example, we discussed how our commitment to digital restorative justice informed our interest in centering these narrative moments on the victims, an emphasis that would impact how we wrote and arranged sentences to ensure that the victims' names were made the subjects of these narrative components. We talked about how there would likely be more information available on aggressors and their defenders in newspaper coverage and encouraged students to ensure that the lives of victims and their families were given more coverage in their narratives. An additional challenge that students faced was our interest in brevity, given the attention spans of audiences and our desire to have the Mapping Violence interface be the beginning of a conversation on restorative justice rather than a resolution or final destination. Working with students to revise and refine these narratives, offering them encouragement when they hit walls in research, reminding them that we were critiquing their word choices and writing rather than their commitments to restorative justice—this was difficult work at times but very important to us.

Due to the disruption caused by COVID-19 in mid-March, we were unable to run all lab sessions for the semester. One major gap in student learning caused by the pandemic was the missed opportunity to talk with a practicing archivist. We had planned an early April visit to the John Hay Library to meet with Heather Cole, head of special collections instruction. While readers familiar with Brown's resources may be surprised to learn that we had planned a trip to the Hay instead of the John Carter Brown Library, given the latter's sizable collection of the histories of colonization and records of racial violence in the Americas, we valued Cole's pedagogical expertise and deep understanding of archival literacy, evident in previous class visits I had arranged with her (among other contexts). As someone who has worked extensively with archivists and archival collections in both digital and nondigital contexts, I feel it is important to have archivists be part of archival literacy and public history initiatives in order to assert the value of our peers in these campus spaces and to introduce undergraduates to the material and professional realities of archival labor.

I made my first trip to a special collections room as a graduate student, and despite my own standing as an early career academic with a relevant research project, I felt intimidated by the physical space of the archive and by protocols that seemed invisible yet clearly understood by my peers in these reading rooms. Although digitization initiatives have removed some of these associations and barriers to access and use of archival materials, we wanted students to understand that the decisions made in these institutional spaces have bearing and impact on what kinds of materials are collected, preserved, and digitized, and Cole's specific role as head of special collections instruction reflects the Hay's investment in encouraging undergraduate use of archival collections on campus. That being said, arranging class visits to special collections can be a way to acknowledge the barriers that remain with regard to undergraduate perceptions of who archival records are for and whether they have to justify their interest in particular materials. Given that our course often includes first-generation college students, several of whom aspire to postgraduate degrees and academic research, Martinez and I frequently bring classes to these spaces as part of semester instruction.

Final Reflections: Data Literacy and Digital Public History in the Classroom

Brandon Locke has observed that for many humanities students, "data is something they hear about a lot, don't see often, and work with much less often."[24] As humanities instructors increasingly acknowledge the value of data literacy through course readings, discussions, and assignments, Locke and other instructors who have worked extensively with data in the classroom remind us of the need to develop approaches that empower students to think critically about historical and contemporary uses of data. Specifically, Locke argues that "data organization" can be particularly important work for students to take up in these spaces.[25] "Not only is [data organization] where many important disciplinary/content-based decisions are made," he notes, "but it's also where students can gain transferable skills that will help them be more critical of data-centric claims, better understand data surveillance and collection, and be able to effectively use civic data."[26]

Locke acknowledges that pedagogical approaches centered on data organization can be challenging to implement in a semester course context, given the constraints of the semester timeline, the presence of additional course objectives and topics beyond data literacy, and other factors. Rather than asking students to "assemble, organize, research, analyze, and produce a product in one semester," he recommends developing workshop and discussion modules with clear, compartmentalized goals, in addition to using accessible forms of scaffolding to provide additional support.[27]

The value of data creation and organization can be introduced to students in humanities classrooms in a variety of ways and forms, For example, Catherine D'Ignazio and Rahul Bhargarva have described their pedagogical investments in "creative data literacy" when teaching for audiences of "non-technical learners."[28] They argue that "data literacy for these audiences should be taught with creative, social strategies over solo exercises and rote learning" and offer a range of collaborative, project-based, and hands-on approaches that require comparatively minimal technical resources, like pen and paper.[29] I find that approaches common to public history outreach and programming, especially when public historians are motivated by desires for an increase in certain kinds of literacy and knowledge acquisition, are helpful contexts to bring to bear when considering creative data-literacy strategies in the classroom.

Like D'Ignazio, Bhargarva, and others, I have created in-class data literacy exercises for high school and graduate students that require minimal investments in digital technology and emphasize creative and even playful approaches to data and its uses. For example, in Media Literacy in the Age of Fake News and Big Data, a summer 2018 course offered through Brown's Leadership Institute, I spent one class session organizing high school students into small groups and then asked them to draft a data set and illustrate a visualization on a whiteboard. I borrowed the idea of asking in-class groups to use data and visualizations to describe themselves from Nicole Coleman, who used this approach as a kind of icebreaker exercise on the first day of her summer 2016 humanities intensive learning and teaching course, Database Design for Visualization and Analysis. I designed this exercise to get students quickly thinking about the possibilities of data-driven storytelling, providing them with the means to tell that story quickly so we could then think through the implications of taking up this kind of work. After completing this in-class exercise, we looked at examples of similar hand-drawn visualizations and forms of data collection from Giorgia Lupi and Stefanie Posavec's *Dear Data*, in part to demonstrate that practitioners in academic and creative spaces beyond our classroom also value these iterative and hands-on considerations of data.

Our classroom work and ensuing discussions of these playful approaches to collecting data and creating visualizations also led to more somber conversations and perspectives. For example, requiring students to share their work with the class at large led to informal considerations of the ethical dimensions and privacy implications of collecting and sharing data with audiences, concerns that led to a larger discussion of the more personal information extracted for a variety of uses by social media networks and smartphone applications. We discussed the limits of certain forms of data collection and visualization and what personal dimensions of the groups were absent. And we compared the limited scope of these data sets to more polished visualizations, reflecting on the authority readers convey to aesthetic choices and sites of dissemination despite a frequent lack of direct access to the data being represented.

We did not choose to deploy these particular kinds of creative pedagogical approaches in the Mapping Violence classroom, given the course subject matter and the lives represented in the project's database. In other courses, I have highlighted the variety of ways that a single data set can be visualized. For example, I have chosen excerpts from Andy Kriebel and Eva Murray's *#Makeover Monday*, in which the authors "find charts that [they] think do not communicate information as effectively as they could"; publish the data used on the visualization; and encourage professionals, students, and amateurs to improve on the original design and share their results on social media.[30] The pedagogical value of highlighting such initiatives is to demonstrate the range of possibilities in data visualization and to identify design trends, tools, and approaches that resonate with contemporary audiences. But these exercises can also be reminders of the distance that visualizations can place between creators of data storytelling, audiences, and the lives represented by the data.

For me, one of the key distinctions between Mapping Violence and other classroom contexts for data literacy is its concerns with a particular historical moment and geographical region. Most of the courses I taught at Brown have been versions of the survey course familiar to many students and instructors in digital humanities. Course titles like Digital Public Humanities, Digital Storytelling, and Digital Archives and Digital Publics document a primary interest in introducing students to a range of approaches, methodologies, and tools. Departments design and offer these kinds of survey courses to fulfill a number of departmental needs. For example, they often serve as required or core components of certificate programs in digital humanities, or they address an absence of digital pedagogy in other course offerings. Many of these courses survey an array of methodologies, digital tools, and use cases, quickly moving from one topic to another. The concept of "Makeover Monday" could be easily incorporated into such a course, where an instructor might designate one of two sessions for an introduction to data visualizations (likely following a week on data). Courses with these titles may center on more specialized subject matter or topics. For example, I taught a fall 2017 Digital Public Humanities course that spent a substantial amount of time working with the Providence Public Library Special Collections Department on digital contexts for archival records of local history.

I continue to value the digital survey course in certain contexts, but I am increasingly convinced that approaches to data literacy may resonate more with students when they are incorporated in courses like Mapping Violence, where digital methodologies are part of a larger set of project-based and collaborative approaches informed by (or, as in our case, extending directly from) public history work. This work is slow, deliberate, and often frustrating, especially when compared to the speed with which sites of digital pedagogy generally deploy visualization tools. But the time we invest in this process is also spent discussing the implications of Mapping Violence's concern for "lives, not metadata." And students have gravitated toward the use of spatial tools to visualize their research processes and to keep track of developing narratives and chronologies.

For example, one student made use of Google Maps in her research workflow to keep track of any spatial reference she encountered while reviewing primary sources. When sharing her motivations and workflow with us and her classmates, she acknowledged that this tool was useful as part of the research process but less effective as a public-facing dissemination of research, given Google's imperialist cartographies and distance from the spatial imaginary referenced in these early twentieth-century documents.

Our public history project work also involved comparing our project-specific work to similar initiatives and practitioners elsewhere. In classwide discussions and one-on-one conversations, we considered and debated the value of spatial histories at the granular level of particular metadata records, perspectives that were also informed by course readings by Richard White ("What Is Spatial History?") and Vincent Brown ("Mapping a Slave Revolt: Visualizing Spatial History through the Archives of Slavery"), among others. We also examined contemporary visualizations like "The Atlantic Slave Trade in Two Minutes," a time-lapsed recording by Andrew Kahn and Jamelle Bouie that students found lacked the attention to the embodied dimensions and investments in specificity that we attempted to prioritize in the data creation of Mapping Violence. It was often helpful to contextualize the pace and approaches taken on our public history project in terms of other active or recent project and storytelling work, connecting our narrow approaches and interests to emerging best practices and common concerns encountered in a wider and still-developing landscape of digital restorative justice initiatives.

The Mapping Violence project's next phase involves the creation of interactive visualizations that begin to narrate the scale and severity of racial violence in Texas from this period, now that we have a more robust collection of spatial data in addition to corresponding metadata and narratives. We view this work as iterative and open to revision, but we are also invested in the value of public history initiatives that advocate for remembrance and reform by presenting narratives and creating public-facing resources. It has taken us half a decade to develop a sample of data designed with our investments in restorative justice in mind. And as we further refine and reimagine this work in project and classroom contexts, we will continue to invest in approaches to data literacy and public history that acknowledge what is unquantifiable.

Notes

1. Mapping Violence, 2014–present, http://mappingviolence.org.
2. Muñoz Martinez, *Injustice Never Leaves You*, 10.
3. McPherson, quoted in Martinez, "Mapping Segregated Histories."
4. Martinez, "Mapping Segregated Histories."
5. Martinez, "Mapping Segregated Histories."
6. Martinez, "Mapping Segregated Histories."
7. Martinez, McGrath, and Rodriguez, Mapping Violence, course syllabus, Brown University, spring 2020.
8. Martinez, "Lives, Not Metadata."
9. Brian Lehrer (@BrianLehrer), Twitter, July 12, 2018, 11:47 A.M., https://twitter.com/BrianLehrer/status/1017435195488776192.
10. García, "Beyond Borders."
11. García, "Border and the American Imagination."
12. National Association for the Advancement of Colored People, *Thirty Years of Lynching*, 11.
13. Wells-Barnett, *Red Record*, 110.

14. National Association for the Advancement of Colored People, *Thirty Years of Lynching*, 6.

15. National Association for the Advancement of Colored People, *Thirty Years of Lynching*, 6.

16. Saidiya Hartman, "Venus in Two Acts," 2.

17. Hartman, "Venus in Two Acts," 12.

18. Hartman, "Venus in Two Acts," 13.

19. J. M. Johnson, "Markup Bodies," 58.

20. Hartman, "Venus in Two Acts," 12; J. M. Johnson, "Markup Bodies," 71.

21. Brown University Steering Committee on Slavery and Justice, *Slavery and Justice*, 3.

22. Brown University Steering Committee on Slavery and Justice, *Slavery and Justice*, 3.

23. For example, see Bauer, "Your Family's Genealogical Records."

24. Locke, "Critical Data Literacy."

25. Locke, "Critical Data Literacy."

26. Locke, "Critical Data Literacy."

27. Locke, "Critical Data Literacy."

28. D'Ignazio and Bhargarva, "Creative Data Literacy."

29. D'Ignazio and Bhargarva, "Creative Data Literacy."

30. Kriebel and Murray, *#MakeoverMonday*, 4–5.

6 The Real Trick Is Holding On to That Energy and Not Collapsing

Teaching Undergraduate Public History on the Verge of the Pandemic

....

ABIGAIL GAUTREAU

This chapter is (mostly) unedited diary entries of my experience teaching an undergraduate introduction to public history course from January to April 2020. This was my first time teaching it entirely on my own with a full class. I teach at Grand Valley State University, and this course was offered on our Grand Rapids campus. Most places would refer to this period as spring semester, but here in West Michigan, spring doesn't start until May, so this was winter 2020. Since you are reading this in the future, you also know what happened in March of that year.

I proposed this chapter after reading parts of Patrick Allitt's *I'm the Teacher, You're the Student*, the text referenced in Evan Faulkenbury and Julia Brock's original call for proposals. I was fascinated by the idea of simply recording immediately what happened in class without trying to explain or justify it. As I wrote in my proposal for this chapter:

> I do not anticipate doing any groundbreaking pedagogy in this class, which is precisely why I feel my contribution to the volume would be valuable. I am in the same boat as many of my colleagues; I am relatively new to teaching and very new to teaching public history. I moved to a new region for this job and have had to build relationships in the community. Having only taken public history as a graduate student, I am figuring out what the goal of an undergraduate public history course should be and what I should expect from students. Although it scares me, I am excited to see what happens when I stop being nice and start being real about what goes on in my classroom.

The process of keeping this diary and editing it has been an exercise in self-compassion but one that has ultimately made me a better teacher. The most challenging part of this process has been resisting the impulse to judge my past self for earlier decisions. It's easy to read these entries in isolation and forget how much was happening at the time. During winter 2020, I was also teaching two other classes, including Research Methods in History for the first time; facilitating a National Council on Public History Working Group; and preparing for a grant-funded trip to South Africa in May. All of that is to say that there are things here that I am proud of and those I wish I had done differently, and I hope that you, Dear Reader, will look kindly on me and perhaps feel less alone if you've experienced some of these struggles as well.

Preparing for Winter 2020

I began working on HST 420: Public History well before January. One of the least glamorous pedagogical challenges is trying to ensure that my classes get sufficient enrollment to actually run. This is especially challenging when there is no graduate program to lend cachet and more difficult still in my particular case, when the course was not originally designed in the catalog to count toward students' history electives. I took a number of steps to ensure that the class would go forward this year, beginning by having it moved from fall to winter term. Grand Valley State University enrolls students for a full year starting in May, and having the class run in the winter meant that I was able to advertise it heavily to students once they were on campus in the fall.

The other major challenge is that we have a fifteen-student minimum across classes, regardless of the maximum. This means that a seminar like Public History capped at twenty must have fifteen students, just like a survey of forty. With falling enrollments overall, this requirement is a real challenge because there is a dwindling population of history majors from which to draw students for upper-division classes. Under-enrolled winter classes end up on the chopping block in late October, and the drop-dead date is usually early November.

This is a particular challenge for public history classes, especially if they are to run an actual project. It's profoundly unfair to line a project up with a community member in July or August, then come back mid-November and tell them actually, no, we won't be doing that project, thanks for playing. Under-enrolled classes are occasionally permitted to run, but it requires special permission from the administration.

By October, I had only five students enrolled, but I had a project lined up and had agreed to write this chapter. I managed to draw four more students by November, so with nine students, the partnership I'd created with a local organization for the project, and the fact of my involvement in this volume as part of my tenure case, I was able to get the class to run. I ultimately ended up with eight students; one dropped the class after realizing it was taught at our downtown campus rather than on the main campus thirty minutes west of town.

The project for the semester was to develop interpretive signage for historic buildings in downtown Lowell, Michigan, a town about thirty minutes east of Grand Rapids. Our project partner was the Lowell Area Historical Museum, under the leadership of its director, Lisa Plank. The partnership emerged from a Meet and Eat organized by the Michigan Museums Association. These informal get-togethers are lunches held at museums around the state, and they are a great opportunity for someone new to the area (like me) to meet local colleagues. When we introduced ourselves at the gathering, I expressed an interest in projects for students, and I was honestly overwhelmed by the interest and support I found. The partnership with the museum ended up being the best fit for the public history class, since it was a historic preservation project (I teach museum studies as well, and it's less difficult to find museum projects for those classes) and since it allowed the students to work independently. The research was mostly already gathered, and because students did not need to work in groups, the project could be scaled up or down easily to suit however many students I ended up with.

I will admit to mixed feelings on not having group projects. I typically create group projects in public history classes because it's how most public history works, and it's how I learned public history. At the same time, the class has gone most smoothly when I haven't had a group project, because the groups add a layer of stress to the proceedings. The other factor I try to keep in mind is that when I was doing these projects, I was in graduate school, and my instructors had assistants and support staff to manage things. This project ended up being ideal because the students were doing similar work, but they each had their own final product. In revisiting these introductory remarks in the aftermath of the semester, I can say that having individual projects was a massive relief when everything went to hell in March.

Wednesday, January 8, 2020

My public history class met for the first time yesterday, with mixed results. I have a new teaching schedule this term, and while some aspects of it are excellent, it also presents new challenges. All of my classes are now Tuesday/Thursday, and Public History is my last class of the day. I teach a U.S. history survey at 10 A.M. on our main campus in Allendale, and then I commute thirty minutes to the downtown campus in Grand Rapids for Research Methods at 1 P.M. (new prep) and Public History at 2:30 P.M. Even though I had Monday to prepare without classes, a first since I began teaching at Grand Valley, I still found myself overwhelmed and a bit shell-shocked by the time Public History started. The first day always feels so long, and I think it's really worse here because we start back so soon after the holidays—we only submitted final grades for fall on December 19, so it's a quick turnaround, especially when you have to travel to see family in that short window. The point of all of these excuses is that Zero Day was not the best.

I did come into Zero Day with a plan; during the fall, I taught a one-hour sampler version of the course as part of a bid to increase enrollment. As part of that class, I did a lesson using two introductory videos for the Whitman Mission NPS site in Walla Walla, Washington.[1] I asked the students to imagine that they were part of a public history consulting firm that had been invited by the National Park Service to redo its introductory video for the Whitman Mission National Historic Site. I gave them a little background on the Whitmans and westward expansion, and then I showed them the original video. After watching the video, we discussed what the problems were and how they might be addressed. I took notes on the whiteboard about proposed changes, and then we watched the new introductory video, which happened to incorporate every suggestion the students had made. I was excited to use this exercise again, thinking it was a slam dunk for a Zero Day activity. I was wrong.

I opened class with introductions, asking students to introduce themselves and share what drew them to the course. I normally have students introduce themselves to each other in pairs first, but I assumed that with just eight, we did not need to do that. We definitely would have benefited from that, because instead, the four students I'd had before felt confident and comfortable, while the newcomers felt put on the spot and remained shy.

Our discussion of what public history is struggled to get off the ground. I cut it short to go over the project for the semester, and then briefly described the syllabus, after some issues with Blackboard. This was also the moment when I realized the syllabus I'd spent hours preparing was missing our site visits. I had based the new syllabus on the one I used the first time I taught the class, which was on our Allendale campus. It didn't include site visits, which meant that after I'd spent hours tinkering with the schedule and readings, it never occurred to me that I needed to add in time for site visits, even though I had already scheduled them with our project partner.

Rounding out this disaster of a first day, the exercise with the Whitman Mission video fell flat. I did not account for the fact that my fall semester students had already been in class and done readings for several weeks when we did the exercise. The students were also likely exhausted from first-week stress, and the exercise simply wasn't set up for success. I always find the first day so stressful, because I think I put too many expectations on myself and my students. Not an auspicious start, but hopefully it will get better.

Thursday, January 9, 2020

Assigned Readings:

Chap. 1, Cherstin M. Lyon, Elizabeth M. Nix, and Rebecca K. Shrum, *Introduction to Public History: Interpreting the Past, Engaging Audiences* (Lanham, MD: Rowman and Littlefield, 2017).

National Council on Public History website: "How Do We Define Public History?," https://ncph.org/what-is-public-history/about-the-field/.

Ronald J. Grele, "Whose Public? Whose History? What Is the Goal of a Public Historian?," *The Public Historian* 3, no. 1 (Winter 1981): 40–48.

The term is off to a slightly rocky start; my partner had a stomach bug I thought I'd managed to dodge, but that caught up with me yesterday evening, so public history class won't be meeting today. I've pushed the assignment deadlines back to accommodate this, and it should be fine.

Tuesday, January 14

Gary Kulik, "Designing the Past: History-Museum Exhibitions from Peale to the Present," in *History Museums in the United States: A Critical Assessment*, ed. Warren Leon and Roy Rosenzweig (Urbana: University of Illinois Press, 1989). (in Blackboard) (READ FIRST)

Michael Wallace, "Visiting the Past: History Museums in the United States," in *Mickey Mouse History and Other Essays on American Memory* (Philadelphia: Temple University Press, 1996), 3–32. (in Blackboard)

Let's try this again! Today went much better, because it turns out that when students come in having done some reading, they actually have a basis on which to have discussions and speak. Who knew? Anyway, today we revisited the question, "What is public history?" and started our discussion of museum history. I always like to start with museums when I teach public history because it's what students are most familiar with. They've all been to some sort of museum, so they know what an exhibit is, or what a museum tour is like. This experience gives them a baseline level of confidence that they can build on, rather than throwing them into the intricacies of the National Register process.

To prep for this class, I reviewed the readings and went through their journals. I assign reading journals that are due the morning before class so that I can read them before we meet. The purpose of the journals is to give them a format for thinking about what they're reading: Who wrote this, and what is their background? Who is the intended audience, and how is that reflected in the piece? What is the author's argument, and do they agree or disagree? What was their favorite and least favorite aspect of the piece? And finally, I ask them to write a discussion question for class based on the reading.

In addition to helping students engage critically, the journals are also helpful as a resource when they go to write their self-reflective essay for the final. The just-in-time format of the assignment is helpful because it lets me spot issues students have with the reading, and it means they are helping to create the class by generating discussion questions. I usually paste the discussion questions into a document that I can use during class.

This is such a small class, and I've had half of these students before, so I had pretty high expectations going in regarding their participation. I did have to pull some teeth to get them going. I can usually count on Mary and Chris to chime in, which they did, and with a bit of prodding, I managed to get everyone else to join in.[2] I also forget that these students often haven't been in a seminar-style discussion before, and that challenge is compounded by the layout of our room, which is set up as a small lecture space. I try to make it a bit less intense by sitting at a table facing them, but it still sets up that dynamic of the students as an audience.

I managed to get everyone in class to speak except for Jason, which was weird because on the first day he told us that he signed up for this class specifically because he wanted to work on our project. He has good friends who live in Lowell, and he was excited to learn more about the town. He also didn't submit any work, which is always stressful and surprising to me—especially early in the term in a 400-level class.

Thursday, January 16

Nina Simon, preface to *The Participatory Museum*, www.participatorymuseum.org/preface/.

John E. Fleming, "The Impact of Social Movements on the Development of African American Museums," *The Public Historian* 40, no. 3 (August 2018): 44–73.

Today's class went well. Since we'd spent Tuesday catching up on the "What is public history?" question, today we did a very deep dive on museum history using the readings that had been due both Tuesday and today. This ended up being a particularly good discussion, because students had to discuss more classic pieces on museum history (Gary Kulik's "Designing the Past" and Michael Wallace's "Visiting the Past" article from *Mickey Mouse History*), alongside Fleming's piece.

One of my major realizations in teaching public history classes has been how heavily my own academic training was informed by historiography (I had Rebecca Conard for both Historiography and Introduction to Public History). While that was appropriate in a graduate program, my students are undergraduates whose training often does not include extensive historiography. I have been trying to find a balance between giving them enough context to understand, say, why the Grand Rapids Public Museum has a mummy in its collections and showing them that the way people wrote about the history of museums twenty years ago and now has changed.

In our discussion today, we built a sort of timeline, examining the parallel origin stories of white and Black museums described by Kulik, Wallace, and Fleming. I've included an image of the whiteboard from the end of our discussion, which ranged from why white museums had more "stuff" to funding to the ultimate purpose of the museums. We distinguished between ideas about history and heritage, aspiration and uplift. While the students found Kulik's work to be dry, they appreciated the way Fleming's article was anchored in historical events, which gave them a better sense of when things were happening.

Today's discussion was excellent, with good participation from nearly everyone. It was also a good reminder to me that one of the other challenges in teaching this class is that students haven't often been asked to carry a discussion, which means that I have to factor in teaching them how to do it. One of the most effective methods I've used in the past is assigning students to lead discussion themselves, because for whatever reason they seem

Whiteboard discussion of museums (courtesy of author).

to feel more obligated to participate when it's a classmate who's prepped the discussion. I want to try this, but I also haven't completely finalized the schedule, which is embarrassing to admit two weeks into the term, but there it is. I've only taught this class once before, as an overload on our other campus; there just isn't a lot of time between the end of fall term and the start of winter . . . excuses, reasons, I'll let it go for now. I'm doing my best, and today we had a good discussion on a tough topic.

Tuesday, January 21

My absolute favorite part of teaching public history classes is field trips. My favorite field trip at the moment is the Grand Rapids Public Museum. It's the second largest museum in the state (after the Henry Ford, of course), and it's an outstanding example of how museums change over time. There are exhibits on everything from science and natural history to the furniture industry, and there are lots of interactive exhibits. I'm fortunate that my department offers to compensate me for admission so that I can cover it and ensure that everyone can attend, and I usually pay the $1 per person out of pocket so that anyone who wants to can ride the historic carousel. What I love most about going, though, is coercing my students into having fun.

When we arrive, the students are, as always, a bit skeptical. They're excited to be there, potentially a bit stressed by having had to show up to a place that isn't our classroom, and unsure of my expectations. I start out by walking around with them, usually through the Streets of Old Grand Rapids, a three-quarter-scale re-creation of Grand Rapids in the 1890s, complete with stores you can go into, though as usual, we aren't there during peak hours, when the stores are staffed by docents who can explain the veritable cornucopia of objects. We then make our way through the museum, and I encourage them to explore without me—to see what strikes their interest, and to keep in mind what we learned about the history of museums. I encourage them to participate in whatever interactives are on offer. My personal favorite is the spun chairs, which I inelegantly climb into in an effort to convince them to enjoy themselves.[3]

This year was special because the changing exhibit is *Toys*, which looks at how play and toys have changed over the years. The museum created period rooms for generations, and some of the toys on display are my own toys that I donated. I spent a lot of time in the exhibit and let the students drift toward and away from me, discussing whether these period rooms were aspirational or realistic and why they think the curators and exhibit designers made the choices they did. I also brought quarters so they could play games in the video arcade at the end of the exhibit.

We had a lovely visit, as usual—the museum visit gives us a shared experience to reflect on going forward, and it's a good reminder for them that this is supposed to be fun. Most of them have been to the museum before, so it's also nice for them to experience it from a different perspective.

Thursday, January 23

Society of American Archivists, "What Are Archives?," updated September 12, 2016, www2.archivists.org/about-archives.

Society of American Archivists, "Using Archives: A Guide to Effective Research," updated March 26, 2016, www2.archivists.org/usingarchives. (Be sure to click all the way through the guide.)

Patricia Galloway, "Archives, Power, and History: Dunbar Rowland and the Beginning of the State Archives of Mississippi (1902–1936)," *American Archivist* 69 (2006): 79–116.

Today was Archives Day One, and an object lesson in how terrible I am at predicting what my students will enjoy. To kick things off, I like to have them read a Society of American Archivists piece on "how to archives," because many of them won't have spent any meaningful amount of time in an archives, though I do sometimes get lucky and have a work-study student who's assigned to the University Archives and Special Collections. I also assigned Patricia Galloway's article on Dunbar Rowland out of sheer stubbornness. It's a very good article on how heavily white supremacy is embedded in archival practice, but it's also not really snappy enough to hold their attention. Once again, just because I think these how-the-sausage-gets-made articles are interesting, that does not mean that my students will enjoy them.

Our discussion involved a bit of teeth pulling today. It's partly that reading practical guides doesn't really lend itself to scintillating discussion, but it's mostly that it's hard to get my all-white students to discuss white supremacy in depth. Instead, the class gets stuck on the level of "oh wow, that's horrible," but then stays up there on the surface rather than diving into how this specific type of white supremacy pervaded the archival profession. I started this discussion with an overview of the "Lost Cause" to try to give them a little more context for who Dunbar Rowland was and why he matters so much, but there's just so much shock that it's hard to have a deeper discussion. I know they can, because they did a great job on the museum material, so maybe I need to find a different article or chapter, or come up with another way of presenting this that will help them break it down more. I'm not ready to give up on this content.

On a better note, I had their reading journals done before class started (again, this is a lot easier when there are only eight of them and one of them isn't doing the work), so it was good to have their feedback before I started. I like this method of homework assessment because it lets me see where the gaps are before class so that I can prepare myself to address them. The discussion question element is also helpful because it puts them in charge of prep, which usually means they have a bit more investment in the class. At the same time, I still think I should switch over to having them lead the discussion, which would mean I would have to finish making up the schedule. You'd think the embarrassment of writing this down for my peers to read would motivate me, but you'd be underestimating my anxiety and backlog of existing work. The issue here, honestly, is not that it's hard for me to decide what we should cover—I have all of that worked out. It's the part where I hem and haw because I'm not thrilled with my existing material, but finding new content is overwhelming because it means the time investment not just in finding new readings on, say, oral history, but also in having to read through lots of them to figure out if they are better than what I have.

Tuesday, January 28

> Marika Cifor, Michelle Caswell, Alda Allina Migoni, and Noah Geraci, "'What We Do Crosses Over to Activism': The Politics and Practice of Community Archives," *The Public Historian* 40, no. 2 (May 2018): 69–95.
> Caswell, Michelle, "Seeing Yourself in History: Community Archives and the Fight against Symbolic Annihilation," *The Public Historian* 36, no. 4 (November 2014): 26–37.

Archives Day Two! So today was going to be a bit of a gamble, because while I had read one of the articles I assigned today a few times, the other I picked without really reading it. I know that there are several schools of thought on this, but I don't really mind taking a chance—I obviously skimmed the article to ensure that it was relevant, and I think we've established that I'm terrible at guessing what my students will or won't enjoy. The upshot of this is that I scrambled through the reading journals before class, and also re-skimmed the article. I am also of the opinion that having finished graduate school, if I can't skim something and lead an undergraduate discussion on it, then someone should revoke my degree.

I have made a change to my schedule that seems to be working well. I used to drive for my full commute, but I've started driving to the downtown campus, parking in the garage, and taking the bus to the main campus in Allendale. While this makes for a longer ride, I do get the time on the bus to read and catch up on things. I can't grade, but I get a solid thirty minutes or so each way to read, and that has really helped me keep on pace.

Today's discussion went pretty well—they were more engaged with this material than with what we read Thursday, though of course the more they read on a topic the easier it is for them to see the connections themselves. Once again, though, the discussion was dominated by Chris, Mary, and Brian, while I had to pull teeth to get Monica, Alex, and Emily to talk. Kevin was out—excused—and Jason once again didn't turn in any work and most likely didn't read. I did finally email him, but I haven't heard back. I tend to be pushier about this with my first-year students than in my upper division classes—I can't actually *make* anyone do anything, but I do send a nice email asking if they have something going on that they'd like to discuss. I think it's obvious I'm asking because they're behind, but I try to frame it as a concern, because it is. Especially since Jason was so keen on the class at the start. It's also easier on my mental health not to assume the worst about students.

The one thing that's been a bit weird about this class has been having Alex in both this class and my Research Methods class, which meets immediately beforehand. Normally it's not a huge deal, but this week I'm teaching Research Methods students about archives, and I'm very curious about what it's like for Alex to sit in Research Methods and learn about the history of archives, and then to sit in Public History and learn about archives in a similar light. It's unfortunate that he's one of my more introverted students, or else I'd really push him for an opinion.

Thursday, January 30

Another field trip! This time we went to the Grand Rapids City Archives. I actually spent all day there, since I brought my Research Methods students too, but it was a lot of fun to get to see two very different archives tours. My Research Methods students got the tour of what an archive is and got to see the kinds of materials one can find and research with at the archives. My Public History students' tour was much more about how the archives functions and how one becomes an archivist. Of course, Alex ended up being on both tours, since he's in both classes, but I didn't feel bad about it. I tour the archives at least once a semester, often more than that, but I always learn something new. Today I really got to learn something new, because I found out they have a fourth floor! Despite my many tours and the number of projects I've worked on with students at the archives, I had somehow never been up there or even heard of it, so that was exciting indeed.

The unfortunate part of today is that because I spent four hours at the archives, I am honestly having a hard time remembering what I did with which class. In any case, it was a really good day, and it's always good to get my students out of the classroom and talking to working public historians.

Tuesday, February 4, 2020

Chaps. 1–3, Norman Tyler, *Historic Preservation: An Introduction to Its History, Principles, and Practice* (New York: W. W. Norton, 1999).

One of the things I definitely want to capture about how I feel teaching this class is that a lot of the time, when I walk into Public History, I am exhausted. I teach my 10 A.M. class, which is a First-Year Learning Community doing all of U.S. history in one term (we play Reacting to the Past games), then I commute to the downtown campus, stuff my lunch into my face, frantically grade and prep the rest of my Public History material, and teach Research Methods.[4] While my first-years are a lot of fun, Research Methods is draining. It's my first time teaching it, and it's a weird class because it's a mix of students who are not actually history majors and history majors who are seniors and should have taken it at least a year ago.[5] They're not always chatty, and they don't find historiography nearly as interesting as I do.

The point of all this is that I'm rarely at my best when I walk into Public History, and I worry that the class won't go well because I'm tired, and that has a way of affecting the tone of the class. But then I went in, and we started talking about the topic of the day. Today that was the first three chapters of Tyler et al.'s *Historic Preservation*. I really like it as a historic preservation textbook—it's not necessarily the greatest, but it's accessible and well-organized and a solid introduction to the topic. So I went in, trying to shake off my exhaustion, and ended up having the most wonderful discussion about the history of historic preservation and different preservation philosophies. It turned out that Kevin had actually been to the Ise Shrine in Japan that the authors describe, and it meant that there was a real sense of connection to the material that doesn't always happen. They asked questions that made me curious about things I didn't really know (as in, very specific questions about historic preservation practice in other countries).

It's hard to pin down what made today's discussion so satisfying, because it was also pretty clear that they hadn't all read as carefully as I would have liked. I'm inclined to think that this means I need to give them more structured questions for these chapters, but at the same time, the lack of an imposed structure gave rise to a more free-flowing discussion. I suppose that's always the hard part—deciding how structured I want things—because when it's left to them, sometimes it's devastatingly slow, but when it isn't, it's magical.

What I really want to share today is that so often I leave my public history class with more energy than when I walked in. It's a special feeling, because I don't always feel that way when I leave class. My public history students—well, about half of them, anyway—always want to stay late. They always have a question, and they will happily stay past the end of class to talk—some of them need to go to other classes and obligations, obviously, but it just brings me such joy to get to talk to these students who are excited about something that I am passionate about. This is my last class at the end of a very long day of teaching, and they leave me buzzing with energy to do more.

The real trick is holding on to that energy and not collapsing when I get home and eat dinner. I've still got a pretty substantial to-do list for today and tomorrow, not least of which is grading their homework, which I completely blanked on. It should have been at the top of my to-do list, especially since I also somehow forgot about the work for chapters 1–3. The just-in-time system is really great, right up until I forget about their work.

I want to hold on to the joy, though, and not get swamped down in the guilt and press of administrative work. I love teaching and working with students—and teaching this class in particular. It's been really wonderful to remember how much I love historic preservation, because it's been a distressingly long time since I've gotten to do any of it. Seeing them discover it is really moving for me. I don't normally go on about my feelings, but that's where I am today, and it's so nice to walk out of a class and feel lifted by the experience and not as though I need to go lie down and put a cold compress over my face.

Thursday, February 6, 2020

Chaps. 4–6, Norman Tyler, *Historic Preservation*.

What a day! OK, so they read chapters 4–6 in Tyler, which is a dry set of chapters looking at the legal basis for historic preservation, ordinances, and how preservation actually works. It's such a good learning experience for me, because it forces me to reassess what I know and explain it in accessible ways. The best example of this today was making a chart on the whiteboard explaining how NPS operates in terms of National Register (NR) versus parks, and how that works out on other levels, as well as what State Historic Preservation Offices (SHPOs) do besides deal with the NR. They had a lot of the same questions I get at community meetings about how the NR affects people, how ordinances and zoning fit into property rights, what a nuisance building is, and so on.[6] It's been a wonderful reminder of how much I love preservation—and really, how much I know about it.

When you're teaching and not practicing as much, it's easy to feel as if you're not a "real" public historian—that it's a skill set you once had but don't use, because it doesn't often intersect with what you do all the time. This makes me want to change that. How can I make public history and especially historic preservation more a part of the classes I teach? How can I bring things into my other classrooms so that I can share what I love with these students? Not that I think my students taking HST 103 for general education are going to be into learning about ordinances, but you know, there're monuments and all kinds of stuff that is genuinely interesting to nonspecialists.

They opened the class by asking me if I liked teaching college or high school better, which was interesting and naturally got me on a digression about what I liked about each.[7] I would never in a million years get to teach historic preservation in a high school, and I think at the end of the day, that's what I like about this. I can teach what I want (within reason), my students are adults, and they're here because they want to be. It's fun.

Prep was pretty minimal today, just reviewing the chapters and grading their homework, which took all of ten or fifteen minutes because there are only eight of them. It's a lot less classroom management, which is really nice. I enjoy not having to prepare lectures and being able to let the class flow organically, although I do think this adds to my pre-class anxiety. If I have a lecture, I know how the class will go. If I don't, then it's up to them, and it might go really badly. I think on the balance, I'm happier letting class happen, so I just need to find better strategies for managing my anxiety/dread/catastrophic thinking. I do think that my public history background has a significant impact on how I view this; I treat my students as stakeholders, and I want them to co-create the class with me.

I'll have to actually write the project up tomorrow—it takes me forever to write up a project. I feel like it has to just gestate in my mind for ages, and then suddenly it bursts forth fully formed—like that creature from *Alien*—in about an hour. The rapidity with which I write it up always makes me think it won't take long, because I forget how much active and passive mental time I spend working on it.

I did finally make a Slack for our class. I have colleagues whose students love Slack and get really involved with it, but mine mostly seem irritated. I can't think of a better way to organize ride-sharing so that the university doesn't know about it, though, so there we are.[8] I've also finally posted the guidelines for their visit to the Meyer May House, which they'll have to do on their own because of the museum's funky hours, and I set up their video chat with Jessi White, a friend of mine who's a historic preservationist for the city of Denver.[9]

Tuesday, February 11, 2020

National Register Day! So once I've had students read about the context and background of historic preservation, I like to get them looking at the way it often actually works in the United States. It's important to me that they understand that it's historical work but that it's also highly technical. I have them read the following:

> National Park Service, *How to Apply the National Register Criteria for Evaluation*, National Register Bulletin, rev. ed. 1997, www.nps.gov/subjects/nationalregister/upload/NRB-15_web508.pdf.
> Michigan SP Garden Bowl, Registration Form, National Register of Historic Places, May 31, 2008, https://catalog.archives.gov/id/25341138. (Focus on the "Statement of Significance.")
> Oak Hill Farm, Registration Form, National Register of Historic Places, February 8, 2013, https://web.archive.org/web/20170802034804/https:/www.nps.gov/nr/feature/places/pdfs/13000125.pdf. (Focus on the "Statement of Significance.")
> Portsmouth Village, Registration Form, National Register of Historic Places, February 21, 1978, https://web.archive.org/web/20180305063712if_/http:/www.hpo.ncdcr.gov/nr/CR0007.pdf.

I let them know that I don't expect them to read all of the bulletin, and I modify the reading questions to help them get that. Basically, I want them to start thinking about what significance means and figure out how to read a nomination. To that end, I have them also look at some existing nominations, and they basically do a treasure hunt—they have to tell me who the author is, the criteria it was nominated under, and why the property is significant. I also have them compare and contrast two district nominations, Oak Hill Farm in West Tennessee (which I wrote, so I'm very familiar with it), and an old nomination, Portsmouth Village off the coast of North Carolina. I think it's helpful for them to really see how the National Register has changed, and part of what we discuss in class is why.

I was really pleased in class that most of them managed to fish out the authors on the nominations—the NR form gets updated fairly regularly, and it seems as though the author page gets moved around and can be difficult to find, especially on longer nominations. During class, most of the students discussed how they enjoyed the Garden Bowl nomination and learned something new. The Garden Bowl is a bowling alley in Detroit, and the nomination does an outstanding job of contextualizing the building and its evolution alongside the changing demands of leisure time and suburbanization.

The class also really got into discussing the Oak Hill Farm nomination and seeing how different it was from the Portsmouth Village nomination. We talked about the differences, and I asked the students to tell me why they thought the nominations were different and what the differences meant. They danced around a bit, so I led them in it.

> *Me*: Which property did they learn more about by reading the nomination?
> *Students*: Oak Hill Farm.
> *Me*: Why?
> *Mary*: It's more detailed. There's a lot more to it.
> *Me*: Like what? Tell me something specific. Which sections are longer in Oak Hill compared to Portsmouth Village?
>   Long pause, they're looking at their notes and skimming back over the nominations. The pause starts to feel anxious. Finally, Chris jumps in.
> *Chris*: The descriptions. The descriptions are a lot longer, and there's more, like, background information.
> *Me*: Great! OK, if you were a researcher and you were going to have to write up a paper about either Oak Hill Farm or Portsmouth Village, and the only information you had to start from was the National Register nomination, which would you pick?
> *Emily*: Oak Hill Farm.
> *Me*: Why?
> *Emily*: There's so much more there—and there's a bibliography that's a lot more current too.
> *Me*: Ding ding ding! We have a winner! So, looking at these two nominations, both districts, how do you all think the National Register nomination process has changed?

Now the conversation is moving—the new nominations are more detailed, there's a lot more information. They are more specific and clearer. So the newer nominations are more useful as research documents, yes? That's a big part of the change. I talk to them about the professionalization of historic preservation and the NR process, and why in some cases that's good

(NRs are a lot more useful to researchers, as they are getting better at reflecting more and different types of histories) and why there are some less good things about it (you really have to be a professional to write an NR, which costs money; SHPO budget cuts mean SHPOs don't have the resources in many places to support the costs of NRs in less affluent areas), and overall it was a good discussion. In writing this, I think next time I might open my conversation with that last question about which one they'd pick to write a paper about. We have our first day of fieldwork on Thursday, so I'm very excited about that.

Thursday, February 13, 2020

It is a truth universally acknowledged that if you schedule fieldwork in February, no matter how nice it was earlier in the week, it will be cold, snowy, and miserable on the appointed day.

My poor students. It had been so nice (dry, upper 30s) all week, and then on the day of our fieldwork, it was snowy and windy and miserable. They were good sports, and everyone managed to show up at the Lowell Area Historical Museum on time to meet Lisa Plank, the director. She gave them the rundown, and then we all bundled up to traipse through downtown Lowell. Once all of the students were good and frozen, we went back and they picked the buildings they wanted to write about and got to work with the materials. A very productive, if frosty, day.

Tuesday, February 18, 2020

> Matthew Lawrence Daley and Scott Stabler, "'The World's Greatest Minstrel Show under the Stars': Blackface Minstrels, Community Identity, and the Lowell Showboat, 1932–1977," *Michigan Historical Review* 44, no. 2 (Fall 2018): 1–35.

Back in the classroom, where it is relatively warm and dry! Today we discussed an article cowritten by my colleague Matthew Daley. Most of my students had read the article before for other classes, so we focused on the parts discussing the impact of the showboat on Lowell's architecture and the way that renovations and restorations threatened that legacy. We had a shorter class today, but I don't mind that since they do so much work outside class.

Thursday, February 20, 2020

> Chap. 1, Thomas F. King, *Cultural Resource Laws and Practice*, rev. ed. (Lanham, MD: AltaMira Press, 2013).
> Ronald W. Johnson, "The Historian and Cultural Resource Management," *The Public Historian* 3, no. 2 (Spring 1981): 43–51.

Today was Cultural Resource Management (CRM) Day! I always enjoy this topic because I'm such a curmudgeon about the difference between CRM and historic preservation (HP)—I tell the students they can go to graduate school either way, but the main difference in my experience is that CRM tends to be anthropologists and archaeologists, and HP tends to be historians and architects. We do the same basic work, and we're governed by the same legal processes; we just have different languages and slightly different methods. I really like assigning parts of Tom King's book because he has such a straightforward, accessible style of writing that's belied by the relentlessly dull title: *Cultural Resource Laws and Practice*.

My students had strong opinions about the chapter. Some of them thought it was great, while others found King's tone abrasive. We talked about who King might be arguing with: Why does it feel like he's arguing? What can you infer from his chapter about the state of CRM and how it's practiced?

They didn't get into the Johnson article as much, and in fairness, that article is nearly forty years old. This is definitely an area of the syllabus that will need some attention before I teach the class again.

Tuesday, February 25, 2020

> Clement W. Meighan and Larry J. Zimmerman, "Debating NAGPRA's Effects," *Archaeology*, 1994, republished online February 26, 1999, https://archive.archaeology.org/online/features/native/debate.html.
> Steven Conn, "Whose Objects? Whose Culture? The Contexts of Repatriation," in *Do Museums Still Need Objects?* (Philadelphia: University of Pennsylvania Press, 2010), 58–85.

Today we talked about the Native American Graves Protection and Repatriation Act (NAGPRA), which requires federally funded institutions to return cultural objects to the lineal descendants of the Indigenous peoples they were taken from. NAGPRA Day is usually a good class because my students get really interested in it. They're often fascinated by history related to Native Americans, and it's something I need to spend more time with. I like to have them read the 1994 piece because it is an important primary source. When I explain what NAGPRA is, a lot of them seem to feel that its value is self-evident, and I want them to understand that that's not, or wasn't always, the case. The Conn piece is a nice one because it engages with some of the museum readings they did back at the start of term and because Conn is a bit of a provocateur. They get stirred up about his claims and opinions, and it really helps drive conversation forward.

Our discussion went well, but I once again left feeling as though I just don't have enough of a grasp on NAGPRA. I'm not great at explaining it, and I really feel my lack of experience in implementation. I guess it's one of the frustrating things about teaching public history; since my actual job is teaching, and most of what I teach isn't public history, I just don't have as much field experience to draw from, and sometimes I feel like a bit of a fraud. I feel a lot of pressure, most of it probably internal, to know a lot about a lot of things, and for that knowledge to be drawn from personal experience. I sometimes feel as though I'm disappointing my students when I don't have an interesting anecdote or some personal connection to the content, even though I realize that is not an achievable or even reasonable goal. I don't know. Maybe I can find a guest speaker who's worked on NAGPRA stuff in the field. I also think that there's more written about NAGPRA and museums than the CRM side, but I'm probably wrong and whoever reads this can feel free to email me and tell me I'm wrong, as long as you also attach a bibliography for me.

This is our last class for a while—they're supposed to go visit the Meyer May House, which is a restored Frank Lloyd Wright house here in Grand Rapids. It is free and open to the public, but the museum keeps weird hours because the Steelcase Corporation owns it and uses it for corporate events. In the past, our class has sometimes been scheduled so that we can go during class, but not this year, so I give them an extra day on the syllabus to make up for having to find their own time for the tour. After that we have spring break, so I won't see them until we meet on March 10 in Lowell.

March 2020...

Well, I think we all know what happened in March 2020. In terms of my class, I came back from a trip to Fairhope, Alabama, on March 8 amid growing concerns about the COVID-19 virus. There were rumors around campus that we were going to shut down, but my class went ahead with our fieldwork day in Lowell on March 10, and that ended up being our last meeting as a class.

I am writing this after the fact, but I remember at the time I was relieved that we had gotten through most of our course content by the time everything shut down. I altered the syllabus dramatically, cutting nearly all the rest of the readings. I tried to keep our final book, Stewart Brand's *How Buildings Learn*, in the syllabus because I wanted to make sure they used the texts they'd paid for, but in retrospect, this was a mistake. I barely had enough focus to read their discussion posts, much less respond to them.

Regarding our project, which was writing interpretive signage for historic buildings in Lowell, the students did complete the assigned work. Shortly after we moved online, I checked in with each of them by phone to see where they were in the process and if they thought they could finish the project. They all wanted to go on, and so they did. We were fortunate that getting a second day of fieldwork meant that most of them at least had images of the documents they needed to work from. It was also fortuitous that even prior to the pandemic, the Grand Valley library prioritized purchasing e-books, so most of the secondary resources students needed were readily available online.

To further facilitate the writing process, I moved the assignment over to Google Docs. This meant that I could comment directly on the work with minimal emailing. I made the deadlines more flexible, and I did my best to support them, though I now realize I was as shell-shocked as they were. This became even more apparent when the semester ended and it took me until August to work up the wherewithal to send their final drafts back to Lisa. I kept thinking I would have the energy and focus to revise their drafts before handing them over, and it simply didn't happen. The drafts were not as strong as I'd hoped they'd be, I'm sure due to the combined stress of the pandemic and the lack of opportunity to collaborate on wording and research. I sent the drafts over as I had received them, simply so that our community partner would have something work with.

I decided to keep the self-reflection essays as the final "exam" because they seemed critical to me at the time. Reflective practice is one of the defining elements of public history practice, and I used the essay to ask students to integrate what they'd learned throughout the semester. The essay itself matters, but not as much as the process of revisiting and synthesizing materials across many subfields into a cohesive whole.[10] With the benefit of hindsight, I'm not sure it was a reasonable request to make of students during a crisis.

To say that it wasn't the end of semester I'd imagined is quite the understatement. In working on this chapter after the fact, all those weeks seem both impossibly distant and achingly close. Revising and writing this chapter has been an object lesson in historical empathy. I know intimately the person who wrote these notes and recorded these thoughts, and yet I am no longer that person and cannot look back without the knowledge of what came after. It's been a little like watching a horror movie, where the protagonist has no idea what's coming and you cannot warn her that she really should stop putting off following up with that student or grading that assignment.

I don't regret undertaking this project; I've learned a lot about myself and my teaching through this process. I am still vaguely embarrassed by my candor; it's not comfortable for me to admit my shortcomings—real or imagined—to my peers, but I hope that in doing so, it's helped you, Dear Reader, find a little more compassion for yourself as an instructor.

Notes

1. The Whitman Mission commemorates the role of missionary settlers Dr. Marcus and Narcissa Whitman in establishing the Oregon Trail. The Whitmans were ultimately killed by the Cayuse, and their deaths instigated the Cayuse War.

2. All students' names have been changed.

3. Spun chairs look like sculptures when upright, but they become chairs that spin and rotate at an angle when tilted. There are excellent videos on YouTube showing them in use.

4. Reacting to the Past is a system of active role-playing games set in the past. This semester I'm using Greenwich Village, 1913, in which labor and suffrage factions compete for the allegiance of the bohemians through persuasive speeches and debate.

5. Several majors (mainly psychology) allow students to take any research methods class, so I have students who haven't had a history class since they did their general education requirements, and students who believe they already know all of this stuff. It's a challenge.

6. "Nuisance building" is a term used by some local preservation/zoning authorities to designate abandoned/derelict buildings that may eventually be taken by the city after imposing fines.

7. I like to talk to my students about what I did before I became a professor. I joke that I've had all the jobs, but before getting my public history PhD in 2015 I did closings in a real estate office, was a summer ranger at Wolf Trap National Park for the Performing Arts, and spent two years as a long-term sub teaching history and English to high school students, among other things. I want my students to know that you rarely take a straight line to end up where you want to be, and that the skills you build along the way can really help you.

8. I let students organize themselves for rides so that there is no liability issue for the university. I'm not completely sure that this is against the rules, but it's a forgiveness-or-permission thing.

9. The Meyer May House is a historic house museum. The house was designed by Frank Lloyd Wright and restored by the Steelcase Corporation.

10. There are many resources available on reflective practice, but perhaps the most relevant to my perspective is Rebecca Conard, "Public History as Reflective Practice: An Introduction," *The Public Historian* 28, no. 1 (Winter 2006): 9–13.

7 Imaginemos Cosas Chingonas

Building the Other Football Public History Project

ROMEO GUZMÁN

My daughter Aura almost missed the game. My phone rang, but I didn't hear it. My wife texted, but I didn't see it. In the middle of the excitement I had forgotten the plan. Carribean and Aura would go to a kid's party, and before halftime, Aura would join me and our friends at Fresno Football Club's playoff game. In the stillness of the stands, I realized my error: I got up, called Carribean, and ran to the main entrance. She had already passed the stadium, but Fresno is a small city, and Fresno Football Club (Fresno FC) plays in a small Triple-A baseball stadium. She pulled a U-turn and drove up to the stadium. My kid got out of the car and ran to the entrance gate. We hugged, stopped by the concession stand for an ice cream and a beer, and headed back to the stands for the start of the second half. That October night we sat along the sidelines, two-to-three rows deep. Our mighty crew included a few faculty, some alumni, friends from a weekly *cascara* (pickup game), and a few students. Some of our friends were also behind the goal, standing next to and singing with the supporters group, Fire Squad. If Fresno FC won, we could postpone the inevitable and extend the end of professional soccer in the Central Valley for at least one more game.

We didn't win.

From the spring of 2018 to 2020, my Fresno State public history course and public history project The Other Football: Tracing the Game's Roots and Routes collaborated with Fresno FC by hosting conferences on and off campus and using home games to distribute knowledge about the history of soccer. Through this work, students working on The Other Football connected with former and current players and coaches and got to hang out at games with students, faculty, and folks whom we had interviewed. Now, without Fresno FC, we'd lost an important collaborator and home for our work. This, as we would come to learn, was hardly the biggest setback. In the spring of 2020, COVID-19 arrived and sent us all online. That same semester, I accepted a job at Claremont Graduate University, in Southern California.

The Other Football became a very intricate and expansive project. It spanned three semesters and also resulted in the formation of an actual soccer team and tournament. To explain all its components, this chapter is organized into four main sections. The first section briefly describes the origins of my public history practice and the founding of the Valley Public History Initiative and The Other Football at Fresno State. The second section focuses on the actual course. I note the readings, in-class activities, assignments, tests, and events. More importantly, I detail how we built a new archive and how we shared our findings. In this section, I quote from student papers and essays to demonstrate how the class worked and to highlight students' contributions to the project. The third section focuses on how The Other Football resulted in friendships and a community that expanded beyond the classroom. Together, we formed a team and organized a tournament-fundraiser to support Central American refugees. Section four is not a happy one; it focuses on the challenges and limits of institutional support. I end the chapter by thinking about the future of The Other Football. It is my hope that if we commit ideas to paper, they might materialize.

Fresno State's Valley Public History Initiative

I arrived at California State University, Fresno, in 2016 as an assistant professor in U.S. and public history. My training, however, was not in public history. I got my PhD from Columbia University in history as a Latin Americanist, with a focus on modern Mexico. My dissertation, like most of my publications, focuses on Mexican migrants and Mexican Americans. While I learned a fair deal about museums and oral history throughout my undergraduate and graduate training, I arrived at a practice and theory of public history through my work with the South El Monte Arts Posse (SEMAP), an art collective codirected by me and Carribean Fragoza and based in South El Monte/El Monte, two working-class cities in Southern California. Founded in 2011 by Fragoza, SEMAP is a collective of artists, writers, educators, and community members dedicated to using the arts to reimagine how we think about and define the use of space. It's a grassroots, DIY collective that applies to and receives grants, but whose work is not defined by grant cycles or academic calendars. In 2012, we were inspired by El Monte's encroaching centennial to find new ways to think about its history and new methods of conveying El Monte's present and past to its residents and the broader public. El Monte's official history, embedded in its official museum and city logo, celebrates and centers the arrival of white pioneers after 1848, effectively erasing the Tongva/Gabrieliño who were here before and the people of color who arrived after.

SEMAP used this historical date as an opportunity to launch the public history and place-making project East of East: Mapping Community Narratives in South El Monte and El Monte, which was funded by the Department of Cultural Affairs of the City of Los Angeles. This initial grant and communal labor helped launch what would become a multiyear and award-winning project dedicated to rewriting the history of El Monte and its neighboring city South El Monte.[1] Through East of East, we collectively created a practice and theory of public history that can be summarized by three central objectives: (1) to build reciprocal relationships between historians (scholars) and the public by placing community members at the center of the historical process, such as the creation of archives and the dissemination and reception of new narratives; (2) to create multiple homes for "primary" and "secondary" sources—or, in other words, to provide multiple forms for history to exist in the world and for folks to connect with the past; and (3) to use the archive and historical narratives to alter the physical landscape and to foster within greater El Monte's communities of color a collective claim to space. I used SEMAP's East of East project as a model to found and direct Fresno State's Valley Public History Initiative: Preserving Our Stories (VPHI). As part of VPHI, I taught courses on oral history and public history, as well as a course titled Fútbol: A Local and Global History of the Beautiful Game.

The Other Football: Tracing the Games' Roots and Routes in the Central Valley

Like many faculty at teaching institutions, I quickly realized how important it is to use courses to think through my own research interests and projects. And, like faculty everywhere, I wrote an abstract for a paper that I had not written for a conference that I was scheduled to attend. Harvard University, Simmons College, and the Athens-based professional team Olympiacos organized a conference titled "Reinforcing, Crossing, and Transcending Borders: Soccer in a Globalized World."[2] Acceptance to the conference included air travel, lodging, meals, VIP entrance to fútbol (soccer) matches, and thinking and learning at the actual clubhouse. In addition to my own research interest, my undergraduate student Tyler Caffee was working on a thesis on soccer in Visalia.[3] I also knew that there were several students who played, had played, or were otherwise soccer aficionados. The course provided an opportunity to meet student interest, become more familiar with the scholarship of soccer, and launch a public history project based in the Central Valley. There were also two very important global and local events in 2018: the Men's World Cup that summer, and Fresno FC's inaugural season, which would run from March to October.

Course Outline and Material

I taught Fútbol: A Local and Global History of the Beautiful Game (an upper-division elective course) in the spring of 2018, 2019, and 2020. Each semester, I included different readings and refined the lectures and in-class activities. The final projects and public engagement activities were only a little different. I created continuity between the semesters by building on the work of the previous semester (or semesters) and centering the archive and community engagement.

Some students enrolled in the course after taking my introduction to public history or oral history course. Some students enrolled in the course because they loved soccer and heard about the course from their classmates, while others found the time slot convenient. As Fresno State is a Hispanic-serving institution located in the Central Valley, many of our students are first-generation students who commute to campus and juggle work, school, and family obligations. Their deep connections to small towns like Visalia, Madera, and Kerman are invaluable resources for building public history projects and engaging underrepresented communities. I constructed the course knowing that I would have a spectrum of students and that the course had to do four things: (1) provide students with a strong understanding of the VPHI's public history ethos and methodology; (2) explore the history of the beautiful game, focusing on the development of the game in the United States while also noting its origins and transnational and global connections; (3) build an archive of soccer in the Central Valley by conducting original research, scanning photographs, and recording oral histories; and (4) share the history of soccer in the Central Valley, both primary and secondary sources, with the community.

In all my classes, I try to make sure my students are comfortable with me and with one another and that they think of their classmates as colleagues and collaborators. I set the tone on the first day of class by putting them in groups of three or four. Taking turns, they all ask one individual one question. So, in a group of four, three individuals will ask one student three separate questions. They all take notes. When they are done, I ask them to introduce someone in their group to the rest of the class. I then ask the groups a series of questions about soccer as a way to introduce the course. I ask, for example: What is soccer? Why should we study it? I then combine their responses to make three big points about the game. One, that soccer is a universal language and that as a language, it has evolved over the years but is understood globally. Two, that soccer is a place where we can study important questions. It's a site, I tell them, where questions of national identity are debated. I offer the French men's national team of 1998 and Mexican American soccer players' place on the U.S. and Mexican national teams as examples. Third, soccer is a global business with tremendous inequality. I offer European academies in Africa as an example of the game's exploitative possibilities, in addition to salaries of Major League Soccer (MLS) players and the U.S. Women's National Team to give them a sense of the pay disparities among teammates, within the league, and across gender. We usually start but don't finish reviewing the syllabus.

The course is divided into three sections: an introduction to how history works and public history, the history of soccer broadly speaking, and research and public engagement. The first section of the course is about three weeks long. The first paper is usually due in week four. To guide the readings and class discussion, I provide students with the first paper prompt during our second meeting: "In order to build a public history project, we must first understand *how* history works. This paper provides us an opportunity to reflect on two things: (1) the production of history; (2) tools, methods, and theories to intervene in this process in order to create new archives and new narratives."

To answer how history works, we read the introduction to Michel-Rolph Trouillot's *Silencing the Past*. By reading Trouillot, students come to understand how power and silence enter the four stages of historical production: "the moment of fact creation (the making of *sources*); the moment of fact assembly (the making of *archives*); the moment of fact retrieval (the making of *narratives*); and the moment of retrospective significance (the making of *history* in the final instance)."[4] Through class discussion and lectures, I draw out the role of the historian. I note that in this four-stage process, the historian does not enter until stage three. The historian plays no role, I emphasize, in the creation of facts or the archive, and is thus dependent on what has already been collected and assembled. I offer Fresno State's special collections as an example. I ask my students if there is a box named Soccer in Visalia. The answer is no.

The course material that follows demonstrates how public history can radically alter the role and place of both marginalized communities and historians in the historical process. This includes lessons on oral history, SEMAP's East of East project and book *East of East: The Making of Greater El Monte*, and The Other Football. I supplement Alessandro Portelli's canonical essay "The Peculiarities of Oral History" with a brief lecture on oral history. The spring 2019 and 2020 classes also listened to a fifteen-minute excerpt from an oral history that is part of The Other Football archive. The takeaway for this class is that through oral history, historians and community members become active agents in the historical process. We not only determine what is "relevant" but co-create a new primary source and new archive.

I follow this class up with a lesson on East of East and a deeper exploration of The Other Football. Students read the introduction to *East of East* to get a good sense of the overall project, and I use class time to give them an overview of how we built the archive. I emphasize SEMAP's public history practice and methodology, noting, among other things, our effort to place community at each of the four stages of historical production. I show them punk flyers that we collected and note that we shared the flyers on social media and in a 1,000-word essay on the online media outlet KCET.[5] My students learn how quickly and easily we can scan photographs and flyers and how they serve as invaluable historical sources. The section on public history ends with an introduction to The Other Football. Students in the spring 2019 course read a brief introduction to the project published on the *Tropics of Meta* blog; listened to Valley Public Radio's audio segment on the project (the station interviewed myself and Tyler Caffee in 2019); and explored The Other Football archival items, which were housed in Box—a cloud storage system that Fresno State makes available to faculty and students.[6] I share the entire archive with students, which is organized thematically in various folders. As "editors," they have permission to upload and download items but not delete or edit files. The second time I taught the course, I invited students from the first semester to present their contributions to The Other Football.

This part of the course always feels quick, and I wish that I could dedicate more time to teaching students how to conduct oral histories. Because I do not train students in oral history methodology in this class, I have to rely on students who have taken my oral history course to conduct oral histories for The Other Football. This first section of the course accomplishes the goal of introducing both public history and The Other Football to the class. With permission from one of my former students, I include here how he understood the role of public history in transforming the historical process: "This paper will outline how the Valley Public History Initiative's The Other Football: Tracing the Game's Roots and Routes revolutionizes the historical process by examining how oral history changes the role of the historian, how public history changes the community's involvement in the historical process, and how oral history reevaluates the silences in historical production."[7]

The second part of the course consists of six to seven weeks and does a few different things: it provides an introduction to the development of the game in England, its emergence in the United States, and its growth in the Central Valley. We pay particular attention to the role of immigrants, especially from Mexico. The core text for this section is Laurent Dubois's *The Language of the Game*. Here is an excerpt from a student's book review:

> *The Language of the Game* truly is a love letter to soccer, and Dubois succeeds in his intentions. He is exceedingly triumphant in not only explaining the various positions of the game but does so in a way that is relatable and goes beyond the game. Dubois seamlessly weaves soccer into the world of politics and culture, and touches on a myriad of relevant topics such as sexism, immigration, innovation, and progress. His use of sources and personal experience combine to create a narrative that is relevant and interesting to both soccer fans and newcomers to the game. Overall, Dubois demonstrates the numerous ways in which soccer is human, it is life, possibility, language, a story, powerful, never ending, an immigrant, a sanctuary, and about more than winning.[8]

Each week covers a different topic but follows a pretty similar structure. I lecture; we discuss the readings (a chapter from Dubois); we do some sort of group activity; and groups of two or three students profile a player, team, coach, or league. In terms of content, this section opens with the origins of the game in England and its emergence as an activity defined by rules and run by official organizations. We then explore the game's arrival and growth in the United States, noting among other things the various reasons for its stunted growth and its popularity among different ethnic/racialized groups.[9] For example, we examine the 1994 World Cup, the MLS, and why professional soccer leagues folded throughout the twentieth century.

Core themes throughout the lectures and readings are gender, race, and immigration. In one class, our exploration of African Americans and soccer in the United States includes the Howard University men's soccer team and their success in NCAA Division 1 in the 1970s. As Spike Lee's documentary *Redemption Song* illustrates, the team was primarily composed of international Black soccer players from Africa and the Caribbean. As these Black soccer players competed and beat all-white teams throughout the country, the team came to embody Black power.[10] We also explore the development of the women's game and examine discrepancies in pay, as well as potential reasons for the women's teams continued success when compared to the men's teams.

The course also considers the development of the game in Mexico, noting its ties to nation building after the Mexican Revolution. Through articles and player profiles, we link migration north to the growth of the game throughout the United States. Building on key works on Mexican Americans and sport, including my own, we look at how migrants created communities through sport. In the Central Valley, a group of international players came together to form an adult amateur soccer league in the 1940s, which included a team by the name of Club Mexico. This team existed for decades and eventually became the basis of the Professional Development League (PDL) team Fresno Fuego, which was founded in 2002. Mexican migrants and Mexican Americans did not just form community in the United States but also created strong links and networks to their home country, and we look closely at how Mexican American players have consistently looked to Mexico to expand their playing opportunities. This includes the Chicana and Fresno native Anisa Guajardo, who played on Mexico's national team; Francisco Alvarez, who played for Toros Neza after playing for Fresno Pacific; and Juan Sanchez (my godfather and college coach), who played for Pumas after his collegiate career with California State University, Los Angeles, under the tutelage of Leonardo Cuellar. It also includes our very own Ernie Vargas (spring 2018 course), who as a teenager moved to Guadalajara to play for Chivas's youth teams.

After the first semester, I was able to incorporate The Other Football archive and local history into the class in a variety of ways. In addition to using the archive to create lectures about the game in the Central Valley, students used oral histories and photographs from previous classes to profile a local team, player, or coach. For example, when we discussed African Americans and the Black diaspora, one group delivered a ten-minute presentation on Melvin Williams, an African American man who grew up in a white neighborhood and played at Fresno City College; on the San Joaquin Valley Adult League; and eventually for the New Mexico Chiles, part of the

American Professional Soccer League in 1990. They used the oral history that we conducted with Williams, which we also published as a highly curated transcript on *Tropics of Meta*. The oral history with Williams was conducted by Juan Fonseca during one semester and edited and transcribed by Marisela Hernandez during another semester. It opens like this:

> I didn't know what soccer was actually. I was coming home from school one day and saw a poster on the wall that they were having tryouts. I told my mom that I wanted to try out. So she brought me back up there, filled out the paperwork, and I went. That was when my brother Keith Earl and I discovered soccer. We played for the soccer team at Wolters Elementary. I was on the C-team in under-10 soccer, playing goalie of all positions. There was one game where our team was losing, so our coach decided to put me out onto the field for the first time. When I got onto the field, I scored about 5 goals. After that, I never went back to goalie.

It ends like this:

> Soccer has been my everything. My whole identity is soccer. Everything I'm about is related to soccer. Everyone I know references me to soccer. For anyone who says Mel, the next thing they say is "Oh the Mel that plays soccer." They go hand in hand. I can't imagine my name without soccer being a part of it. There is nothing about me that's me without soccer. It's what I do. Soccer is everything, and that has never changed for me. Soccer was my first love. I hadn't played soccer before the third grade, but I was athletic. I started off playing goalie. It was at that first or second game where our team was losing, and my coach took me out of the goal and onto the field. I scored a bunch of goals, and we caught up and won. That was it. My whole life changed that day.[11]

I considered removing the student presentations from the course, but the group presentations allowed students to conduct research and to connect their specific player, coach, or team to themes from the class. It also gave them a chance to practice skills they would deploy for their final class projects.

There are two big assignments for the second part of the course. A 1,000-word book review of Dubois's *The Language of the Game* and a take-home midterm. The prompt for the take-home midterm is fairly open and invites students to combine different readings, primary sources, and group presentations. The prompt reads as follows: "'Once,' wrote Oscar Handlin, 'I thought to write a history of the immigrants in America. Then I discovered that the immigrants were American history.' The Harvard professor and Pulitzer Prize winner was referring to his 1951 *The Uprooted*, perhaps the most well-known and read history book on U.S. immigration. This quote, while overused and a bit cliché, nicely characterizes the history of soccer in the United States. Using lectures, student presentations, and readings, write a 4-page essay that examines the relationship between migration and soccer in the United States."

This section covers a lot, and students often felt as though they did not get credit for everything they learned. I scaffold both papers, but it is always hard to test students on all the course material. One early criticism of the course, and particularly this section, was that we read a lot about soccer but never watched it. Students who were new to soccer said "they didn't really get it." After the first course (spring 2018), I showed more soccer clips throughout the semester. On at least one occasion, we watched a game in class. Although the Dubois book is indeed written for the fútbol aficionado and novice alike, students really enjoyed watching soccer together. Another Fresno State professor and I also bought two seasons tickets for the 2019–20 season and gave these away to students. The only condition was that they post from The Other Football's Instagram or Twitter account (@historiapublica).

If I had to summarize the goals of this part of the course it would be to provide students a language to describe and understand the game across both time and space and get them excited for local history, particularly contributing to and building The Other Football archive.

Building the Archive

Parts one and two of the course provided students with the context and language to research the history of fútbol in the Central Valley and to help build The Other Football archive. In the third part, which is about six weeks, students worked on building the archive by researching the history of soccer in the *Fresno Bee* and in high school and college yearbooks, scanning photographs provided by community members, and conducting oral histories. The final often included presenting our research to the larger community. Students who took the course in 2019 or 2020 had fewer subjects to pick from but had the benefit of seeing what other students had done and, in some cases, using the existing archive to write an essay. I graded holistically and tried to keep in mind students' plan and process, the number of primary sources they added to the archive, the quality of the scans and inventory forms, what they produced from the archive, and the challenge of their specific research subject. I'll discuss this section in terms of research—how I structured the work and what students found—and then explain how they presented it to the community.

I provided students in the spring 2018 course with a very clear and defined list of options. Working in groups, students were asked to research the history of men's and women's soccer teams at Fresno City, Fresno State, and Pacific University. In addition, they could research the history of professional soccer in the Central Valley. I allowed some students, particularly those who had already taken an oral or a public history course with me, to research the development of the game in their community. My undergraduate advisee Tyler Caffee, for example, focused on the development of the game in Visalia. Another student, who was part of Fresno Fuego's Fire Squad, interviewed the founders.

To structure the groups' work, I asked them to dedicate one week to coming up with a very detailed research plan/calendar on Google Drive. They had to note who was going to look where and when. They were also required to keep a time log of hours and tasks completed. Throughout the rest of the semester, I checked their Google folders and documents. We also continued to meet.

The benefit of researching collegiate soccer was that there was a clear identifiable database. Groups could find and download articles about their respective teams in the *Fresno Bee* and the respective campus newspapers, and search for photos in the various yearbooks. It was relatively easy to locate when a university founded a team, under what conditions, and a team's relative success. To facilitate and aid student research, I conducted an oral history with Jaime Ramirez, who played at Fresno Pacific, was the first coach from the PDL team Fresno Fuego, and coached both the men's and women's team at Fresno Pacific. Indeed, he was the first head coach of the women's team. "El Profe," as he is affectionately and respectfully known in the Central Valley community, also contributed beautiful photographs of both the men's and women's teams at Fresno Pacific.

In the second and third semester, the themes expanded. Students added different high schools and additional local and regional leagues and teams. This included, for example, the Portuguese Club House and team in Tulare, which was founded in the 1960s. As in the first semester, I continued to offer to conduct oral histories with relevant players or coaches.

Over the course of a few weeks, students organized the articles they found in Google Drive based on the source—such as the *Fresno Bee*—and also uploaded photographs from the yearbooks, which they scanned. They maintained a list of items and worked together to note what they found. As a way to check on their progress, I held a little contest for extra points during class. Each group was given fifteen minutes to identify the "coolest" archival find and to create a quick PowerPoint to present their finding and offer an initial analysis. At the end, each group voted for the coolest find. One group found that Fresno High School had a team in the early 1900s. Another group presented a photograph of the Edison High School boys' and girls' teams: both were founded in the 1970s and were composed predominantly of African American youth. Were the players, the group asked, inspired by the Howard University men's soccer team from the 1970s or were they inspired by the Brazilian soccer player Pelé?

In Google Drive, students and groups provided weekly updates, which I followed closely. I helped groups that were struggling and nudged individuals that were not doing enough work. Everything—articles, scanned photographs, copyright forms, and so on—were originally uploaded to Google Drive. For the final exam, students were asked to take their archive and upload it to Fresno State's cloud storage system (Box), along with a finding aid that briefly summarized the scope of the material and number of items. This worked fine for most groups, but there was always one or two groups that had compiled a pretty massive number of *Fresno Bee* articles. In addition, students found it tedious that they had to upload material to Google Drive and then to Fresno State's Box. I agreed with them, but I used Google Drive as a first draft; I could see the collection and decide whether or not it should be uploaded to Box. For example, I could discard any photographs that did not have release forms, photographs that were too blurry, or items that we did not have the rights to.

Public Engagement, Outreach, and Final Projects

The Other Football, like all my public history work, seeks to center community members in the entire historical process. In some ways, this is a bit more challenging in a university setting. The campus and curriculum are set up to center students. However, we worked hard to center community members and to find creative ways to engage them throughout the semester and with the final projects. The first two years I received funding from the College of Social Sciences. It's a lot easier to be creative and engage the community when one has funding. Instead of organizing our community engagement and public-facing events by semester, I'll describe them based on whether they were on or off campus.

On Campus

To connect with students and faculty across the college, we organized an official launch for The Other Football in the middle of the semester and in the Social Sciences quad: a space between four buildings that houses trees, some grass, and benches.[12] We set up a booth with flyers advertising our end-of-the-year conference, information about the project, and books on soccer. Through technology services, we set up a large monitor and a microphone. On the monitor, we played a PowerPoint that introduced the project. One of the students emceed the event, which included playing music from his laptop. The event was anchored by a quiz, Fresno FC's visit to campus (the team set up a booth next to ours), and a juggling contest: we invited faculty and students to use their feet, thighs, chest, or head to keep the ball aloft. The students divided juggling contestants into advanced and novice soccer players. The person who juggled the most in their respective category won two tickets to a Fresno FC game. The quiz, created by students using course content, consisted of multiple-choice and true-or-false questions. The prize for the two highest scores was a Starbucks gift card (Starbucks is an official vendor, which made it possible to justify it as an expense). Somehow, the faculty won the gift cards (boo).

The event was a success. We had a good crew of faculty and students in attendance, as well as the local independent and leftist newspaper the *Community Alliance*.[13] A few students who attended the event, such as McKay Kozielski, eventually enrolled in the course. More importantly, the event provided a space outside the classroom for students and faculty to hang out and chill. Fresno State is a commuter campus, and it's important to be intentional about creating learning opportunities and experiences that might otherwise be difficult for students to attend.

In addition to juggling and hanging out in the quad, we organized two conferences on campus. We promoted both conferences through social media and by distributing flyers throughout the community. The first conference lasted two days and focused on students' final projects, along with one keynote panel. Most of the students worked in groups to organize and present ten-minute PowerPoint presentations. Topics included the history of collegiate men's and women's soccer at Fresno City, Pacific University, and

Fresno State; the history of the game in places like Madera and Visalia; the history of professional men's and women's soccer; and the Fire Squad fan club. We used part of our College of Social Sciences funding to provide lunch on both days of the conference. In addition to student presentations, we had Jeremy Schultz (Visalia native and general manager of the Fresno Fuego and the Fresno FC in its inaugural season), Jaime Ramirez (Fresno Pacific coach and the first coach of the PDL Fresno Fuego), and Francisco "Cisco" and José Antonio "Tony" Alvarez (the brothers who were founders and owners of the Fresno Fuego) do a panel on the history of soccer in the Central Valley. They discussed their own personal trajectory and how they all came together to work on the PDL team Fresno Fuego. Their talk was fire (pun intended), and it was standing-room only. Students enjoyed the conference, and they got some great feedback. Lee Herrick, Fresno City faculty and Fresno's poet laureate (2015–17), attended most of the talks on the second day and congratulated students on their research and work. One big challenge was attendance: we had really good numbers around lunchtime and for the panel with Schultz, Ramirez, and the Alvarez brothers, but we had lower numbers in the morning and afternoon sessions. A few students suggested that we try to spread out the talks by the "famous soccer" players as a way to get more bodies into seats throughout the day.

The second conference focused on Fresno Fuego, fandom, and women's soccer, held off campus on a Friday and on campus the following day. Friday's panel was held at Tioga-Sequoia Brewing Company before a Fresno FC game and included the Alvarez brothers, Jaime Ramirez, José Luis Delgadillo, and Jeremy Schultz. The brewery let us use their private reception room, which holds about seventy-five people. Students greeted folks at the entrance and set up a table with The Other Football flyers and materials. Half of them left the brewery early for the stadium in order to set up tables to distribute trading cards. Most of them wore red or gray The Other Football T-shirts, which were designed by local artist Tony Carranza and printed through Fresno State's print shop (every student who attended the Friday or Saturday conference received a shirt). The panel explored the earlier years of the Fresno Fuego, including their roots as the Sunday league team Club Mexico and Fuego's hard-fought games against MLS teams like Chivas USA and the LA Galaxy.[14]

Immediately following the panel, everyone in attendance walked over to the stadium to watch Fresno FC play against Orange County. Faculty, students, and a few friends sat together. It was a must-win for Fresno FC. Orange County scored two goals within the first twelve minutes of the game.

With eleven minutes left in the second half, our team was losing 2–0. Christian Chaney got the squad within range by scoring a beautiful diving header off a cross and making it 2-1. The captain, an Argentine player in his early thirties named Juan Pablo Caffa, tied it up with a free kick from outside the 18-yard line. The stands erupted, and folks clapped, yelled, and hugged. A few of us headed back to Tioga-Sequoia for one last beer.

The conference continued on campus the next morning. Lacking any foresight, I scheduled the fandom panel for the morning. Pedro Navarro (a local activist and player), Kathryn Johnson (Fire Squad member, Tioga-Sequoia employee, and alumna), Edward Stewart (Fire Squad member), and Chris Step (Fresno Skulk) discussed how and when they fell in love with the game, the ethos and mission of their fan club, and their position on the use of the Mexican chant that includes the homophobic word *put** at Fresno FC games. As the opposing goalie gets ready to take a goal kick, fans yell "Ehhhh put*." The origin story places the birth of this chant in Guadalajara, Mexico, at a Chivas versus Atlas game in 2003. Regardless of its origin, fans in Mexico and the United States have popularized this chant and even taken it to the World Cup, resulting in both controversy and fines.[15] Navarro and Stewart explained why they are against the chant and do not use it. Another interesting point of contention discussed was about the lack of collaboration between the different fan groups. One person in the audience, for example, asked why they cannot all sing the same songs.

The panel on fandom ended with a surprise visit from one of Fresno's most loved local players. Christian Chaney was born in Fresno (1994) and attended and played for Fresno City, for Fresno Fuego, and professionally in Mexico and Armenia. He was a big signing for Fresno FC and was one of a handful of local players who consistently got playing time. His reputation as a local player has been cemented by his commitment to one of Fresno Fuego's most cherished traditions: walking over to Tioga-Sequoia for a beer after the game. I cannot remember how we first invited him to the conference. We might have messaged him on Instagram or Twitter or seen him at Tioga-Sequoia after the 2–2 tie. What I do remember is that we prepared just in case he took us up on the invitation. We already had an enlarged eight-by-eleven-inch Chaney trading card. We framed that one, set aside a dozen or so regular size cards, and neatly folded one of our T-shirts. Chaney arrived and joined the panel on fandom, sitting next to his fans. After the panel, he signed trading cards, took a few selfies, and headed out. From outside the library, he posted a story on Instagram: he gave us a shout-out as he held his trading card and wore The Other Football T-shirt.

The second panel on Saturday brought together coaches and players involved with women's soccer at the collegiate and professional level. Edna Ortega, who was in the 2018 course, delivered a fifteen-minute presentation on the history of women's collegiate and professional soccer in the Central Valley. She used her own research on Fresno City and browsed the archive to include the other colleges and professional teams. Our panelists—Timothy Carroll (head coach of the Fresno FC Ladies, the sister team of the Fresno FC), Oliver Germond (Fresno City head coach), and Maria Magaña (Fresno City alum)—discussed the challenges and opportunities for women's soccer in the Central Valley. One coach told a funny story about stealing benches from one campus so that his players could have somewhere to sit during games. Carroll gave a particularly impassioned speech about the loss of the Fresno FC Ladies after just one season. Despite winning the 2018 Pac North Division title in impressive fashion (six wins and two draws), the franchise placed the team on hiatus (it also placed the U-23 men's team on hiatus). He also encouraged the fan clubs to do more to support women's soccer. The makeup of the panel reflected the dominance of male coaches in women's soccer. The coaches, both male and female, emphasized the importance of creating pipelines for women to become head coaches. This panel was followed by Josh Nadel's keynote on the history of women's soccer in Latin America. Students in my courses read selections from Josh's first book, *Fútbol! Why Soccer Matters in Latin America*, so students were excited about his second book, coauthored with Brenda Elsey, *Futbolera: A History of Women and Sport in Latin America*. You'll have to read the book, but for some players, the struggle to play included cross-dressing and passing as boys.

Trading Cards at Fresno FC Games

The most popular and, perhaps, most innovative aspect of The Other Football project was combining primary and secondary sources by creating trading cards about players, coaches, and teams. We created the first set of trading cards in the first semester and continued through the second semester. The structure was straightforward. An individual student or group of students was asked to use an oral history or other relevant primary sources to compose a brief narrative and to list the teams that the person played on, coached, or managed. We created a style guide to consistently spell and capitalize certain words. In addition to writing the text, students were required to generate or find an image for the front of the card. To streamline the process, I provided the class a blank form via Google Drive. Once they

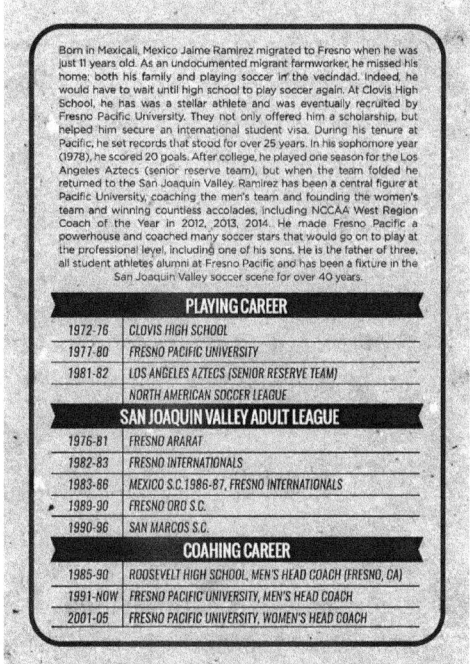

Jaime Ramirez trading card, front and back, Valley Public History Initiative (courtesy of author).

had a good draft, I looked it over, made some edits, and moved it from the student's Google Drive folder to a new folder. I then shared this folder with the designer, Tony Carranza, who created a uniform design for the trading cards and took the text and images from Google Drive to make each individual card. Tony also found creative ways to make up for low resolution or otherwise poor-quality images. I submitted the cards to the print shop on campus. These cards then became part of the digital archive.

I realized very early on that one of Fresno State's biggest assets for public history is in-house printing, which makes it very easy to print posters, images on foam board or canvas, chapbooks, and even T-shirts. In addition to trading cards, we printed The Other Football T-shirts: one in gray and one in red. I usually distributed these at the end of the semester to students who volunteered to hand out trading cards at Fresno FC games. I'm also pretty sure that anyone who wanted one got one, but my memory might be betraying me here.

In total, we created about twenty-four trading cards and printed at least 5,000 between 2018 and 2019. We distributed these at the local Sunday league, at youth games, and at indoor leagues where The Other Football team played (more on that in the next section). Through our partnership with Fresno FC, we were also able to distribute them at the club's home games. We would arrive at the stadium early and enter through the two glass windows reserved for staff and workers. Fresno FC provided me with about a dozen tickets every time we distributed trading cards. A group of three students would gather at each of the entrances, while another group and I sat next to a table, where we displayed cards and old archival-looking books about the game, as well as flyers and information about The Other Football. After students distributed the few hundred or so cards we'd printed up, most would head to the stands to watch the game, while a few of us stayed back to hang out at the table. At the end of the half, we'd pack up and watch the game.

The partnership with Fresno FC allowed us to have fun, to enjoy fútbol, and to engage an eager public. It also granted us a lot of credibility with the Central Valley soccer community and made it easier for me to pitch the significance of public history to my students and university. The collaboration with Fresno FC was in part thanks to Jeremy Schultz, whom Tyler Caffee interviewed for his senior thesis in the fall of 2017 and profiled in an essay that we published on *Tropics of Meta*. When Fresno FC bought Fresno Fuego, Schultz became the general manager, which gave us instant access. Of course, Schultz had a lot of important things to take care of, and our main point of contact became Angel Moreno, a Fresno State alum. At our first meeting, me, Moreno, and a few students explored ways we might collaborate. From that first meeting, Moreno and I spoke over the phone and exchanged emails. Through Moreno and distributing cards, we quickly got to know the Fresno FC staff, including Chuy, the ticket rep.

Forming Community Outside the Classroom

Some ideas, to borrow from the Mexican archivist and historian Diego Flores Magón, do not have authors. They are so good that they belong to the collective and not the individual. They grow organically and connect a project to its past while pointing to its future. Public history, like the beautiful game, has a degree of improvisation and individual talent, but ultimately, it is a collective endeavor.

After just the first semester, The Other Football community expanded beyond the classroom to form a team. Its movement from the classroom to the fútbol pitch was the result of watching Fresno FC games together, handshakes and chit-chat in the hallways, and a genuine effort by young faculty (in this particular case, me and adjunct history professor Joe Orbock, who regularly contributed to the VPHI projects) to engage and mentor students. It was also, at least in part, the result of one faculty member joking with the students about their relative skills on the pitch.

Professor Orbock and undergraduate students Carlos, Ernie, Juan, and Rigo made up the core of the team, which we named Joaquin Murrieta's All Stars. The team was rounded out by me and Carlos's younger brother and friends. We practiced a few times before our official match with the Mellysport Futsal soccer league, which was located on the periphery of Blackbeard's Family Entertainment. We wore black shorts, black socks, and red dry-fit jerseys that Carlos's dad made for us and sold to us at cost. The words "Historia Publica" ran across the chest in white font, and numbers adorned the back. It quickly became apparent to us that the league was a strong one, composed of teams with former and current college players. I ended up doing more coaching than playing, and together the squad came to play some good fútbol, defend our name, and put up a battle. We got to know one another but also became friends with some of the other players and teams and developed a relationship with the owner and former soccer player Melvin Williams, whom we ended up collaborating with and whose story appears earlier in this chapter. When Mel first refereed our games, none of us had any idea that he had played professionally.

That core group formed a co-ed soccer team for Fresno State's fall 2018 intramural league. While alumni could not play, creating a co-ed team provided us a chance to reach out to women soccer players and create a more inclusive team. While we did a lot better than in the Mellysport Futsal league, the rules of the co-ed league were a nice reminder about how little most white Americans know about soccer. The pitch was too long, the goals were neither small nor big, and the referees knew little to nothing about the game. We opted to play only one season. The Other Football team continued to play under Professor Orbock's direction in a newer indoor futsal league with pristine fields (my family welcomed a new baby, so I was unable to attend with any regularity).

Futbolistas con Refugiados

By connecting on the futsal court and hanging out in the Fresno FC stands, we created a space to think together outside the classroom. As the Central America caravan made its way to the U.S.-Mexico border, we asked ourselves

Group photo from tournament-fundraiser, Fresno, California (courtesy of Peter Maiden).

about the role of soccer in raising awareness. The Fire Squad had stood firmly against the homophobic "put*" chant but was very quiet about other political issues, including the presidency of 45. As we learned more about Central American refugees and the efforts by Mexicans on both sides of the U.S.-Mexico border, we asked ourselves, "What would Sócrates do?" A few of us had started reading and learning about this tall, lanky central midfielder who was a doctor, a philosopher, and the captain of Brazil's national squad during the 1980s. He marched against dictators, advocated for players' rights on and off the pitch, and wore a headband during the 1986 World Cup in Mexico that read "Mexico sigue en pie" (Mexico still stands).[16]

After walking more than 2,000 miles during the fall of 2018, the caravan of Central Americans arrived in Tijuana and found themselves a temporary home at the Unidad Deportiva Benito Juárez (Benito Juárez Sporting Complex). Very quickly, a network of Southern California Raza activists began collecting donations and making regular trips down to the border to deliver material goods. As news of their efforts populated our newsfeed, we arrived at the idea of organizing a futsal tournament to raise funds for Central American refugees. This tournament was part of The Other Football network, but because we were raising funds and playing soccer (a potential insurance issue), we did not promote or align it with The Other Football or

Fresno State. Each team that played in the tournament donated fifty dollars, and the finalists received custom T-shirts made by Carlos's dad that read "Imaginemos Cosas Chingonas" (Imagining the impossible).[17] The winners received shirts and two copies of Joshua Nadel's *Fútbol! Why Soccer Matters in Latin America.*

Six teams participated. Four of the teams were co-ed, and together the six teams were composed of players from multiple generations and included Central Americans, Mexican migrants, Mexican Americans, African Americans, Asian Americans, and white Americans. Activist Pedro Navarro-Cruz and Professor Orbock helped secure the teams and tapped into their cascara and soccer networks. Fresno State students José and Juan refereed all the games. Between games, Fresno State professors Anabella España-Nájera and Luis Fernando Macias provided brief but concise lectures on the history of Central America, U.S. empire, and the asylum process in the age of Trump. They were joined by Saúl Sarabia, one of the Southern California Raza activists.

While I was worried about how to effectively combine soccer and lectures/discussions, it ended up working out well. "I feel like the players and teams were really concerned and interested in learning from the professors about the history of Central America and from the organizer Saúl Sarabia a firsthand perspective on what is going on," reflected one of the players.

The End of the Other Football?

In the spring of 2020, I taught Fútbol: A Local and Global History of the Beautiful Game for the third time. In this case, there was absolutely nothing charming about the third time. The ownership of Fresno FC was unable to create a stadium for the team—a United Soccer League requirement for all new franchises—and decided to leave town. With Fresno FC gone, we were left without our biggest partner (and audience). That same semester, as most of you reading this know, COVID-19 arrived. At first, administrators and universities greeted it with optimism: perhaps it would fade away. Indeed, in the early days, we walked around campus without masks, washing our hands over and over again. However, it quickly became apparent—to most sane folks at least—that COVID-19 was serious and that moving all classes online was the only safe option. I also accepted a job at Claremont Graduate University (CGU) in Southern California. That spring semester was so new and different that no one outlined how to officially depart. Indeed, I took my campus laptop with me to Los Angeles and left my campus office intact. Before departing, I emailed my department administrators, folks in the library whom I had worked with on digital collections, and the tech folks in the College of Social Sciences. As things got settled, I requested continued access to my Fresno State Box, where the entire archive was housed.

The fall semester arrived, and Fresno State and CGU remained online. Throughout the summer, I had checked my Fresno State email. I checked again in September and there was nothing new. My permanent away message was still responding to each and every email, notifying the sender that I'd left Fresno and that I could be reached at my new email. I logged out and then logged into my Fresno State Box. When I arrived at Fresno State, I founded the Valley Public History Initiative, which included, among other responsibilities, creating digital storage (Fresno State's Box) for all my public history projects and oral history courses, as well as copyright release forms for images and oral histories that we collected. In addition, per the library's request, I signed an agreement with the library to donate the collections. Before I left, VPHI's Straight Outta Fresno collection was successfully transferred from my Box to the library's CONTENTdm.[18] However, over 3,000 items of The Other Football still resided in my Fresno State Box.

I logged into my Fresno State Box that September day, and instead of 3,000 or so items organized in a series of folders, I saw nothing. Or, to be precise, I found a Box that had zero folders and zero items. I yelled a number of expletives and then became contemplative: Was it my fault? Did I bear the blame? I had emailed my department administrators, folks in tech, and the librarians, but had I placed an official request to extend my access to Box? I had offered a possible transition plan, which included having adjunct faculty—collaborators and co-directors—take over my classes, as well as future collaborations between CGU and Fresno State. Blame, of course, would do me no good. I quickly realized this and started composing—from the Fresno State–issued laptop I was allowed to mail back—an email to the chair and the main person in the campus's technology division.

As I waited for a response, I imagined having to explain to the Fresno Fuego founders, players, and coaches how I had lost the archive. How the oral histories that we conducted in their offices, in their homes, and at the local brewery had vanished into the ether. How it was not necessarily my fault but that it was absolutely my responsibility. I imagined telling my students who drove to Tulare to scan and archive the photographs from the Portuguese club that their work was gone. And then, as I was remembering my students' labor and faces, I recalled that I had shared the entire Fresno State Box archive with Ryan, a student in my spring 2020 course, and made him an editor. That semester Ryan took the entire archive, created a copy, and organized it thematically (yes, I know this is not how archivists prefer to organize archives, but for teaching purposes it works nicely). Ryan graduated that semester, but we were connected via social media. I jumped on Facebook and messaged Ryan: "Call me as soon as you can. Please." He called me a few minutes later. I explained what happened and asked him if, as an alum, he still had access to Box. He opened his laptop, punched in his username and password, and—much to our relief—found the entire archive just as he had left it.

I asked Ryan to go buy an external hard drive and to download all the folders. We had "lost" the archive once, and I didn't want to lose it again. I also contacted folks at the CGU library to explain what had happened and to ask for help. In the end, Fresno State's solution was to grant me access to the archive for a few days and to have me download all the items and save them somewhere, anywhere. Then, at a future date, to share the collection back with the Fresno State library. Fortunately, the staff at CGU provided a clear path. I shared the Fresno State Box with CGU staff, and they quickly absorbed it into CGU's storage, relieving me of any future nightmares.

The point here is not to shame individuals and institutions. Fresno State is a large institution that is in the process of figuring out how to help and work with faculty on digitally born projects. The university was absolutely great with a previous project, Straight Outta Fresno: From Popping to B-boys and B-girls, which we hope will be up on its digital collections soon (and which moved smoothly from my Fresno State Box to CONTENTdm). This potential disaster, however, can serve as an important lesson for faculty at institutions that are underfunded or new to digitally born archives/public history projects. If possible, libraries should shoulder the burden of digitally sustaining and preserving collections as they are created. Ideally, this would include storing the digital archive and providing a clear and direct path to publishing the digital collection. But perhaps more importantly, the joy and responsibility of seeing a public history project come to fruition as a digital collection should be shared.

Toward a Conclusion: "Imaginemos Cosas Chingonas"

In Latin America there is a saying that goes like this: "Les pesa mucho la gamiseta." The literal translation is "Their shirts are too heavy." This, of course, is such a bad translation that it almost serves as a betrayal. It is a simple saying and serves an even more basic function: it creates distance between a player and a team. The individual player or team is somehow not worthy of wearing the jersey. They lack the heart or commitment to the values and ethos that the shirt is collectively understood to embody. This saying can only ever be used to disrespect a player, but I want to hold on to it, to think through it a bit. Perhaps, even subvert it.

If we take the player out of the saying, we are left with a shirt, a shirt whose weight can be measured in previous struggles, victories, and hardships. The weight of the shirt, in other words, is formed collectively and temporally. In this way, it's not too different from The Other Football: the project grew and expanded through the individual and group effort of students. Each oral history we gathered or photograph we scanned added to our collective desire and commitment to preserve, document, and narrate the history of the game in the Central Valley; to see professional football arrive, stay, and thrive; to honor the labor and work of those Sunday league coaches and pioneers of fútbol teams and leagues, particularly women's soccer.

But what happens when you take off the shirt? Can one remain committed to a place from afar? If public history is meant to transcend the divide between the public and the university, can it also bridge the gap between universities? If my goal as an educator is to create community outside the classroom, what does that look like now? I'm not sure, but I remain hopeful. The COVID-19 vaccine has arrived, the original founders of the Fresno Fuego have bought a new PDL team—the Central Valley Fuego Football Club—and in the fall of 2022 I am teaching a public history course on fútbol at CGU. Together with a few alumni, we've started building a digital archive of The Other Football: https://futbolencalifornia.com. If professional soccer found its way back to the Central Valley, maybe we can connect that valley to the San Gabriel Valley.

Notes

1. In addition to oral histories and digitized photographs, East of East resulted in an edited book, thematic bike rides, ethnic studies curriculum at the high schools, murals, a ten-minute documentary about lost murals, public talks and readings, and a digital archive. See Guzmán, Fragoza, Cummings, and Reft, *East of East*.

2. For more on the conference, including the program, see https://globalsoccerconference.wcfia.harvard.edu/summary2017.

3. After attending the conference, I published "Field of Dreams," and Tyler Caffee published several short sections of his master's thesis on the academic blog *Tropics of Meta* (www.tropicsofmeta.com).

4. Trouillot, *Silencing the Past*, 26.
5. Parra, "Punk Flyers from El Monte."
6. Tsutsui, "'Roots and Routes' Event Highlights Valley's Soccer History."
7. Unpublished essay in possession of the author.
8. Unpublished essay in possession of the author.
9. David Trouille's article on soccer in Chicago works particularly well as a reading assignment in this section. His focus on Chicago allows students to see larger national patterns and, I hope, inspires them to think of Fresno and the Central Valley's deep multiethnic history. See Trouille, "Association Football to Fútbol."
10. Holley, "Redemption Song."
11. Williams, "My First Love."
12. Most of the public engagement aspects of the class occurred at the end of the semester.
13. See Maiden, "Fresno Soccer History."
14. The Fuego, an amateur team at the time, played against professional teams in scrimmages and in the U.S. Open Cup. The team's fourth-round game was covered in the *Los Angeles Times*. See Gutierrez, "Galaxy Rallies to Beat Fuego in U.S. Open Cup."
15. For a detailed history and exploration of the chant, see Hidalgo and Vargas, "Ehhhhh Pu! . . . what?"
16. See Downie, *Doctor Socrates*.
17. If Sócrates originally guided our thinking, it was now the Mexican forward Chicharito's provocation that challenged us. For the Mexican national team, imagining the impossible meant believing they could beat Germany, the reigning World Cup champs. As players, scholars, and children of migrants, what futures can we imagine? What *cosas chingonas* do our people deserve?
18. In collaboration with Sean Slusser—Fresno State adjunct professor and co-director of Straight Outta Fresno—and Claremont Graduate University, we created an Omeka site to showcase some of the archival items. See https://digitalclaremont.net/straightouttafresno/intro.

8 Seven Weeks of Heaven

Teaching an Undergraduate Introduction to
Public History Course in Half a Semester

JENNIFER DICKEY

Most of my teaching career has involved teaching public history to undergraduate students at a large (40,000+ students) state university in Georgia. For more than a decade, I have had the good fortune to teach nothing but public history courses. The advantage of this is that I get to channel my energies into teaching courses about which I am passionate, and I get to work with undergraduate students as they are beginning to discover this thing called public history. The disadvantage, if there is one, is that a public history course may require extensive and extraordinary preparation and coordination on the part of the instructor, especially if it involves a student project with an outside client. While each course is unique, there are commonalities across the semesters that undergird the structure and format of all my classes. I strive to get my students to engage with one another and with our community, to be interested in the ways that they encounter the interpretation of history outside the classroom, and to understand the processes by which those interpretations are created.

My introduction to public history course, which I have taught over a dozen times in the past twelve years, serves as the gateway to our undergraduate public history program at Kennesaw State University (KSU). The course is one of two core requirements—the other is an internship course—for an eighteen-hour certificate program. It is the course I use to introduce students to the fundamentals of theory and practice in the field. It is one of my favorite courses to teach because it allows me to explore the many modes of public history. I have taught this course in a variety of formats—as a traditional fifteen-week course, a seven-week course, and a two-week Maymester course. The latter, which I have taught twice, I often refer to as public history boot camp. It is an immersive, five-hour-a-day course for which I allot time in the classroom for group work and other hands-on components. My favorite format is the seven-week version, because it allows me and my students to focus on a single course for a concentrated period of time. I have no illusions that this is the only course that my students are taking, but for the first seven weeks of the semester, it is the only course that they are taking with me. That allows me to get to know them better—we meet twice a week for two hours and forty-five minutes—and allows them to focus on one public history project for those seven weeks. I pair the intro course with my museum studies course, which I teach during the second seven weeks of the semester. Usually about 75 percent of the students who take the intro course also enroll in the museum studies course, which creates a great sense of camaraderie and helps build a cohort, something that is often difficult at the undergraduate level. Students who enroll in this course take away a deep and wide understanding of public history and the work that public historians do as well as an understanding of the importance of public history in American society. What follows is an account of my introduction to public history course for fall 2019.

The Course and Its Objectives

According to the KSU catalog, HIST 3325 "exposes students to how Americans think about the past, as well as its commemoration and public presentation. Special focus will be placed on the ways in which historians transfer their writing, research, and analytical skills to professions outside of academia. Major subfields and professions within public history are examined, as are the current issues and controversies within the field." This is a course description that was written in 2001, when the public history program was established. While the course description is rather broad and vague, I have found that it serves a useful purpose and allows me, or anyone else who may teach the course, the flexibility to shape the course as we see fit. Furthermore, having experienced the joys of pushing new courses and program changes through the many layers of the university's bureaucracy, I have wisely chosen not to fiddle with things that seem to be good enough.

The course objectives, on the other hand, are my own creation. While I have tweaked them over the years, the list of objectives is designed to be achievable and measurable and to contain every professor's favorite "verifiable verbs" that will pass muster with the powers that be who review such things. For my fall 2019 course, I listed the following course goals:

- Identify the major forms of public history
- Explain the origins and evolution of public history as a profession

- Discuss the variety of careers in the field
- Analyze the main principles and current issues of public history
- Evaluate how historiographical trends are reflected through public history
- Assess the problems and issues associated with implementing public history projects and programs
- Examine the place of public history in discussions of the contested past
- Compare the role of public and private memory in shaping interpretations of the past
- Develop a public history project

I assess students' ability to do these things through class discussions, group or individual presentations, and written assignments. Students also get a chance to assess their teammates and themselves through a peer-review process. My hope is that by the end of the semester, every student will be able to check off each of these goals as completed. An unwritten but not unstated goal for the course is that students will become more thoughtful and engaged citizens in their communities. I also spend time enlightening my students on the basic skills and abilities that they will need to get a job in the field. Drawing on the 2017 report *What Do Public History Employers Want?*, as well as from Philip Katz's "Public History Employers—What Do They Want?" (which summarizes a 2003 report from the American Historical Association), I emphasize the importance of communication skills, both oral and written; the ability to do historical research; historical knowledge; and the ability to speak in public.

Additionally, I explain that I will serve as a reference for my students as they move on to graduate school or into the workforce, and that the work they do in my class forms the basis of my recommendations on their behalf. The most frequent question that I am asked by potential employers is about how well this person works as part of a team. My assessment of this ability comes from the performance of students on group projects. I find that much of a student's success is predicated on his or her ability to work well with others, and I often see this soft skill as a lead indicator of whether a student is well-suited for a career in public history. On the first day of class and throughout the semester, I remind students that I am aware of how much they hate group projects and public speaking, but that being able to do both of these things are fundamental to their success in the world. I am trying, then, to teach them about public history—what it is and why it matters—while developing and improving their written and oral communication skills as well as their ability to work as part of a team.

Experiential Learning and the Depot Project

Experiential learning is a popular concept in education—the notion that students learn best by doing and then reflecting on what they have done. Such hands-on work is essential in public history, although there is much disagreement about how much of this can be done at the undergraduate level. Often, undergraduate students do not have the requisite skills to complete a project over the course of a semester, in which case the professor may end up doing a lot of editing and polishing. My philosophy is that even if the students cannot complete a project that is ready for prime time, I am teaching them the process. Doing public history work is collaborative and iterative, and it is something that may take them years to master. My classes are the beginning of that process. I am a firm believer in giving my students the opportunity to do a project that will have a life beyond the class and an audience besides me. I also accept that for an undergraduate class, I need to do a lot of work in advance to gather research materials and make some executive decisions about resources, themes, and topics. This is doubly true when I am teaching a seven-week course.

I spend a great deal of time working with organizations inside and outside the university to develop projects to which my students can contribute. I am fortunate that KSU has a Department of Museums, Archives and Rare Books (MARB) that supports my efforts to find worthwhile projects. For fall 2019, I worked in tandem with our special projects staff in MARB to develop an exhibit project for an outside client in a neighboring county. The client was interested in developing interpretive programs for several historic sites within the county, so two MARB staff members and I fleshed out a proposal for one of the smaller projects—an exhibit in a former railroad depot—that could be completed in two phases by students in my two fall classes. The Depot Project would entail the creation of a fifteen-panel exhibit for the inside of the recently restored railroad depot located in a small community, Tate, that had once been the epicenter of marble quarrying in the United States. The MARB staff and I spent the early part of the summer gathering research materials and discussing some basic themes that we thought the exhibit should explore. We developed a "big idea," to use the exhibit terminology made famous by Beverly Serrell, and an outline, which we shared with the client. I then wrote the text for the introductory panel, which was reviewed by MARB staff and the client, and handed it off to our in-house graphic designer. By the time the course began in mid-August, our researcher at MARB and I had developed a list of topics, compiled research materials, and produced a beautifully designed introductory panel.

In the Beginning . . .

Because the intro course is offered in the fall, because it is one of the required courses for the program, and because it has the word "Introduction" in the title, it is often the first public history course that students take in the KSU public history program. Since I only teach courses in the public history program, that means it is also the first course that they take with me. Often I have met with the students, either individually or as a group when I gave a presentation on the public history program as part of my recruitment efforts, before they enroll in my classes. I am, however, notoriously bad at remembering names. A face-to-face meeting in my office with an individual student is no guarantee that I will know that student's name in the classroom. Even with small classes, I struggle to remember names. For what it's worth, I do the same thing with my neighbors and acquaintances at parties, so this is not something that afflicts me only in the classroom. Putting students into groups early in the semester—usually during the second course meeting, when the drop/add cycle is over—helps me associate names and faces. As I have discussed earlier, group work is fundamental to public history work, so my weakness is masked behind this need to get them quickly into groups for the work that we will do during the semester.

My fall 2019 class has fourteen students, only one of which I have had in a previous class. I begin the first class by introducing myself and asking the students how many of them are pursuing the public history certificate. About half of them raise their hands. I know that all but three of the students are history majors, and if they are not in the certificate program, they are likely taking the course as an elective. Sometimes students enroll in my courses because it fits into their schedule; sometimes they do so because they have heard good things about my classes. Sometimes they enroll for other reasons. Whatever the reason, I expect them to be engaged and participate with the same amount of fervor as do the students who aspire for public history to be their life's work. I ask the students to introduce themselves, including a bit about their educational trajectory, hobbies, pets, or any other tidbits that they would like to share. Friendly debates about cats versus dogs and *Star Trek* versus *Star Wars* emerge quickly and serve to get everyone chatting. I am struck by one student's comment that she previously attended my undergraduate alma mater and hated it. I make a mental note to revisit that story once I know her better.

After a review of the syllabus and a short break to stretch their legs (each class session is almost three hours long), I launch into my opening lecture about the field of public history. We talk about how the public learns history and the difference between what historians do in academe versus what they do outside the academy. While some of the students enrolled in the course because they aspire to be a park ranger, a curator, or some other sort of museum professional, most of the students had no idea about the many places where public historians work and the kinds of work they do. I remind them of the wise words once spoken by Dr. Connie Schulz of the University of South Carolina: in order to be a good public historian, you must first be a good historian. I conclude the day with three case studies that illustrate the possibilities and the perils of public history: a state historical marker with factually incorrect information, a Confederate monument in front of a county courthouse, and two markers commemorating the same event created by opposing sides in a military conflict. Each case study prompts students to think about the goals of the course and how history on the landscape shapes what the public knows and believes about the past.

As is almost always the case, the students are dismayed to find that they have been lied to by something cast in bronze and erected by the state government. The historical marker in Rome, Georgia, proclaims a historic house to be "Martha Berry's Birthplace," when in fact Martha Berry was born fifty miles away near Gadsden, Alabama. They quickly recognize the myth of the Lost Cause embedded in the inscription on the Confederate monument in front of the Dekalb County Courthouse, which will be removed in June 2020, and unanimously agree that, in opposition to what is presented on the monument, slavery was the underlying cause of the American Civil War. While they may know less about the Vietnam War and the Tet Offensive, they recognize the philosophical difference between the commemoration of individual sacrifice presented on a marker erected by the U.S. government remembering the individuals killed on the grounds of the U.S. embassy in Saigon on January 31, 1968, and the notion of collective sacrifice by the unnamed fighters who "heroically fought and died for national liberation" on the monument erected by the Vietnamese government about twenty feet away but outside the former embassy grounds—two sides of the same story. The first day concludes with a flurry of students approaching me with individual questions about possible internship locations, upcoming classes, and how to get to and from field trips without missing other classes.

I begin our second session addressing some of the questions I got at the end of the first class, most notably the field trip transportation question. One of the reasons that I requested that my classes meet for the double session (two hours and forty-five minutes as opposed to seventy-five minutes) is so that I can incorporate field trips into the course. I have experimented with sending students to visit historic sites and museums on their own versus having us go as a group, and there is no question that the group field trips are more successful in terms of stimulating discussion and student engagement with the issues on which I want them to focus. The site reviews that students have produced following such visits over the years have convinced me of the value of this shared experience, as have the discussions we have had back in the classroom. The students' course evaluations confirm that the field trips are highlights of the class. Consequently, I make every effort to incorporate class visits to public history sites into my courses. The location of our university combined with ingress/egress issues make it impossible to get anywhere off campus and have a meaningful amount of time on site within a seventy-five-minute class period. I explain to the students that I have allowed travel time at both the beginning and end of class for all our excursions outside the classroom. I am mindful that many of the students have other classes either before or after my class, and I do not want to be the professor who thinks that my class is more important than anyone else's. Also, I encourage them to carpool, which not only is helpful in terms of having them arrive en masse but also requires less parking drama and reduces emissions.

After dealing with the field trip and other residual questions, I launch into a presentation about the Georgia Historical Marker Program. I am in the final stages of polishing a peer-reviewed article for publication on this very topic in *The Public Historian*, and that article is the assigned reading for the day.[1] All the students are familiar with the historical markers that dot the roadsides around the state, but none of them have ever given any thought to how those markers came to be. When and why did the program start, and who decides what stories are worth telling? In the past I have worked with staff at the Georgia Historical Society (GHS)—the organization now charged with managing the marker program—to have my students create additional content about markers in Northwest Georgia for the GHS website. Each student would research a marker, then write an essay providing more detail and context on the topic, which would be posted on the GHS website. I would invite the GHS staff person who coordinates the program to join our class by Skype to discuss the significance and value of the marker program as well as the importance of doing research for the contextual essays. This semester, however, the final project is the depot exhibit, so I use the marker program as an entry point into the history of the county for which we are developing the exhibit. We look at the seven markers located in the county and discuss how they relate to our project. Two of the markers relate to topics that we will cover in greater detail in our exhibit—Federal Road (erected in 1954) and Georgia Marble Company and the Village of Tate (erected in 1999). The students agree that the Federal Road marker may be misleading in its interpretation of the acceptance by the Native population of the intrusion by white settlers. They also agree that although the Georgia Marble Company marker packs a lot of information into 106 words, there is much more to be said about the marble business and the Village of Tate itself.

Lastly on our second day, I finalize the groups in which the students will work for the semester. From experience I have concluded that the perfect group size is three. It is big enough that students will have to grapple with different personalities and work styles and figure out how to divide up the work, while giving everyone enough to do to make them feel like they are contributing. Groups of four or more often lead to factions arising or someone in the group not pulling their weight. Groups of two can be tricky because a stronger student often carries the load while a weaker student may step back and ride on the strength of the other; thus, there may be less leveling of effort. I generally decide on the number of groups based on how many students I have in the class, divided into groups of three. This semester, however, I created six groups. Perhaps driven by my optimism that I would get eighteen students in the course or my desire to have student groups present on at least six different chapters from each of the assigned readings, I proceed to assign the students to groups based on where they happened to be sitting on the second day of class. This is not the best decision I have ever made by a long shot. The result is two groups of three students and four groups of two students. In my defense, I was also trying to create enough groups to make the math work for the Depot Project. Could I have created fewer groups so that I had no groups smaller than three? Yes. Should I have done so? Probably. The results at the end of the semester will be uneven and require substantial reworking by me before they can be presented to the client, but this is an account of what I did, not what I should have done. I review what the students need to think about for their first group presentations, which will happen during our next class session. I review each group's assignment and the questions that they need to address in their presentation. I introduce them to Tony Horwitz through his website.[2] His short video about how and why he wrote *A Voyage Long and Strange* provides a nice introduction to the way Horwitz worked and how he combined archival research with field work to explore how we remember the past and why myth often trumps fact in collective memory. I encourage the students to spend the last few minutes of class getting to know the others in their group and sharing their contact information—cell phone numbers, email addresses—so that they will be able to communicate beyond the discussion board in D2L, our course management system, if necessary.

Group Efforts

Our second week of this seven-week course begins with students delivering their group presentations on assigned chapters of Tony Horwitz's *A Voyage Long and Strange*. This is a text that I have used on and off over the last twelve years. While his most famous book, *Confederates in the Attic*, remains a staple of many public history courses, I have found Horwitz's exploration of the "mislaid century" between the arrival of Columbus and the arrival of the Pilgrims to be a revelatory experience for my students. Horwitz explores the history and the myth in an interesting and humorous way that helps students understand that the history they see all around them—on markers, at historic sites, at festivals—is as likely to be based on fiction as it is on fact.

Not all of the student presentations are what I would consider top-notch, but each group has managed to produce something that is at least visually interesting and addresses the major questions posed to them about what happened in the past and how that past is memorialized. My instructions about how to create an effective PowerPoint, it seems, have been mostly successful, with each group providing good images that capture the "public history" of their story. The students are noticeably nervous on their first trip to the lectern, but at least they are not alone. Part of my logic behind having them give group presentations early in the semester is to get them working together quickly and to get them in front of the class as part of a team rather than on their own.

Unfortunately, not all of the groups have gelled as I would have hoped. Whether it is a matter of time—we have only been together for a week, after all—or a matter of personalities is not immediately clear. I am hoping for the former but fear it may be the latter. The breakdown in one of the groups made up of two students is obvious during the presentation when one member seems unknowledgeable about the topic on which she is presenting. Later, during my office hours, her teammate comes to see me to discuss the communication problems that arose as they were working on their presentation. To her credit, this student, while obviously frustrated, states that she is determined to make this partnership work and has offered to carpool with her partner, who does not drive, to the site of our upcoming field trip. I am encouraged by this development and impressed with this student's empathy and willingness to work at this relationship. Another student approaches me after class to express his distaste for public speaking and his frustration with his partner, whom he found to be a bit "strange." As I noted earlier, such eccentricities have a way of leveling out in groups of three or more. In a group of two, not so much. I reiterate that among the things that we are all learning in this class is how to work with others, and that this ability, especially the ability to work with someone whom you would not likely associate with personally, is extremely important. The stakes for the group presentations on readings, of which there are two, are low. They count for 10 percent of students' grade. But they provide an opportunity for students to figure out how to work together in advance of developing and delivering their final project.

We conclude the class with a discussion of how Horwitz, after a three-year voyage of his own, returned to Plymouth with a changed perspective on its meaning and significance. The students are alternately indignant and amused by the misappropriations of history that they have uncovered during Horwitz's journey. They are also becoming suspicious of the history that they encounter on the landscape, which I think is a healthy thing. They are beginning to question things that they have long taken for granted, a curiosity that I encourage. We wrap up with a review of our field-trip plans to the nearby county, where we will visit the former home, now a wedding venue, of the president of the Georgia Marble Company along with the depot in Tate. Carpool plans are made, with most of the students agreeing to ride with their group member(s) to the site.

The field trip proves to be an adventure, as we get a tour of the Tate mansion by its current owner, who seems very eager to sell the place. This is not a traditional historic site tour, but it does get the students inside a historic building that would not otherwise be accessible to them unless they were willing to pay many thousands of dollars to get married there, and they get a chance to meet some of the local folks who are spearheading the project. The students are excited about getting inside the building and are appropriately wowed by the site. We also visit the depot that will eventually house our exhibit. Recently moved about fifty yards from its original location and restored to its nineteenth-century appearance on the exterior, the depot is an empty shell. County leaders have debated what to do with this building, which has no climate control or restroom facilities. It is located near the county elementary school and, were it not for the lack of restroom facilities, would be an excellent field-trip destination if some interpretation were introduced to the site. While the restrooms are beyond the purview of me and my students, the interpretation is not. In preparation for our site visit, I have shared with my students the National Register nomination for the Georgia Marble Company and Tate Historic District along with other resources, such as entries in the *New Georgia Encyclopedia* and assorted short articles about significant events in the history of the area. My goal is for them to arrive at the site informed but not overloaded and to have them walk away inspired to learn more. The students arrive on-site mostly on time, are appreciative of the time and attention given to them by the local community leaders, and seem enthusiastic about the project.

Within two weeks, we will be at the halfway point of the semester, so we will spend the entirety of week three working on the exhibit project. Our Tuesday session, which meets in the KSU archives, is devoted to exploring the process of exhibition development and digging into the research materials that the MARB special projects staff and I have compiled. Several years earlier, the leadership of the Georgia Marble Company, now a wholly owned subsidiary of the Canadian corporation Polycor, donated the company's papers to the KSU archives. That donation was the genesis of the relationship between KSU MARB and the county leadership, and those papers form the bulk of the research materials that my students will be using while developing the exhibit for the depot.

For many of the students, this is the first time that they have done archival research. I often liken doing research at the KSU archives to doing archival research with training wheels, and I mean that in the best possible way. The staff at the archives does a tremendous job of teaching the students the basics, from no food, drinks, or ink pens, to how to access the materials. Staff members have pulled several boxes of materials that they think will be most relevant to our project and have prepared a short presentation on how to do archival research. Most of the students seem to enjoy the experience of digging through acid-free boxes of papers and photographs and appreciate the tangible nature of this type of research, even though some of them are overwhelmed by the sheer volume of materials and become frustrated at the needle-in-a-haystack nature of doing such research on largely unprocessed materials. The frustration is largely drowned out by the squeals of delight that erupt when someone comes across a particularly interesting item, such as an old company brochure, a photograph of the Lincoln Memorial (made of Tate marble) under construction, or documents related to a labor dispute.

The trip to the archives merely whets their appetite for the project, but there are other resources that they need to explore as well. Most of those have been collected for them and made available through D2L. I created a module with research materials broken into topics that includes primary sources as well as secondary sources, such as National Register nominations and excerpts from a book published by a local historical association. In a seven-week course, we simply do not have time for students to scatter far afield in their search for sources. The students have already been introduced to our big idea (How did a small community in rural Georgia become a pillar of America?), and they sign up for individual topics that they will research over the next couple of weeks. Each student must submit a first draft of text for their topic next week, before they begin working in their groups to revise and refine their text.

While it is important for the students to be able to do historical research, it is equally important that they learn the process by which they should create an exhibition. Whether it be for a museum large or small, the fundamentals of exhibition development are largely the same. I introduce students to the basics of interpretation using Freeman Tilden's six principles of interpretation, first laid out in his 1957 work *Interpreting Our Heritage*. More than sixty years after it was first published, Tilden's principles, with their emphasis on revelation, provocation, and making interpretation relevant to the visitor, still hold up. I also use excerpts from Beverly Serrell's *Exhibit Labels*, which I describe to my students as the exhibit-text bible. Serrell lays out the ten commandments of exhibit-label writing in the introduction, and she spends the rest of the book elaborating on how those commandments can lead to an excellent exhibition.[3] Her notion of the "big idea" has become part of the vernacular among those of us who curate exhibits. From the big idea to the word count for image captions, Serrell lays out the process in clear, simple language. The students soon learn to "write short" in a world where most of their professors have encouraged them to "write long." They soon learn that it can be harder to write a 120-word exhibit panel than it is to write a twenty-page paper. My hope is that they learn how to sort through myriad events to determine which are the most important, and learn to distill complicated ideas and events into simple but powerful language that can convey a rich and layered meaning. Hopefully, they also learn the value of having many voices participate in the creative process, how to embrace new ideas and interpretations, and how and when they might need to let go of their own ideas in favor of someone else's.

This is a lot to pack in during a single semester, much less a single class period, but we give it a go during week three. We spend a day looking at research materials in the archives, and a day at an exhibition in a depot-like welcome-center building in a nearby city, so that students can get some sense of what the final product might look like. The existing exhibit that we visit and the proposed exhibit on which we are working, while for different communities, have some thematic overlap. Evergreen topics such as education, religion, commercial and industrial development, and race relations are common to both. I think it is useful for students to see how to tell a complicated story, such as segregation in education, in a single exhibit panel. While that panel certainly cannot tell the whole story, it can present an unvarnished overview of how things were. With the proper combination of images and text, a powerful story can be told in a small space. The students spend about an hour in the exhibit taking notes and gathering in small groups to discuss what they see. They leave the site simultaneously energized and terrified about their own project.

After three field sessions—the depot site visit, the archives, and the welcome-center exhibit—we return to the classroom for week four. The first session of the week focuses on James and Lois Horton's *Slavery and Public History*, an epic collection of essays, mostly in case-study format, that the students find especially eye-opening. I ask the students to read the introduction, the first three chapters, and the epilogue, and I assign each of the six groups an individual chapter on which they are to present to the class. First published in 2006, *Slavery and Public History* has, in some ways, become dated. The site of the President's House adjacent to the Liberty Bell in Philadelphia, for example, has evolved considerably from what it was when Gary Nash wrote about it in his chapter, "For Whom Will the Liberty Bell Toll? From Controversy to Cooperation," and the interpretation at Monticello is dramatically different from what Lois Horton writes about in "Avoiding History: Thomas Jefferson, Sally Hemings, and the Uncomfortable Public Conversation on Slavery."[4] Rather than look on these texts as outdated, I encourage students to consider them as starting points for a mini-research project about the site that is the topic of their assigned chapter. I ask them to read the chapter, then find out what has happened at the site in the years since the book was published. Some of the groups ace this assignment and come to class with rich presentations loaded with images of what has happened at the sites in recent years. Others barely scratch the surface of what is out there about their site or topic. While I see evidence of ongoing communication breakdowns in one of the groups, I am pleased to see that their presentation is actually quite good, with clear representative images that help illustrate the key points of the essay. I also see on the discussion board that the frustrated but empathetic student has persisted in her efforts to communicate with her partner, and those efforts seem to have borne fruit. While both of them still need to work on their public speaking skills, they seem to have worked out their interpersonal issues, which allows me to breathe a sigh of relief.

Taking on Tough Topics

I am fortunate that one of our curators in MARB was on staff at the 9/11 Memorial Museum in New York City during the early stages of the museum's creation, and I always invite her to speak to my class on one of the days closest to September 11. I provide the students with several reviews of the 9/11 Memorial Museum, including Rick Beard's review published in *The Public Historian* as well as reviews from the *New York Times* and the *Washington Post*. The last two are both very harsh, which I think is a valuable perspective for the students to see. Our curator brings a much more personal perspective to the class with her insider's view of what it was like to work on the project. She gathered images and stories about each of the individuals who was killed during the attacks, and her work is on display in the *In Memoriam* exhibition. Most of the students are excited to meet a real live curator, even though they have now spent four weeks with me, a curator in my own right. But Adina Langer's work on this national museum that commemorates and interprets an epic event that changed their world puts her in another category as far as they are concerned. I am delighted to turn over the class to her. Afterward, I wrap up the day, which can be very sad and heavy, as I always do: with Wade Goodwyn's NPR review of the Broadway musical *Come from Away*. Goodwyn's review is quite possibly the most exquisite such piece I have ever encountered. He perfectly captures the essence of this story about the aftermath of 9/11, and his review allows us to end the discussion on a high note.[5] I remind students that the first drafts of their exhibit text, which were submitted electronically before class, have been posted online so that they can review one another's work over the next week. We will discuss these submissions as a class in week six, after the students have had a chance to read all the panels.

As we move into week five of the semester, we begin a unit that focuses on the National Park Service (NPS) and the history of the modern U.S. civil rights movement. An understanding of the role and significance of the NPS is fundamental to any understanding of the field of public history in the United States. As I tell my students, the NPS might not quite be the 800-pound gorilla in the public history field, but it is mighty close. Between the sheer number of sites over which it has responsibility (over 400) and the national scale and scope of those sites, the NPS is the biggest, most important player in the public history field in America. And then there is its role in historic preservation, a subject on which we barely scratch the surface in my intro course, because I teach another course titled Historic Preservation, in which I delve into the details of that field. I provide students with links to a short history of the NPS as well as *Imperiled Promise: The State of History in the NPS*, a report produced through the collaboration of the NPS and the Organization of American Historians in 2011. As the report weighs in at 146 pages, I have no illusions that the students will read the whole thing. Together we look at the findings and recommendations presented by historians Anne Mitchell Whisnant, Marla Miller, Gary Nash, and David Thelen—a combination of optimism at the excellence of some of the work being done at NPS sites and despair at the overall lack of financial and philosophical commitment to fulfilling its mission of leaving its sites "unimpaired for the enjoyment of future generations" and its aspiration to "become the nation's largest outdoor history classroom."[6]

We segue into a discussion of the American civil rights movement and how sites associated therewith have been interpreted by the NPS, which sets up our Thursday field trip to the Martin Luther King Jr. National Historical Park (MALU) in downtown Atlanta. Before we wrap up the day, we watch an episode of *Eyes on the Prize*. This semester I show them episode 2, "Fighting Back," which tells the stories of the effort to integrate Little Rock Central High School and James Meredith's enrollment at the University of Mississippi. The students are horrified by the screaming white protesters outside Central High School and dismayed but also amused by the white college students who think that football should be played even if the university has to be closed down because of the violence erupting all around Oxford, Mississippi. These events seem like ancient history to my students until I remind them that they happened during my lifetime. Much of what the public remembers about the American civil rights movement has been shaped by *Eyes on the Prize*, at least until recently. It was and is a powerful series that captures many of the sights, sounds, and stories of the movement and in some ways has reinforced a narrative about civil rights in America that begins with Emmett Till and ends with the passage of the Voting Rights Act. There is so much more to the civil rights story, and there are now many public history sites around the country where the story is told. We talk briefly about some of these sites, like the Legacy Museum and National Memorial for Peace and Justice in Montgomery, Alabama, and the National Museum of African American History and Culture in Washington, D.C. I wrap up with instructions for our Thursday field trip and a reminder to read the newspaper articles and introduction to the 2011 strategic plan for MALU. The implication, while unsaid, is that what they will see in downtown Atlanta may not represent the latest in civil rights scholarship or museological techniques. It is, however, an important civil rights site that is rich with opportunities for teaching students how to assess public history in practice.

Created as the Martin Luther King Jr. National Historical Site and Preservation District in 1980, MALU includes within its boundaries an NPS visitor center (opened in 1996), the historic Ebenezer Baptist Church, a historic fire station, Martin Luther King Jr.'s birth home, and a number of other historic residential buildings. Within the district boundaries is the King Center for Nonviolent Social Change, which is the headquarters for the nonprofit created by Coretta Scott King following her husband's death in 1968. The NPS and the King Center do not always work well together, but their geographical proximity and similar focus on remembering the life and work of Martin Luther King Jr. combine to offer an excellent opportunity for my students to take a close look at two competing yet complementary exhibitions. The NPS exhibit, designed by Ralph Applebaum Associates, is a compendium of photographs, interpretive panels, and videos. The exhibit has no artifacts. The main exhibit at the King Center is a display of personal objects owned by Dr. and Mrs. King. One exhibit relies on technology and design to tell the story, while the other relies on artifacts. The contrast between the two is striking—one exhibit offers a broad, impersonal civil rights narrative that is rich in context, while the other provides no context but is rich in personal insights. I always leave the site feeling like I want the two organizations to pool their resources to put together a single exhibit that combines context with King's personal journey.

I prepare my students for what they will see by giving them access to the MALU strategic plan, a map of the site, and the mission statements of both organizations, and I require them to use Beverly Serrell's Framework for Assessing Excellence as they work their way through the two exhibits.[7] Their assignment is to write a review that compares the two exhibits. I have used this comparative review assignment for many years, both with and without Serrell's framework, and I have learned that when they use the framework, their reviews are more thoughtful and analytical. When I do not require the framework, I get a lot of "my fun day at the awesome historic site" papers. The framework is invaluable in getting students to think beyond the thrill of being on a field trip and actually assess the exhibits in terms of the criteria—comfortable, engaging, reinforcing, and meaningful—that make an exhibit "excellent." I ask them to keep their reviews short: 750–1,000 words. Most of my students will likely not go into academia; however, if they do work in the public history field, they might find themselves writing reviews for publication. It is important that they know that such things as word limits are real and are seriously enforced by review editors at scholarly journals.

Much to my delight, on what turns out to be a sunny if somewhat warm day, all the students arrive on time with a hard copy of the framework in hand. We visit both exhibits and do a quick walk around the historic district while I give them a bit of history about the neighborhood and the development of the area since the establishment of the NPS site. I stay behind to answer questions and am pleased to see several students go back into the visitor center to make a second pass through the *Courage to Lead* exhibit. I have visited MALU, which bills itself as Atlanta's "top tourist destination," many times, but I never get tired of taking my students there. Most of them have never been, and it is exciting for me to watch them explore the exhibits with a sense of purpose.

The penultimate week of our semester is a bit fragmented. I was asked by the director of campus internationalization to incorporate a lecture on World Heritage Sites in Cuba into my fall class in support of our on-campus Year of Cuba programming. Consequently, we meet on Tuesday in a larger classroom in the library for this lecture, which is open to the public. Much to my dismay, the air-conditioning system in the library is not working, so the large but packed classroom quickly becomes oppressively hot. Perhaps this is in keeping with the topic, I observe, as I whirl through images of Cuba's nine World Heritage Sites for forty-five minutes in what feels like a tropical environment. After taking a few questions, much of the audience leaves the sauna-like classroom, but my students stay behind to turn in their MALU papers, which are overall quite good, and offer their suggestions and edits as a group on the text panels for the depot exhibit. We realize that we have some overlap and some gaps in our topics, so we realign the panels to smooth out those problems. The students will now work within their groups to revise the text for final submission on the last day of class.

For our Thursday class session, we visit our on-campus history museum. A recent excursion by me to the Tule Lake National Monument in northern California has inspired me to incorporate a unit on the commemoration of Japanese internment into my class, and the KSU Museum of History and Holocaust Education has among its on-site and traveling exhibits a student-curated exhibit on that very topic. We gather at the museum for an introduction by the museum's director, who explains why we have a World War II and Holocaust Museum at KSU (it has to do with accusations of anti-Semitism against the administration that date back two decades), and members of the museum education team provide an overview of the work that they do, mostly with K–12 students, as well as a tour of the Japanese internment exhibit. One of my former students is part of the museum education team, which the students find both inspirational and aspirational.

The museum staff will team-teach a museum education course in the spring, and I want to introduce the students to the team now and encourage them to take the course. Museum education is a great entryway into the museum field, and it is the path by which many of my students get their first jobs. I share with the students an excellent article, "Tule Lake Today: Internment and Its Legacies," by Shelley Cannady, an associate professor in the College of Environment and Design at the University of Georgia. A native of Tule Lake, Cannady offers a personal perspective on what it was like to grow up in an area that was once the site of incarceration of thousands of innocent civilians as well as insight into the preservation and interpretation of this National Historic Site.[8] I include photographs from my own visit to the site. I also share tips that I picked up in conversation with the NPS ranger at the site about how to get a job with the NPS, the key to which was being willing to move to a remote location for which the NPS could not find any other applicants. I also introduce students to the International Coalition of Sites of Conscience, and we discuss the challenges of preserving and interpreting sites, such as Auschwitz, that shock the conscience.

We begin our final week with a unit on the controversy at the National Air and Space Museum over the proposed *Enola Gay* exhibit, supported by Richard Kohn's "History and the Culture Wars," which provides a comprehensive account of what happened. We also explore the Truman Library & Museum's *Decision to Drop the Bomb* exhibit, as well as Martin Harwit's August 1994 editorial in the *Washington Post*. I preface the *Enola Gay* exhibit discussion with a bit of background on the controversy over the National Museum of American Art's 1991 *West as America* exhibit and provide the students with excerpts from the comment books. These case studies, the *West as America* and the *Enola Gay*, bring together many key issues embedded in the course goals—how historiographical trends are reflected through public history, problems associated with implementing public history projects, the place of public history in discussions of the contested past, and the role of public and private memory in shaping interpretations of the past. We have, of course, encountered these ideas throughout the semester, but the *West as America* and *Enola Gay* stories bring them all together in a dramatic way that stimulates discussion and piques students' interest in learning more about such fraught public history episodes. I allow time at the end of class for students to work with their groups on polishing their exhibit panel text, which is due at the beginning of the next class.

Closure

Our final class session is spent reviewing the exhibit text for the Depot Project. Each group has submitted their text and a list of suggested images for their two panels. In spite of our iterative process, which has involved feedback from me as well as from their classmates, some of the text is still not ready for prime time. The students have clearly learned to "write short," but some of them have not yet mastered the art of writing clearly and concisely. The MARB staff and I will need to do some additional polishing before we can deliver the text to the client, but I had expected as much. Still, the students seem excited about the topics that they have researched and written about, and some of them have come up with terrific images that we can use on the panels. We fiddle with the order of the panels as a group, and the students see how their piece of the story fits into the whole. We also spend some time talking about the upcoming Georgia Marble Festival, which the students will attend in lieu of having a final exam.

The Georgia Marble Festival is held each year on the first weekend in October in a park near the county seat. During our early negotiations with the county leaders about the project, they mentioned the festival as something that might be of interest to the students. In addition to the traditional funnel cakes and arts-and-crafts booths that are a staple of such festivals, tours of local historic buildings and the marble quarry were also available. As part of the effort to raise awareness about our public history partnership and the interpretive programs that we would be developing for the county, we agreed to staff a booth at the festival. The hope was that our presence would generate interest and excitement among the local population and hopefully lead to raising money to help pay for the exhibits. While the students would not be responsible for asking passersby for money, they were expected to be able to talk about the history of the county and the contents of the exhibition that they had helped develop. We had on display the introductory panel, which provided an overview of the exhibit and introduced visitors to the story that we would tell in the depot. The students would staff the booth in two-hour shifts. MARB staff and I would also be on-site and would cover the booth while the students took the quarry tour. Although our stint at the festival did not result in a financial boon to support the exhibit, it bore fruit of another kind. A local business owner who was staffing a nearby tent came to talk to us about our project and revealed that she was in possession of a number of items related to the history of the community and the depot itself that might be useful in the exhibit. I will follow up on this lead as we move into phase two of the development of this exhibit with my museum studies students in the second half of the semester.

No one will be surprised to hear that the students much preferred going to the Marble Festival to taking a final exam or turning in another paper. They got to engage with the public, talk about their project, tour the marble quarry, and eat funnel cakes. By this time, the students had bonded over their shared experiences, and the Marble Festival experience reinforced this bond. In spite of the overcast and somewhat chilly weather, we ended the semester on a high note.

Student evaluations indicated that the "real-world" project and the field trips were greatly appreciated, while the group presentations, not so much. This was not an unexpected outcome, but I anticipate that I will continue to include all three of these things in my future classes. This is not the first time I have received such feedback at the end of a semester. On more than one occasion, however, I have had students come back to me months or even years later and report that although they hated them at the time, the group work, in retrospect, was one of the most beneficial things we did. As I peruse the student evaluations, contemplate the assignments and class discussions, and look back at the course goals, I am able to check off everything on the list. The students have, at a minimum, read, written, and talked about the main ways that the public encounters history outside the classroom, how the public history profession has evolved, possible career paths they might pursue, current issues in the field, how historiographical trends make their way to the public, the possibilities and perils of public history projects, the place of public history in discussions of the contested past, and how public and private memory manifest themselves through public history. They have also had the experience of being part of a team that helped produce an exhibition that will be on display to the public for years to come. The course is exhilarating and exhausting for me. For the students, hopefully it is more of the former than it is of the latter. Based on the rate at which students continue to enroll in my classes, I believe this to be true.

Eleven of the fourteen students from the intro course will join me for the next seven weeks in my museum studies course. The Depot Project will carry forward, and the museum studies students will revise the text, find more images, write captions, and work with a graphic designer to bring the exhibit to fruition. By the end of the second seven weeks, we will have the panels completed and ready to go into production. Everything seems to be going full steam ahead for a spring 2020 opening.

Notes

1. Dickey, "'Cameos of History' on the Landscape."
2. Tony Horwitz's website, tonyhorwitz.com, no longer exists as of March 2022.
3. Serrell, *Exhibit Labels*, 1–3.
4. Horton and Horton, *Slavery and Public History*, chaps. 5 and 7.
5. Goodwyn, "*Come from Away* Musical."
6. Whisnant et al., *Imperiled Promise*, 1.
7. Serrell, *Judging Exhibitions*.
8. Cannady, "Tule Lake Today."

9 Keeping the Tensions Present in the Public History Classroom

JULIA BROCK

For the last forty years, public history has put its students on a path to professionalization within the academy. This course seems necessary for practical reasons—public history work requires specific skills to steward and interpret the past—yet it contains potentially dangerous contradictions. Recent internal critiques of public history point to an acute awareness that our work takes place in the context of a predominantly white middle-class field, the practitioners of which come from programs that are run predominantly by white people (I am included in that group). GVGK Tang, for example, has articulated arguments and raised questions meant to challenge those of us in positions like mine who are training students in the context of the modern university.[1] Past critics of public history also question the push to professionalize. In 1980, as public history was crystallizing as a distinct subfield of academic history, writers like Howard Green raised questions about public history in the pages of the *Radical History Review*. Green wrote of professional public history as posing "a serious threat to existing networks of amateur and local historical work."[2] We train new generations of professionals who may displace "uncredentialed" cultural workers more knowledgeable and with greater stake in community histories. We also train new generations in the twenty-first-century college or university, which undoubtedly has consequences for our field.

This chapter reflects on the tension that emerges from the institutionalization of public history training and the more socially transformative claims our field makes about itself. In its ideal form, public history work operates within a clear set of practical and ethical parameters—of collaboration with partners, of the oft-cited principle of sharing authority, and of critical reflexivity. We hold a commitment to complicated and compelling history that incorporates multiple perspectives and lived experiences, even in the face of discomfort from our partners who might want a simpler, cheerier view of the past. Professionalization—the work of the modern university—is bound in structures that do not necessarily align with this ideal. My home institution, the University of Alabama (UA), was created in 1831 to reproduce a white ruling class, a mantle it only grudgingly, and imperfectly, began to shed in the late twentieth century. Like other institutions of higher education in the twenty-first century, it is now melding to the model of the "corporate university" explored in depth by Christopher Newfield.[3] Given these contexts, Randy Martin of Imaging America has questioned whether universities and communities, however defined, "can partner on equal terms toward a mutually beneficial vision of society."[4] Similarly, I often question whether institutionalized training of public history students, where we connect our practice to communities outside the classroom walls, facilitates the "spread of the university beyond the university," in the words of Stefano Harney and Fred Moten?[5] I suggest that it does, and this contention means I must attend to the lessons of my own practice as a public historian and draw from the insights of those who work at the intersection of critical pedagogy, antiracism, and praxis. But with this as my goal, I confront the question, Can I identify how I reproduce power structures that entangle the classroom and the "community," and if so, what do I do with that knowledge?

I use my work in this collection to explore whether I can align my public history classroom with the critical pedagogy.[6] There's much to say on that front, but one insight helpful to me comes from Naeem Inayatullah, a professor of politics at Ithaca College. In an admittedly polemical piece, he suggests there is rarely any teaching or learning that happens in the classroom (or, if so, it is learning at the expense of teaching), only a series of encounters between students and teachers.[7] I find the idea of the encounter, as I understand it, well-suited to public history teaching. An encounter is open ended, can harbor multiple meanings for the individual, and has no predetermined learning outcome to assess. Encounters don't just happen with other people, be they students or colleagues, but can be emplaced. In fact, meaningful encounters with the past is a principle goal in public history practice.

I'd like to offer from my own classroom a few encounters that try to actively address the multiple tensions that are bound to teaching public history. In the fall of 2019 I offered an introduction to public history class. My writing and reflection began during that semester in a course journal and continued into the spring and summer of 2020, as the murders of Ahmaud Arbery, George Floyd, Tony McDade, and Breonna Taylor prompted nationwide protests led by Black Lives Matter organizers and other Black activist groups against police brutality. Reflection continued as I prepared another introduction to public history course in the fall semester of 2020. Amid the upheavals of the COVID-19 pandemic, I taught this course face to face as my university returned to campus despite mounting cases in our region. In this context, I wished to challenge myself to sharpen my own sense of responsibility in daily work. Journaling about my desire to craft a critical public history pedagogy incorporated of-the-moment responses and internal mulling, and is part reflection and self-accounting.

Every public history course is structured in some way by academic calendars—our semester covered fifteen weeks, with biweekly meetings of an hour and fifteen minutes. I think about the course's architecture as being arc shaped; we begin with introductions to the field, define the scope of public history work, learn the landscapes on which public history is practiced and experienced, build understanding and comprehension through conceptual reading, and finally tie these components together with a collaborative project. The approach is linear, though with a reflexive and reflective edge and reminders that we attend to our social commitments and responsibilities. The early introduction to the field and its ethical considerations act as a refrain as we plan and implement our project work.

I think of my approach as being all in. Our profession has debated the introductory course; whether or not it's best to conduct a career-driven survey, a journey through methodological literature, or application via a community project.[8] I try to do all of these, which, on the critical side, sometimes ends with a fear that I overwhelm students. In the fall of 2019, the all-in approach brought visits by practitioners, including those working in queer community archiving, cultural resources management, local museums, and campus public history initiatives, and introduced literature that covered a survey of the field (Lyon, Nix, and Shrum, *Introduction to Public History*), dark tourism and unsettled pasts (Miles, *Tales from the Haunted South*), archives and power (Trouillot, *Silencing the Past*), and the complication and joys of collaborative, creative work (Sergel, *See You in the Streets*). The semester included project workdays geared toward a collaboration with a historical site and weekly reading responses and writing assignments that asked students to engage with public history in their immediate present. I employ no conventional examinations in the course; it's an upper-level class designed for majors and runs as a seminar with a practicum module.

This class also included a graduate section with four students. I'm relatively new at this university and so have the opportunity to expand public history offerings to MA and PhD students. I was concerned, however, that the course might not serve all of its enrollees fairly. Those worries didn't dissipate entirely, but I found that graduate presence enriched discussion and, instead of intimidating undergraduate students, evoked more serious engagement and willingness to speak. Graduate students, themselves in early training as teaching assistants, were encouraging of the others. They reciprocated in the class project as mentors of small groups of undergraduates.

Our class collaborated with Old Cahawba Archaeological Park, a historic site near Selma that preserves the landscape of Cahaba, Alabama's first capital (1820–26). Old Cahawba is an 800-acre park that includes evidence of the original street grid of the town and several traces of the built environment, including cemeteries, former quarters of enslaved people, a church, and an intact home from a later era, when the nearly abandoned town became a sanctuary for Black men and women and their families, as well as a hotbed of Republican politics. The class researched and wrote draft narratives for a walking tour at the park that focused on these Black families who remained in Cahaba during and after Reconstruction.

These details constituted the brass tacks of the course, and in them emerged the conflicted senses of purpose I grapple with as an instructor for an introduction to public history course. My experience suggests an uneasy relationship between teaching public history in the classroom, which tends to rely on a traditional teacher–student hierarchy, and the potential of doing public history work, which in its ideal form is nonhierarchical, collaborative, collective, and sometimes spontaneous (or at least with some kind of organic iteration), and labors to preserve something meaningful about the past. How do we teach when, as Karen Buenavista Hanna reminds us, the university was not created for everyone and, as Tang has suggested, the most important voices, the ones who are doing the grassroots work of public history, are excluded from the university space?[9] We find ourselves in the public history classroom because of structures (without and within) that embolden some and silence others and limit the choices we can actually undertake. The ideal of public history as egalitarian collaborative work is not at the forefront of university pedagogy, and thus it's difficult to know what is attainable.[10] Perhaps the best we can do is reject idealism and attempt to bring to the surface the tensions of professionalization in the classroom and in the field. It's a tall order. The introduction to public history classroom is often the first time college students get the notion that one can study history and put it "to work in the world," to borrow the tagline for the National Council on Public History.

In the fall of 2019, I attempted to engage these tensions into my course in three key ways: by focusing on the policies and practices that produce and reproduce what becomes the material stuff of public history; by engaging with the historical landscape of campus; and by including an applied component, wherein students work in service of a nearby historic site, a "ghost town" of early Alabama history.[11]

Because our work relies on collaboration, I introduced (via the Lyon, Nix, and Shrum textbook) and problematized early the ethic of "sharing authority."[12] On the first days of the course, we discussed this and other responsibilities of multivocal work, including reflexivity, listening and hearing, and understanding one's position (vis-à-vis privilege and identity) in the context of others in the classroom and community. These are, in the end, lived practices. I try to model these principles during the semester through collaborative decision-making, particularly when it comes to the class project, which is uncomfortable for students who expect highly directed and enumerated guidelines or rubrics for every assignment. Yet a conversation about ethics had to foreground all the content and labor to follow.

From here we moved into a survey of the places where public history is practiced and, especially, the policies (federal, state, and local) that have defined what from the past is preserved. I incorporated short lectures, readings, and conversations with public history practitioners to illuminate the ways that public history policy is shot through with exercises of power. In the introduction to archives and archival practice, for example, we read Trouillot's *Silencing the Past*, we visited campus special collections, and we hosted Joshua Burford and Maigen Sullivan, the founders of the Invisible Histories Project (IHP)—a queer, community-based archiving initiative that focuses on southern LGBTQ history.[13] I'm not alone in using Trouillot in the introductory classroom; now over twenty years old, it continues to deliver a powerful unveiling of the silences inherent in the production and reproduction of history, including the sociohistorical construction of archives.

Students found the text provocative and lucid and took that engaged reading into conversations with the archivists. In the UA special collections visit, they heard archivist Kate Matheny discuss her professional responsibilities and daily duties. Matheny also introduced and explained collections policies so that students could better understand why the repository acquires and maintains its holdings, and how expanded and revised collections policies are changing the scope of what the archive acquires. The IHP staff spoke to how the marginalization and criminalization of LGBTQ people in the South leaves a gaping absence of queer life in the archives.

IHP works to reclaim space for histories that have been silenced by dominant society and also to transform archival practice more broadly. The module on archives was particularly successful; the paired reading with practitioner conversations gave immediacy to the conclusions of Trouillot.

We spent time working through municipal, state, and federal policy as well. When we talked about recent removals of Confederate monuments, it was easy to point to Alabama's recent law that no monument over forty years old can be removed and name it as a ploy by those in power to protect Confederate "heritage." We covered the 1906 Antiquities Act, the 1966 National Historic Preservation Act, and the 1990 Native American Graves Protection and Repatriation Act (NAGPRA) to assess the work of federal agencies in preserving cultural resources. For the latter, we read Chip Colwell's *Plundered Skulls and Stolen Spirits*, a survey of the passage of NAGPRA rendered by someone who witnessed the movement to pass the historic legislation and, as a curator at the Denver Museum of Nature & Science, saw its many successes and some painful inadequacies.[14] The reading gave us a chance to discuss earlier federal practices that created the need for NAGPRA, such as the U.S. Army Medical Museum's theft of Native bodies to populate its collections. We visited the UA Office of Archaeological Research to learn how that organization partners with Muscogee, Choctaw, and other First Nations in its cultural resources management work, especially as it relates to NAGPRA and repatriation. Once again, hearing from practitioners proved crucial to helping students see how policies work (or don't work) on the ground level. I noted in my class journal for that week that my decision to include both reading and class visits with practitioners left too little time for reading discussion (especially given that the class met once a week for two-and-a-half hours); I used student reading responses as a way to engage more with their ideas and takeaways from the material, but my notes make it clear I was rethinking my own all-in approach to the course.

I organized the course schedule so that we surveyed public history on the broader landscape before returning to our own campus. I incorporated an examination of our institution's history into the course itself—the actual history as well as the "approved" history that students learn through stories the institution deploys to students, staff, faculty, and prospective students and their families. We also learned from the work of UA scholar Dr. Hilary Green, who has created multiple public history projects (including a walking tour) that foreground the post-emancipation lives of enslaved workers at UA. Her work not only reveals how slavery was central to the founding and growth of the school but also tracks the effort of the university to conceal and banish that past, as well as its more recent halting efforts to acknowledge it in response to student and faculty demands. Students' time with Green, along with their assigned site reviews of the Gorgas House—a building constructed by skilled enslaved craftsmen and now a campus museum—helped them deconstruct the ways that the institution has created a usable past over time. It's increasingly essential that we combine teaching public history with looking critically within our own institutions—there is a subgenre of public history that focuses on campus history and a growing body of scholarship on slavery at the university to support an examination of public history under our feet.

Students were energized by the module on campus history because it cast new light on their university. Their questions for Green on her walking tour were rapid fire, especially as she spent time explaining her own methodology using sources that can be found in the campus archives and pushing the stories of enslaved UA workers beyond freedom and into Reconstruction. In our discussion after the tour, students compared what they had learned on early campus tours with their parents or in first-year orientation—tours that whitewash campus history—with the painful intimate details of enslaved lives at UA. In fall 2020, the intro class had even more to discuss given the events of the summer, which led to student petitions to university administration that have hastened the move by administrators to rename buildings that honor racist men.

Our class project is the final piece of the course. Though I have concerns about attempting a community-based project in the introductory class, I've not yet eliminated it, because this kind of applied practice lies at the heart of public history work. I wrestle especially with fitting any kind of project into a fifteen-week semester, given that I'm already loading so much into the class. I understand the need to deliver something useful to community partners, and it's a lot to ask of students just encountering the field to take on the obligation of external expectations (the technical efficiency expected of professionals). Instead of completely eliminating an applied project, I attempt to manage the scale of what we do. In previous intro classes, I've asked students to bite off more than they can chew—multicomponent interpretive plans or polished and packaged walking tours, for example. These days I work with partners in advance to define a role for our class that is more manageable and that, ideally, the next class offering could pick up and build on.

The Old Cahawba Archaeological Park project was a step in that direction. We framed our work as a first phase of a larger effort to expand Black history tours at the site. Fueled and enriched by the westward expansion of slavery and the dispossession of Native Americans, Cahaba, even after it lost its status as the capital in 1826, was a wealthy place. That wealth vanished after the Civil War, when planters lost the fortunes they'd invested in owning people, and white Cahabans largely picked up and moved to Selma. Black Cahabans, however, remained, and the town became a stronghold for Black Republican political activity.

Visitors to the park can wander the original street grid and encounter what's left of the physical fabric of the city. Owned and staffed by the Alabama Historical Commission, a part of the state government, the park offers self- and docent-guided tours. Conversations with site director Linda Derry in the summer of 2019 helped to focus our work on the first draft of a walking tour that focused on the post-emancipation Black community. Derry wanted to know, in particular, more about the Black families who remained, as many visitors are descendants of Cahabans and are interested in genealogical connections to place.

Though the project was preconfigured by my conversations with Linda Derry, I wanted to model the kinds of public history ethics we'd covered earlier in the semester. I introduced the project and its basic parameters to the class but left a good deal of the outcome to be shaped by student research and creativity. In some modest way, this approach also offered to disrupt the fundamental power dynamics of the class—me as instructor setting all the course boundaries and students complying and responding to receive a grade. Public history, in my understanding, is about co-creation. I did not want to be seen as having the final say in what we produced for Old Cahawba. I wanted students, who also met with the site director during a visit to Old Cahawba (the department supported a van rental), to think through how they might respond creatively to the site's needs and the site director's priorities. My primary mode of disruption, as naive as it sounds, was to leave much of the work open to the students' interpretation, a kind of liberty in a looser structure.

This method caused some consternation among students, who perhaps do not seek the liberty that I wanted to thrust on them. By late September, graduate students expressed concern about not knowing what the final project would be or look like in the end—in short, they wanted to know what their workload was and how they would be assessed. By the time we were focused solely on the project (the last six weeks of the class), undergraduate students also wanted more from me in terms of guidance. I resisted their desire to have uncertainty addressed by discipline. I encouraged and assured them but also reminded the class that the work we do forms in conversation, by mutual decision-making, and by our own creative spark. If that assurance didn't help, the research project did—I watched as they became absorbed in finding the details about Black Cahabans and ultimately created narratives to incorporate into a walking tour. Graduate students became wonderful mentors to the undergraduates, many of whom did not know how to access databases such as Ancestry.com and Newspapers.com, where we found valuable information about Cahaba families. Hilary Green stepped back in, too; an expert in Reconstruction studies, she helped frame some of the broader historical context of post–Civil War Alabama and where to look for additional primary sources. The "applied" portion of the class is the best vehicle with which to model collaboration.

In the end, students chose their own foci for the project. Though we spent time in our tour script addressing the politics of Reconstruction in Cahaba, the researchers were ultimately drawn more to the quotidian, the everyday work of building lives in freedom. They followed the path of families such as the Lightnings, whose story began with a name given in mockery by an enslaver to a purportedly slow-moving enslaved boy. The Lightnings, who now reside in Indiana, and other Black residents of Cahaba, such as the Moseleys, Hatchers, and Lundys, took part in binding their families together, in sometimes setting off on a new course by leaving partners and children behind, in building churches and schools, and in settling in nearby communities and eventually growing a multigenerational connection to central Alabama. They did so in the face of violent white response to Black political and social gains, as hard-won as those were. Students stressed to Cahaba staff that these families and their stories were the connective tissue of the place, and without understanding the everydayness of their lives, visitors to Cahaba could not appreciate what the families had built and endured. They met the work with creativity, engaged research, and their own sense of interpretive import. Yet they remained resistant to embracing authorship of the project's outcome. Their encounter with a public historical site and its history underwrote a desire for structure and a set of parameters. I relented—or, perhaps better, I responded to the needs of my collaborators.

On the final day of the class, students presented these narratives to site staff, and we passed along our research files and student narratives for the site's use. The director and assistant director were, I think, pleased by the student's enthusiasm and their work in recovering family stories. We also sketched out a potential tour path and guiding themes for an expanded tour. At this writing, as the COVID-19 pandemic shut down the site for eighteen months beginning in March 2020, it is unclear if our research and ideas have been incorporated into programming at Old Cahawba. Staff did request that I join an advisory board for the site, which might be interpreted as one marker of their reception of our work.

I ended the course by asking students to define public history, and I've listed, with student permission, a few of these definitions here:

> Public history is the process of both helping to create and discovering meaningful (that is, what people already consider meaningful) encounters with narratives and artifacts of the past, by historians and the public in nonacademic settings.
>
> Public historians are simultaneously recorders of the past and mediums through which historical narratives are taught and connected to a public audience.
>
> Public history is very generally the act or field of bringing history, in both a traditional and a nontraditional sense, to the public outside an academic classroom setting. It often becomes a form of advocacy or even activism because every story a public historian portrays is limiting the scope of another story. To do this work a public historian must be collaborative and understand their role in the shared authority of bringing what is often stories of stakeholders or communities to life professionally. This field is very layered, often with challenges of advocacy, politics, funding, and ethics in a unique way that many other professional fields do not encounter.
>
> Public history is history outside the classroom. At its core, it is the collaboration between communities and the historian to preserve narratives and make history accessible. This shared authority is the process by which narratives are developed. Public historians are stewards of collective memory and present it in a way that allows audiences to connect with history and learn it on their own terms.

I see in these that there remains work to do on my end to lend greater texture to their understanding of the notion of sharing authority (or "shared authority," as several frame it here). Some students continued to see the exchange between public historians and partners as more one-way. Almost no one mentioned the tensions that I see as so apparent in the introduction to public history classroom, perhaps because I failed to bring them to the surface in an adequate way. No one specifically mentioned an emphasis on a more substantive understanding of the university's past, or the encounter with history in their own public history project. But in these definitions, I do see a reflection of course themes (and the defining features of our field): collaboration, the politics of historical production ("every story a public historian portrays is limiting the scope of another story"), stewardship, and service. Reflecting on the class, I am once again reminded of Inayatullah's notion of the encounter: "We enter the classroom to encounter others. With them we can meditate on the possibility of our own learning."[15] Perhaps the encounters that students have in the course—with one another, with the past—will resonate in ways that I hope.

Notes

I would like to thank Sara-Maria Sorentino and Filipe Robles at the University of Alabama for providing insightful feedback that helped shape this chapter.

1. GVGK Tang (@gvgktang), Twitter thread, March 19, 2020, 11:21 A.M., https://twitter.com/gvgktang/status/1240659617073561602. This thread was Tang's presentation for the 2020 National Council on Public History virtual conference and titled "Gather, Connect, Amplify: QTAPI Testimony and Grassroots Community Building." See also Tang, "We Need to Talk about Public History's Columbusing Problem."

2. H. Green, "Critique of the Professional Public History Movement," 165.

3. Newfield, *Unmaking the Public University*, 29.

4. Martin, "Linked Fates and Futures."

5. Harney and Moten, *Undercommons*, 37.

6. For meditations on pedagogy and the radical possibilities of the public history classroom, see Elizabeth Belanger, "Radical Futures: Teaching Public History as Social Justice," and Rebecca Amato, Gabrielle Bendiner-Viani, Dipti Desai, Denise D. Meringolo, and Mary Rizzo "Radical is a Process: Public History Pedagogy in Urban Universities," in *Radical Roots: Public History and a Tradition of Social Justiec Activism*, edited by Denise D. Meringolo (Amherst, Mass: Amherst College Press, 2021), https://doi.org/10.3998/mpub.12366495, accessed October 12, 2022.

7. Inayatullah, "Teaching Is Impossible."

8. See, for example, Meringolo, "Cry for Help."

9. Hanna, "Pedagogies in the Flesh," 231; Tang, Twitter thread.

10. Filipe Robles, a graduate student at UA who commented on the chapter, wrote in response to this section: "When I read your assertion about idealism, what comes to my mind is Marx's sentence, 'Everything that is solid melts into air. . . .' Neither is public history perfectly egalitarian nor does the university need to always be hierarchical." Included with his permission.

11. "Home," Old Cahawba, https://cahawba.com/, accessed October 12, 2022.

12. The term "sharing authority" has been used and misused since its introduction by oral historian Michael Frisch. More recently, Aleia Brown has questioned

its utility in light of a public history practice that centers around care for Black lives. See Brown, "An Ethic of Care in Black Public History," Thread Reader App, https://blackfreedomproject.notion.site/AN-EVENING-WITH-ALEIA-BROWN-TWITTER-CHAT-e3e6215cb08340fdbe455a2499164e93, accessed October 12, 2022.

13. See "About Us," Invisible Histories Project, https://invisiblehistory.org/about-us/, accessed October 12, 2022.

14. Colwell, *Plundered Skulls and Stolen Spirits*.

15. Inayatullah, "Teaching Is Impossible," 18.

10 A Journey at the Center of Public History

THOMAS CAUVIN

Teaching public history courses has been among my best experiences as an educator. I have been teaching history at the university level for almost ten years, and I can honestly say that the more it includes public history projects and practices, the more I enjoy the course. Being part of international public history networks, I am often asked by colleagues from countries where public history as a university field does not exist what benefit they could have in teaching such courses.[1] An academic answer would be that it is fundamental for students to acquire special skills and practices to be able to work in, for, with, and among different publics.[2] A more personal answer would be that public history courses are always fun to teach and (generally) fun for students to attend. Public history courses are also very much connected to our present environment through partnerships, contacts with a variety of audiences, and consideration for present-day issues. I consider public history teaching to be project-oriented experiences that foster learning-by-doing approaches. As a result, my public history courses change every year, despite what curriculum rigidity of the catalog would let students think. Due to the rich variety of practices, projects, and even definitions of public history, courses vary from institution to institution, from colleague to colleague, from year to year.

Nevertheless, teaching public history can also be quite challenging. In spite of available teaching resources—some from the National Council on Public History (NCPH)—as well as published textbooks, handbooks, and other companions, we as instructors often struggle to teach public history. In this chapter, I present how I designed and taught an introduction to public history course for undergraduate students in the fall of 2019. The class was composed of three main parts: definitions of the field, discussions of specific issues and practices with invited professionals, and the production of two public history projects. I ask you to follow me on a journey through the different phases of my teaching, the construction of a syllabus, the organization of sessions, the small successes and achievements, the remaining challenges, and my doubts and moments of contentment. But before that, I will present my personal understanding of public history and how it impacts what I want to share with students, colleagues, partners, and audiences.

My Approach to Public History

As instructors, our previous experiences, preferences, and careers contribute to explaining how we understand, practice, and teach public history. Teaching public history is, for me, an opportunity to reflect on my own work in a self-inspection process. I am never the exact same historian before and after I teach a public history course not only because it asks me to reflect on how I perceive the field but also because I leave a large part of my teaching open to negotiation with partners, guests, and students. Every time I teach a public history course, I test new assignments, collaborations, and types of projects. In the end, those collaborators—including students—force me to adapt my practices.

I consider the creation of tangible products to be a critical aspect of public history. Much more than courses on representations of the past in media (TV, monuments, or museums, for instance), I strongly feel that public history courses should be based on hands-on experiences that allow students to both create projects and engage with nonacademic audiences. This priority has to do with me teaching in the United States, too. In Europe, for instance, much more attention is generally paid to the historiographies and theories of history in public.[3] This discrepancy raises a long-discussed question about public history training: the relations between theory and practice.[4]

Making things even more challenging, public history includes a broad range of practices. I recently compared public history to a tree—"public his'tree—a system in which all the different parts (roots, trunk, branches, leaves) are interconnected.[5] Although the metaphor has some flaws—it may let students think that there is direct process from collecting sources to using history, or that some practices are exclusive to some part (for instance, not only is oral history about collecting sources, but it can also belong to interpreting and communicating history)—it helps visualize the multiple practices, steps, and possible actors of the overall public history process. Students should be aware that doing public history can include steps and practices beyond what they might expect from theory-based learning, such as the traditional interpretation of primary sources (the trunk), and include some practices less often associated with the job of historians. Those include

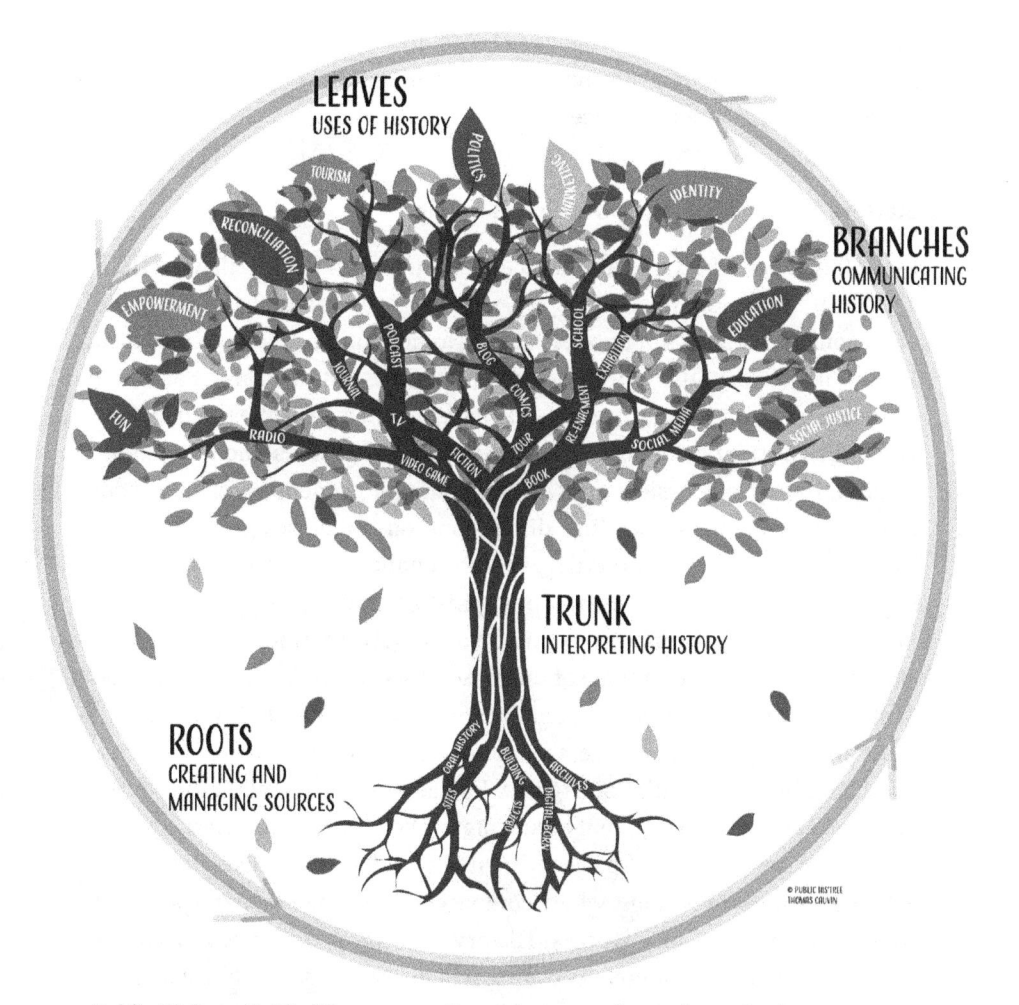

Public His'tree: Public History as an Ecosystem, 2019 (image by author).

creating and preserving sources (the roots), communicating history through a multitude of media (the branches), and paying attention to the various public uses (leaves) of history. Understanding public history as an interconnected system can help students understand the multitude of actors, the need for collaboration, and why learning skills matters.

Based on this understanding of public history, the specificity of its teaching very much deals with a focus on communication and engagement with the nonacademic public (the branches of the tree). In 2019, I therefore decided to ask my students to communicate history to nonacademic audiences

A Journey at the Center of Public History 203

through several kinds of media. In order to do so, students had to develop and offer their research through an episode of a podcast and a wall panel to be disposed in a public space.

Starting the Journey with Some Ideas in Mind

In the fall of 2019, I offered a course called Practices of Public History (HIST 479) for undergraduate students at Colorado State University (CSU). Like other courses, Practices of Public History was not limited to history students. History majors usually represented 50 percent or so of this class. I also had a good number of communication, journalism, and even some English, law, and political science majors. This wide range of profiles encouraged interdisciplinary discussion and practice among students—for instance, communication majors leading discussions on panel design and public speaking—but it can at times trigger some challenges. In the evaluations, some students confessed that not being history majors, they were far less interested in sessions on careers and fields of public history. This can be a caveat, but I do think that some of the career discussion—in particular, those dealing with CVs, cover letters, and internships—benefited all students.

As an undergraduate course, we capped the class at thirty-four students, but it has never been full. Colleagues who had previously taught the course had between fifteen and twenty students in their class. This relatively low enrollment fits the type of project-oriented work we undertake, but it nevertheless raises questions when compared with some other (popular) courses, such as Military History, History of Ireland, or History of Witchcraft. Although this is somehow common to many courses, public history is still relatively unknown among students. In fact, the large majority of my students had never heard of public history and barely knew about careers that history majors can get beyond school teaching. Teaching public history often requires a lot of clarification on what the field is and how students can benefit from it.

Building a public history class can therefore start six months before we actually meet in the classroom. To spread awareness and augment enrollment, I started to canvass colleagues' classes as early as the spring of 2019, explaining what the course—and public history—was, what types of projects we would undertake, and the possibility of connecting with local partners and internships. Canvassing my fifteen colleagues' classrooms was time-consuming, but doing so sparked interest. Eventually, twenty-four students enrolled. Public history requires lots of explanation about why public engagement matters for historians, but the fact that history can be practiced and performed outside classrooms is a very convincing argument for students who like history but do not want to teach or get a PhD. In addition to enrollment, a public history course requires thoughtful consideration regarding collaboration, projects, and even spaces in which to practice public history.

To build my syllabus, I pictured my students at the end of the semester and the knowledge and skills they should ideally master. I first wanted to familiarize them with the many facets of public history and to provide enough information for them to decide whether this could be a field they would like to study and work in. My strategy would have been slightly different in a department where a public history undergraduate concentration—with several public history courses—exists. Being the unique course devoted entirely to public history, I felt responsible for providing a generalist approach to the field.

Being that most public history careers are outside academia, I decided to include discussions with professionals on career choices, jobs, and salaries.[6] The latter was actually very useful. If some students had only a vague idea of how much a schoolteacher makes, they had no idea how much university faculty, museum staff, or National Park Service rangers make.

Regarding the balance between theory and practice, I wanted to cover some theoretical public history debates through class discussions and offer history projects for nonacademic audiences. For those projects, students would have to adapt their research to a public audience. While most university students write essays and design projects for their instructors, I find it crucial for public history students to be able to communicate and explain their research to public audiences. In targeting public audiences, my students would be confronted with two main issues. First, their audiences might not know much about the historical topics. Second, and more challenging, is that these audiences might not even be initially interested in the research. I wanted students to leave their comfort zones and be confronted with the requirements and challenges of public history, but also to experience the fun and pride of working for broad audiences in collaboration with partners who may have specific requirements, objectives, and guidelines. Working with partners forces students—and they often dislike it at first because they have to take into consideration additional requirements—to be flexible and accept compromises in their work.

The course was therefore divided into three main parts: (1) definitions of public history, (2) an overview of public history practices with professionals from the field (guest speakers), and (3) two public history communication projects (a podcast and wall panels). Of course, even in the process of following a rough itinerary (defining, going deeper with professionals, and then building projects), the nature of public history would inevitably force students to deal with multiple assignments. For instance, although the two projects were to be presented in the last two weeks of the semester, students had to start their research as early as week five.

Defining or Not Defining: This Is the Question

There are many ways in which students can explore the field of public history. One long debate in pedagogy and among professionals is over the definition of public history itself.[7] Through the International Federation for Public History, I have often been part of conversations on whether or not we should provide one definition of public history.[8] Internationally, one single definition may limit the field. On the other hand, not providing any definition makes any discussion quite confusing, as there is no basis for understanding. Teaching an introduction to public history course faces a similar challenge.

The situation in my class was even more challenging, since not everyone possessed the same backgrounds and skills in history. I found it useful to start the semester with an informal class conversation on what history means to them. Although students had two short pieces to read, I wanted the discussion to be based on their personal understanding.[9] My objective was for the class to understand history as a process—with steps, analysis, and sources—different from the past itself. We did not have much time to cover this vast topic, but we had a great experience that focused on memory, history, and sources.

In order to go further on history being a process with multiple steps, I assigned Michel-Rolph Trouillot's *Silencing the Past*. This is a fantastic book for exploring the differences between history and the past. Trouillot brilliantly demonstrates how the multiple steps in making history—as early as deciding what constitutes an archive—allow for interpretation but also result in silences about the past. We discussed the book during an entire class session. In relation to public history, the book was also useful for visualizing the various actors in making history—not only the historian interpreting primary sources but also the individuals who select and preserve sources. To me the book also revealed how history belongs to the public realm, how history can empower some public actors—including historians—and how others are underrepresented in the construction of history. It finally highlighted how students, when they produce history, will have their own responsibility in selecting topics, sources, and events.

Having some understanding of how we construct history through various steps and with various actors, the class then prepared a discussion on public history. Each student had to create an approach. I organized a class discussion on what public history is or can be to explore whether—and if so, to what extent—it differs from what we said about history. I offered some resources from the NCPH on defining the field and a post of their choice among the *History@Work* blog.[10] I also asked them to read the introduction of my public history textbook, so even I became part of the debate.[11] I wanted students to think about several questions: What is public history? Where do we practice public history? Who does public history? Why do we do public history? The objective was not to achieve a strict definition of public history but to have a forum in which students propose, explore, and argue for multiple approaches and ways of doing public history. I thought that this way, students would get a preliminary understanding that they could shape over the semester.

Being early in the semester, this class discussion felt at first a bit artificial. Students reused many of the same arguments from the readings. However, the fact that they chose different projects from *History@Work* fleshed out the discussion over concrete examples. Plus, I had decided I did not want to lead the discussion, having one student chair it instead. I intervened through questions every now and then, acting as a participant more than an instructor—easier said than done, as we teachers have a tendency to monopolize the floor. After the class discussion, students had to write a two-page paper on what public history means.

Students' definitions evolved throughout the semester through exposure to examples, projects, and guests. I like asking guests to present their vision, practice, and public history projects. The first guests I invited into the classroom were actually two graduate students from our own master's program. They briefly introduced themselves, revealed why they were in a public history program, and explained how they saw the field. Defining public history in front of twenty-plus undergrads turned out to be a difficult but fun experience for the two graduate students. The discussion was very lively and included many personal details—for instance, why one chose to enroll in a public history program after having taught in middle schools for years. The fact that the two graduate students had different paths, different focuses—historic preservation and cultural resource management—and different understandings of the field made the conversation very useful.

The next step in the journey of discovering public history was another discussion with a guest. I had asked my students to read and review Ari Kelman's *A Misplaced Massacre*. Kelman's book deals with the long and contested creation of a national park devoted to the massacre of Cheyenne and Arapaho people in 1864 by federal troops.[12] He details the many steps in creating a public history site and the intense discussions, debates, compromises, and arguments between the various actors of the project. The book exemplifies the collaborative dimension of public history—doing history with groups, communities, and partners—but also shows how difficult and challenging collaboration can become. It was also interesting to choose this book because the Sand Creek Massacre took place in Colorado, just two hundred miles from CSU.[13] For the discussion, I contacted Kelman, who agreed to have an online session with my students.

The experience was fantastic in many ways. Being able to explore a book with the author provided a unique opportunity to discuss not only the contents but also the writing process. Kelman was straightforward on the reasons he chose that topic, the challenges he had confronted, what he was happy with, and what he would now do differently. It helped students understand the construction of history, the need for multiple drafts, and constant reviewing. Kelman himself, a great orator with a keen sense of humor, made this discussion one of the best moments of the semester. In order to prepare our discussion, students and I attempted to map all major actors involved in the creation of the national park. This attempt ended up in a very complex design and network of power relations—and proved that it is not only historians who play a role in building public history. The map and the discussion allowed us to reflect on the definition of authority, expertise, and power in public history—ideas quite advanced for an undergraduate course.

Public History: An Umbrella, an Archipelago, and a Tree

If it is important to have a sense of what public history is, I also wanted my students to explore specific practices. Public history is a general term that includes many types of practices. As such, it has been metaphorically defined as an umbrella and more recently as an archipelago or a tree.[14] Needless to say, it is impossible to cover all the various subfields and practices of the field in one semester, so I selected four for weekly focus: historic interpretation, historic preservation, archives, and museums. These choices derived from what I considered to be the four most important fields of practice at that time and for those particular students. Furthermore, CSU has a strong focus on environmental history and historic preservation, and archives and museums would be the main types of institutions providing our students with internships.

The broad range of practices explains why it is quite difficult to select books for an introduction to public history class. For this class, I decided to use the textbook I published in 2016, *Public History*. Using my own book gave me the advantage of knowing exactly what I wanted my students to read. Since I designed the book's chapters to introduce fields such as museums, archives, oral history, and historic preservation, I used these sections to familiarize my students with the practices. In addition to my textbook, I organized discussions with professionals. Contacting potential guests and preparing the discussions explain why it was necessary to build the syllabus early on. I find the presence of professionals both exciting (making the discussions much more concrete and acute) and rewarding for students, who can connect with day-to-day public history practices. Sessions usually lasted around thirty minutes, with a ten-minute presentation in which guests provide details on their role and activities, followed by a forum for questions and answers.

I designed the week around historic interpretation using readings from my textbook along with extracts from Freeman Tilden's book *Interpreting Our Heritage*. I devoted the first session of the week to the process of interpretation and how interpreting the past for a large nonacademic audience affects the process. This was followed by a conversation with Nick Sacco, park ranger at the Ulysses S. Grant National Historic Site. I have known Nick for a while and have asked him several times to present his work to my students. I always enjoy how clear and educational he is. As a former public history graduate student, he can also talk about the connection between public history training and careers. Students appreciated the opportunity to discuss the everyday activities of a park ranger. Talking about the challenges of interpreting historic sites to a wider audience, students had questions on how to react to difficult questions and assertions from the public—for instance, the Lost Cause narrative and claims that the U.S. Civil War had nothing to do with slavery. Nick explained that he never tries to confront those comments head-on but rather invites participants to discuss how they know what they know and engage with historical sources.

Another session was about museums and public history. I asked two former students of mine (from my days at the University of Louisiana at Lafayette) to join the class and talk about their experiences working in museums.

Both are young professionals who know the challenges of moving from a public history graduate program to a public history job, but their profiles are different. Meghan Sylvester directed a small local history museum (Iberville Museum in Plaquemine, Louisiana), and Adam Foreman was the student program specialist at the National World War II Museum's education department in New Orleans. The two provided different approaches to the museum field and what students could expect from a museum career. For the week on archives, I asked Lesley Struc, who works at the Fort Collins Museum of Discovery, to explain her work in local archives. As a former student of our CSU graduate program, Lesley had much experience in managing archives as well as designing internship experiences for our students.

Megan, Adam, and Lesley briefly talked about their jobs, described what public history practices in museums and archives look like, and gave their personal thoughts on public history careers. The latter point was the issue my students were most interested in. This interest was something I had already noticed. In previous class evaluations, students had expressed the wish to have more information on careers and internships. Students were particularly interested in discussing one issue: the competitiveness of the field.

The difficulty of getting a job, the competition with students who have other types of degrees (particularly in library and information science for jobs in archives), and the need to get additional internships (often nonpaid) rightly worried some students. I had not foreseen the substance of questions that followed the guest talks, but it led to an intense and honest discussion on nonpaid internships. In Fort Collins—a rather small college town in Colorado, where the number of partnering institutions is quite limited—finding paid internships is easier said than done, especially for undergraduate students. Contacting, discussing, and guaranteeing paid internships from local partners is not impossible but requires lots of time and energy. This is why some of us in my department had asked for the creation of a specific internship coordinator position.

I had prepared two sessions to discuss internships (what to look for, where to find them, and how to apply), CV and cover letters, and, if time allowed, mock interviews. For those students who wish to pursue public history training, it is critical to have internship experience—a deciding factor in our selection of graduate student applications. One objective of the class was to equip students with the necessary knowledge of what to look for in terms of an internship. I asked Lesley Struc to help provide advice and feedback.

The session we co-led was practice oriented, with tips on how to prepare one's application.

Questions on what an internship is, how to apply for one, and how to actually earn one were quite common.[15] Students also inquired about salaries in public history. This originated with one of our guests, who shared salaries for entry-level positions in her institution. It turned out that students had no idea how much schoolteachers, instructors, or museum and archive staff make. I think salary expectations should be a discussion we have not only with our undergraduates but also with our graduate students. This could be very useful, as some graduate students who apply for jobs have to propose and negotiate their salary—a quite disturbing reality if one has never thought about it. Although the figures vary from state to state and from institution to institution, I shared how much I personally earned, how much some schoolteachers were making in Colorado, and some additional figures I had collected from anonymous former students who now worked in the field. Providing entry-level salary information for archives and museums is more difficult, as each institution has its own grid. I conducted some online research and shared what I found with my students, but I wished I had had more time to prepare. All in all, I think these discussions helped students understand what to expect from public history careers—even though wages are only one aspect of their career choice. Although I find that public history provides many possible opportunities, it is important not to make false promises. Coming from Europe, where student education does not cost as much as it does in the United States, I sometimes felt helpless when students asked me how they could reimburse their student loans with unpaid internships or entry-level wages from jobs that could turn out to be extremely competitive.

Beyond the Classroom: Communicating History

It is necessary for public history students to confront audiences beyond the classroom. But one should not lose sight that public history is not mere communication. My students always conduct original research using archives and other primary sources. When doing so, I often ask them to focus on local history. First, it helps them to discover and learn about where they live—even if only temporarily. Second, it builds local networks of partners, history buffs, amateur historians, and audiences. When teaching in Louisiana, I offered projects on the Cajun French heritage, and in Colorado, I once offered a class on the history of beer.

For this class, I tried something new. The idea was to have students choose individual research topics, but I wanted to somehow involve local residents in finding ideas for topics. Before the semester started, I used a Facebook group whose members (around 12,000) discuss, share, and comment on histories and memories of the city. I simply asked what events, buildings, characters, or topics from Fort Collins's history they would like to know more about or thought worthy of exploration. I collected suggestions and kept track of the likes so I could order the topics by popularity. I came up with a list of about forty-five possible topics. When the course started, I proposed that list to students as a resource for choosing their research topic. I briefly introduced the topics with some basic details: where the site was, when the event took place, what it dealt with. This was challenging, as while I wanted students to have the information they needed to choose their topics, I did not want them to have so many details that it would provide them with a way to present their research.

Done early in the semester, the choice of topic was important, as each student would keep the topic until the end. I provided the number of likes from the Facebook group so that students could get an idea of the public's interest. The public engagement with local communities in finding, choosing, and exploring topics could be developed more, but this provided a first opportunity to connect students with local residents. Having selected their topic, students had to learn about its history. It is crucial that the course contains some original historical research, in which students use and engage with primary sources. Because we had a limited amount of time devoted to researching and collecting information, I structured the research through several specific steps. Guiding them through requirements saved time for the production of the two later projects.

Students had to collect and read secondary sources about their topic. I provided some online repositories and local history blogs. Next, they had to find primary sources, including at least five historical photographs, one map, and three written documents from a list of online archives. Finally, I encouraged them to find someone who knew about their topic for a discussion. This last requirement was supposed to offer them an opportunity to collect information and memories from local communities. However, it turned out to be too optimistic. The time needed to find, contact, and have a discussion with someone was not feasible for our calendar.

After having compiled and collected information, students wrote individual 4,000-word research papers about their topic, the historical context, the main actors, and the collected documents. Quite traditional in its design, this assignment gave students the necessary historical knowledge about their topic. Ultimately, 4,000 words were more than enough; the challenge was to downsize their research for their public history productions. These research steps required some time, and I had to give students until week five of the semester to finish their research papers. However, as the research paper served as the basis for the two projects, it was important that the research could be undertaken early enough in the semester. In the end, students liked being the single expert on their topic and explaining to the class why their research mattered. The class sessions in which they all presented and shared their research became true conversions about local history. For example, one student had spoken to the descendants of the historical character she was researching and received bags of what they called "historical trash." Those bags were actually full of everyday objects from the early twentieth century that other students used for their own research.

My goal is for my students to leave the class not only with new knowledge and skills but also with something more concrete that they can show, share, discuss, and be proud of. This product can take several shapes (some years it is a short documentary film, and others, it is a public tour). This year, the products would communicate the historical research students had undertaken. Facts, events, primary sources, and interpretations would remain the same but had to be adapted to a different medium with a different audience. Whereas I was the only audience for their research paper, the two projects would be produced for a general and nonacademic audience in Fort Collins, who might have no idea about the topic. Communicating historical research to nonacademic audiences is a very important skill for public history.

In order to discuss the communication of history, I contacted Torri Yates-Orr. Trained as a TV host and media producer, Torri created the social media series #OnThisDayInHistory, short (three-minute) history videos that became quite popular on Twitter. Part of the History Communicator group that developed through the NCPH, Torri graciously agreed to share her knowledge with my students. I asked my students to watch some of Torri's videos and prepare questions about how she worked and the challenges of communicating history through short videos on social media.

We discussed with Torri not only the amount of research she does to prepare her videos but also how she finds topics that resonate with current events and public interests. This was very useful for students, who began to understand how much they would have to modify and adapt their research for it to become public history work. Torri and my students also discussed the modes and ways of communicating to nonacademic audiences. Students would not have to produce three-minute videos, but the tips were useful all the same. The communication process—vocabulary, public speaking, interaction with audiences, and visual documents—would be something students would have to learn and practice for their research to be engaging. One good example was the class discussion on evidence that followed the guest presentation. As for Torri's videos, many public history projects do not include footnotes—unlike the students' research papers. This practice puzzled several students, and we explored how the medium affects not only the form but also the content of the research.

You Shall Not Leave My Class without a Product:
The Land Grant Chronicles: History at CSU

In order for my students to explore public history forms of communication, I looked for possible ideas and partners on campus and in Fort Collins. One possibility was to create a podcast. At CSU, we were fortunate to have a professional campus radio station (KCSU) complete with podcast managers. After several meetings to discuss opportunities for collaboration, we decided to work together. KCSU offered help with the logistics—that is, recording and editing podcast episodes. I remember leaving the meeting with a feeling of success, having connected several partners on campus, provided an opportunity for students to share their work, and ensured that a final product would be available. It was also a relief not having to ask students to master the technology and skills to create an entire podcast. While the overall process is not extremely complex, creating a podcast would have meant borrowing materials, setting up an online space, and taking care of editing episodes—a daunting task for a class project.

With the support of KCSU, I included steps in the syllabus for students to transform their research into single episodes. We listened to various history podcast episodes and discussed what made them good—or not so good. Besides the topic, we focused on storytelling, public speaking, adding personal stories and anecdotes, picturing the past for listeners, and communicating history to an unknown audience. Collaborating with KCSU also aimed at showing students how partnerships can affect the production of history. Considering the amount of work required for them to do the editing, KCSU agreed to help us under two conditions. First, episodes would not go beyond ten minutes overall. Second, although all students would be able to record their episodes, only ten (out of twenty-four) would be selected for editing and would be aired live. The selection of the ten best episodes would be done by myself and the podcast managing team (two staff members).

This collaboration allowed me to focus in class on two specific skills: script writing and public speaking, both very important in communicating history to large nonacademic audiences. Although I had no particular experience in writing scripts for podcasts, I had taught script writing for documentary film production. I also taught myself through tutorials and examples of script writing for podcasts. Next time, I would probably approach colleagues from the English and communication departments for help. Script writing is challenging, especially for history majors who have been trained to write in specific academic ways. Moving from their 4,000-word research papers to a script for a ten-minute episode was very challenging. My previous experience told me that students would need lots of rewriting and multiple drafts before getting something satisfactory. We started by discussing together the dos and don'ts of public history writing. By comparing the first page of an academic article, a blog post, and the first minute of a podcast episode, we pinpointed a few rules: avoid jargon, be straightforward, avoid long sentences, and communicate in active tense. I introduced students to the Gunning Fog Index, which calculates the level of readability of a text. Although it should not be taken as a definitive solution, this tool attributes some figures connected to education level, and pinpoints some flaws (like long sentences). We had fun comparing students' first drafts, ranking them from the most to the least public-history-friendly works. Another step was to share and discuss the introductions in peer-review sessions. If we had more time, we would have had more of those sessions.

Students ended up with three to five drafts for their scripts—quite normal and in line with my previous courses on documentary filmmaking and public history writing. I had to read about a hundred drafts in two weeks—definitely one of the busiest times of the semester. The process of writing and rewriting was a challenge for students who were not used to having so many drafts for a paper. Nevertheless, I found it to be one of the most interesting ways of learning. It showed students that history (especially history writing) is a constant construction process that requires back and forth. My only concern was that I was the main source of review. I tried once or twice to have students read one another's scripts, but this was quite time-consuming. I wish I could have involved partners—KCSU podcast managers, for instance—but they were already doing lots of work, and

I did not wish to add to their plates. One possible idea for the future would be to open the process of review to online communities; involving members of social media groups through private access to scripts would be exciting.

The other skill I wanted students to practice was public speaking. Very often, oral skills are not given enough credit in history education. How many times do we offer opportunities for students to practice their oral skills? I am not talking about class discussions but about ways to enunciate clear historical arguments to nonacademic audiences. This is indeed a key skill used not only by tour guides but also by park rangers, museum staff, audiovisual professionals (radio and TV presenters), community workers, and educators. Being clear, convincing, and engaging will certainly help students in their future jobs.

In class, we explored communication skills for which communication and English majors were unsurprisingly better equipped: when and how to breathe, pace (speaking too fast was one common mistake), and how to engage with the audience. We also covered issues related to history production, such as how to depict the past for listeners, how to use primary sources, and how to adapt complex ideas to public storytelling. Moving the focus from writing to speaking also modified how the class functioned. It was clear that some students whose writing skills were not the best were more at ease with public speaking. Others were very shy and feared those sessions. We also had one conversation on public speaking and anxiety, and I offered some tips for easing anxiety. Although I thought I had provided a safe learning environment—providing tips, offering individual tutoring—it was clear I could have been more proactive, since some students did not confess their fear and anxiety until after the events took place.

Collaborating with the campus radio station gave students a small preview of what partnership entails. As for other public history courses, flexibility and the capacity to make compromises are key skills for students. The campus radio station agreed to edit and host our episodes, but they had some demands, too. For instance, KCSU asked to be the only space where the selected episodes would be available; students could not upload their episode to their personal website (or anywhere else). More demanding was the requirement for us to create a podcast series in the midst of the semester. Indeed, KCSU was very happy with the episodes and proposed that instead of airing individual short stories, we come up with a specific podcast series—with a title and a short description—in which to group all of them. While we had a great class discussion—how to create a title that could encompass all topics, how to engage a local audience while being marketable for broader online publics—the request showed how evolutionary and unpredictable collaboration can be.

Choosing a title for the podcast series was part of the creative dimension of public history teaching. The whole class took part in the decision-making. We thought about several possibilities for a title, discussing not only titles but marketing strategy. We submitted our titles to the whole department (colleagues, staff, the history club) through an online vote. The class had the ultimate decision to choose three options, which we submitted to KCSU for feedback. We ended up with *The Land Grant Chronicles: History at CSU*, which referred to CSU being a land grant university, storytelling, and local history.

For many students, recording was the most stressful moment of the semester. Although the class had previously visited the radio studio and met with the producers and sound engineer, it remained a new experience for all of them. In order to ease their anxiety, we had decided that they would go one at a time, accompanied only by the podcast manager, who would take care of the recording so that students could focus on their script. Due to the high number of recordings—twenty-four in total, divided into three series of eight students—they had only one opportunity to record their episode (although editing would allow some cuts). I decided not to enter the studio with students to limit the group pressure. Students actually entered in twos, the second student listening to the recording of the previous one. From what I saw and from the class feedback, all students found the recording—and the production of each episode—very rewarding. Ultimately, the station managers loved the episodes, so instead of selecting only ten, they edited all of the recordings. KCSU agreed to air all twenty-four the following semester (two episodes each week).[16]

In-Stall History

The second project was born from a discussion with Chilean colleagues. I was involved in an international discussion on how to set up an introduction to public history course in some Latin American countries. During this discussion, a colleague from Chile said she had asked her students to come up with proposals for new formats to display their topic in public spaces. One of her students proposed having panels in public restrooms. Although the proposal was a basic first draft, it struck me as something I wanted to explore with my students.

The idea was for my students to communicate their research topic—the one selected at the beginning of the semester—through one panel in one public restroom in Fort Collins. They could opt for restaurants, bars, coffee shops, breweries (most popular in Fort Collins), museums, or libraries. Due to the special—some would say strange—location, students had to be very careful and thoughtful about the contents and design. It also forced them to work outside their comfort zone, as they would be engaging with a specific but anonymous public. I admit I did not go into too many details in the syllabus, as I wanted the class to construct the project together. I requested intermediary steps, such as proposing, contacting, and securing possible sites; designing panel drafts; and installing panels. Over a discussion on social media with public history educators, Rebecca Wingo proposed calling the project "In-Stall History," a brilliant idea that I immediately shared with my students.

Due to the unusual space, we had an informal and honest class discussion at the beginning of the semester to explore students' feelings, expectations, and worries about the project. I designed the discussion as three parts: all the questions they had about the project, what assets and advantages such a project can have, and what could go wrong. The last part of this discussion was a problem-solving process. Students had mixed feelings about the project, and some were openly reluctant to design a panel for restrooms. They had valid questions, such as about installing them inside restrooms rather than in "more public" spaces, such as libraries, restaurants, and stores. I did hear their comments, but I thought and still think that the project had some advantages. First, it was as if students worked as consultants answering a demand (mine) from a client for a product: they had to adapt to a request. Second, it forced them to rethink their work to fit in very specific places. They had to think not only about the contents of the panel (based on their research) but about how the space and public affect their production. Most restrooms being gendered, their panels would certainly have a specific audience. Students had to design their panels to be easily and quickly accessible, as people generally do not spend much time in public restrooms. The light, height, and doors were also criteria to consider.

Students were responsible for finding sites, and they had to follow certain steps, such as proposing three possible sites, contacting and securing a place, and installing their panel in the restroom. One of the interesting aspects was students having to convince managers to accept a history panel for installation inside their restrooms. Students had to prepare arguments explaining why history panels could be an asset for restaurants, breweries, public libraries, and other types of stores. The links between history, business, and customers were something I wanted students to explore. We ultimately had an interesting class conversation on the value of history for businesses and other for-profit companies.

For some students, though, it turned out to be quite difficult to secure a site. Although we had talked about possible ways to contact managers and explain the project (stating that it would be for a university class project and perhaps not mentioning the restroom in the first contact), it could be stressful to randomly contact stores and propose history panels. Besides, class history projects were not a priority for managers, and some of them did not return student calls. For three students, the search became quite time-consuming, and one of them only secured a place at the very end of the semester. On the contrary, some students simply contacted places they knew—because they worked there or knew someone who did—and secured a site very early. In retrospect, I could have helped students by providing a preliminary list of places they could contact. Another problem was that I should have provided a clearer perimeter. The only condition I gave was that the site had to be in Fort Collins. It turned out that some of the sites were far from others. As I had to visit all the sites for their final assignment, it became quite cumbersome for me during the final week.

The project offered opportunities to reflect on the relationship between public history and space. Student panels related to space in separate but connected ways. Students had to conceive, explore, and understand their research in space. From our class talks, we had to figure out to what extent the choice of a site—restaurant, brewery, library—connected to the research topic. In other words, would some sites be problematic or more appropriate for some topics? To give just one example, could research on a cemetery— or other sacred places—be displayed in a public restroom? In a more flexible way, how would a topic on a sacred site have to be adapted to be displayed in a public restroom?

Another piece of discussion focused on how best to select a site to connect with the research topic. I invited students to think about possible sites that could mean something for their research. One option was to propose the panel to a site close to where the historical event took place. One student working on the 1997 floods in Fort Collins placed her panel in a store right where most of the damage took place. Another solution was to focus on the topic. One student proposed her panel about the long policy of alcohol prohibition in Fort Collins to a craft brewery. Another interesting example came from a student who did his research on George Strauss's cabin—one of the oldest remaining buildings (built in the 1860s) in northern Colorado. Among the various possible ways to interpret the site, he chose to focus on the cabin being burned down due to arson in 1999. The high school students who burned down the cabin invoked stories of ghosts associated with Strauss's family as a reason for exploring the site. My students proposed that the Strauss panels be placed at the pizzeria in front of the high school and adapted the student's research to the urban legend surrounding George Strauss's cabin (thus restoring the truth about George Strauss, who had no family), his life in the nineteenth century, and how rumors and myths can impact the present.

Space also mattered due to the specificity of having panels in restrooms. Students discussed how this specific space could affect the contents they would provide. One challenge was the fact that public restrooms may not be sites where people want to spend too much time or even engage in discussions about the past. Through their panels, they had to catch people's attention and get straight to the point. We explored resources on exhibit and communication design, including journalistic approaches such as not waiting until the last paragraph to explain the key argument. I limited panels to 250 words maximum, already quite significant in terms of museum standards but still challenging for students in comparison to traditional essays. Students considered the other specificities of their sites: Was the panel geared for a specific gender (and if so, would they have specific gendered audiences that they might consider in their content)? How small was the space? How would the light (or absence thereof) affect the design? We explored traditional rules of design, such as eye-vision height, text size, color, and F-pattern reading. Each space (and therefore each situation) was different and required specific negotiation. This showed students how public history projects may have to adapt to specific audiences and spaces. In contrast, the podcast project, for which students produced and rewrote multiple drafts and rearranged text and photos, led to some interesting discussions in which we moved away from the oversimplified view that fact is fact and history is history. Instead, we explored more complex arguments about how space and the process of communication affects history production.

A Journey That Never Ends: Self-Reflection

Public history encourages self-reflection—both for students as well as instructors. I usually conclude my public history courses with a self-reflective assignment, allowing time for students to discuss how their projects and practices contributed to rethinking public history theories and debates we encountered at the beginning of the semester. In a theory-practice-theory triptych, I want students to leave my class with their own understanding of the field, as it helps avoid the same ready-to-use definitions of public history. In this final assignment, students had to comment on their initial definition of public history, to explore how their approach had (or had not) changed, and why. I specifically asked how—and if so, to what extent—the two projects fit the theories of public history. Instead of an academic essay, I invited them to adopt a first-person writing style and not shy away from personal views and feelings.

The self-reflective papers included many personal stories and opinions on public history. Two students presented critical views of the field—attitudes that I had not detected in the class discussions. In that sense, the absence of group pressure in this assignment allowed students to express ideas that I would have otherwise missed. Their critical views were not failures—convincing students that public history is the track to follow was by no means my objective—as we need more critical discussion in the field. But they did raise some issues. First, as this was the final assignment, I had limited opportunities to discuss their paper—in individual feedback or through class discussion—and this felt a bit frustrating to them. Some of the criticisms were more due to personal stands—"the public does not know what I (history major) know about the past"—but the better-constructed arguments deserved more class discussion. For instance, one student argued that public history is more communication than history, as the search for objectivity is challenged by the collaboration with publics and groups for which objectivity is not a goal. Even though I do not agree with the argument, it is indeed a key debate in public history and would have been a great topic of discussion. As a thought for later, it could be interesting to confront students with long-standing arguments against public history (from colleagues—mostly historians—who see public history as a neoliberal trend in universities or as a sort of memory construction devoid of rigorous history methodology). It could also be a way for students to reflect on (and perhaps get engaged in) history training in higher education. How and where would public history stand in their four-year education? For most senior history majors, public history goes against some of the most honored history principles: always quote your primary sources as footnotes, never use first-person style, and get rid of any connection with the present.

Students had two other opportunities to provide feedback. They filled out the traditional university-based course evaluations, but because I like to explore some of their feedback, I also arranged a class discussion. Having this conversation before final grades—in a process that cannot guarantee anonymous comments—can be intimidating and challenging, and can also present ethical concerns. On the other hand, it can encourage students to provide constructive criticism—not simply highlighting what does not work but also contributing to finding solutions. Their comments are often useful for future courses. For instance, in 2018 a majority of students asked for more sessions on public history careers, something I included in my 2019 course.

Student involvement could even go further with direct participation in the design of future class syllabi. The students would not have to design a syllabus from scratch but could reshape the current one according to what they liked, what they found effective, and what they identify as missing topics. Rather than passive end-of-the-year evaluations, in which feedback and criticism are usually not very constructive, students could transform their input into concrete pedagogy and assignments. This would also ensure that introduction to public history courses evolve and adapt to training strategy, community partners, and student expectations.

Students had mixed feedback about the two projects. Projects made the overall workload quite challenging—75 percent of the students thought so in the evaluation. It was perhaps too optimistic to ask students to produce both an episode for a podcast and a panel for a public restroom. I do not think the main issue was the workload per se but rather the energy that two different projects required. Although the research was the same for both, the media, the space, and the required skills were so different that it forced students to switch gears often. Alternatively, I could try to separate the two projects during the semester. However, I still think that the flexibility, the time management, and the organizational skills that the projects demanded are critical to work in the field of public history.

Despite the challenges, students valued the projects. Having two physical products that they could share with their friends and family was extremely rewarding. Having a link to their episodes is also valuable for their CV and future job applications in that it shows concrete examples of what they can do. I remember some colleagues telling me that they had seen (and learned from) some of my students' panels in town while having dinner in a restaurant over the weekend. Projects contribute to making history alive, engaged, and shareable beyond university campuses. Projects can also be fantastic opportunities to create collaboration. After this class, the campus radio station proposed to continue the collaboration to keep *The Land Grant Chronicles* alive. Several colleagues—as well as our history club—expressed interest in making podcasts with and for students. In the long run, we could also have a rich network of history panels throughout the city—and not only in public restrooms. A local ethnic association and a long-established restaurant contacted me, as they were interested in designing and hanging similar panels about their local history and heritage.

As an instructor, there are a couple of rules that emerged through this class. First, project-oriented courses imply long office hours. This is not something new but is extremely important all the same. Project-oriented courses are, for many history students, not the norm. Individual meetings to both accompany the progress of the project and reassure overwhelmed students are necessary. While flexibility and time management are key skills for public history students, these courses can often be accompanied with periods of stress (especially when the process of production depends on partners). Being used to this way of working, I perhaps did not pay enough attention to the need for anxiety relief. I proposed some workshops on anxiety in relation with the podcast and public speaking, but this should have been extended to project management. Working ahead with university student services could facilitate those steps.

I define a successful class through its impact on students—the knowledge and skills they learn—and on communities. In that sense, this Introduction to Public History course was definitely a success. Students learned not only about the local history but also about nontraditional ways to communicate their knowledge to a variety of publics. Perhaps even more important, they were proud of their achievements and contributed to making history relevant in Fort Collins's public space. As an instructor, witnessing my students' pride when they heard that the radio station was impressed by their podcast episodes, wanted to air them all, and proposed starting a regular series was priceless. I consider teaching public history as bringing about fantastic opportunities to create spaces of co-production and public discussion about the past. The fact that colleagues listened to the episodes and decided to assign podcast production as a new assignment in their classes (not necessarily public history courses) demonstrates that good student projects can not only inform about the past but also inspire new ways of doing and communicating history.

Notes

1. See the International Federation for Public History's website at https://ifph.hypotheses.org.
2. Cauvin, "Undergraduate Public History Teaching."
3. Rousso, "Applied History"; Cauvin, "Rise of Public History."

4. Thomas, "From Theory to Practice to Problem."

5. Cauvin, "New Field, Old Practices."

6. "Scale of Fees," Professional Historians of Australia, 2022, www.historians.org.au/scale-of-fees.

7. Weible, "Defining Public History."

8. Cauvin, "New Field, Old Practices."

9. Stearns, "Why Study History?"; "Why Should You Study History?".

10. The *History@Work* blog is hosted by the NCPH; see https://ncph.org/history-at-work/.

11. Cauvin, *Public History*.

12. Kelman, *Misplaced Massacre*.

13. See the Sand Creek Massacre National Historic Site website at www.nps.gov/sand/index.htm.

14. Cauvin, "Campo nuevo, prácticas viejas."

15. International Federation for Public History, "Internship and Public History Training."

16. All episodes of *The Land Grant Chronicles: History at CSU* can be found on the KCSU website at http://kcsufm.com/category/podcast/land-grant-chronicles/.

11 Do Public Historians Need Grades?
Ungrading during a Pandemic

KRISTEN BALDWIN DEATHRIDGE

In recent years, I've asked myself several versions of this question: What are grades *for*? Particularly when I think about the ways that public historians do their work in the world, I find that I'm less and less certain of the answer. How we teach in the classroom should prepare students for the future in a way that I don't think traditional grading does well enough. This chapter explores a semester teaching an upper-level undergraduate course, Introduction to Digital History, from January through May 2021 at Appalachian State University. The chapter consists of my reflections, beginning with course planning and moving through my weekly thoughts after each class meeting. I opted to use an "ungrading" approach to the course. In essence, ungrading relies on student self-assessment—students write reflections on their process and learning and propose their own grades for the course, while the professor provides narrative feedback and assistance.[1] As I will discuss further, public history work often requires approaches that are self-reflective and that share authority. Ungrading models this.

This is the third version of the course for me, and it relies heavily on what I learned from the Doing Digital History 2016 Institute for Advanced Topics in Digital Humanities, run by Sharon Leon and Sheila Brennan and sponsored by the NEH.[2] I created the course for our university and use the following catalog description: "This course prepares you to use and understand a variety of current and emerging digital technologies in the service of doing history. In addition to learning about these technologies, students will also consider their usefulness, and what digital history means. The focus is on building a sense of possibility, contingency, and agency in the world of the digital humanities. Students will complete one or more digital projects." The course objectives are as follows:

- In this course you should learn skills that will help you in your other history courses as well as in your job search. This course will broaden your modes of research and communication.
- This course should help you to overcome the fears and intimidation associated with digital technology.
- This course will introduce you to some of the key digital tools and products used by historians.
- This course should help you to understand the differences in input and output technologies for historians, and what constitutes digital history.
- This course should enable you to build a sense of possibility, contingency, and your own agency in the world of the digital humanities.

I was trained as a public historian, but until the Doing DH 2016 Institute, I had no formal training in digital history. At the same time, much of my training did require digital tools, and I learned the potential uses of social media while in graduate school and on the job market.[3] I know how important these things are and wanted to be deliberate about how I teach them.[4] Each time I've taught digital history, I've changed some of the readings, switched out assignments, and otherwise revised the course. This semester has been no exception, not least because I taught it during the COVID-19 pandemic. This time, there were twenty-one people registered for the class, with a cap of twenty-five. One audited. In the past, the course has been full, but considering the constraints of this semester and the subject of the course, this was a good-sized group to have.

Digital history itself is part of the amorphous digital humanities, and I teach it acknowledging this while also working from a public history perspective. Some of the other chapters in this volume discuss the difficulties and shifting nature of defining public history, and digital history proves similar, but there is clear overlap that is often at least as much about intent and implementation as it is about specific methods—or, in the case of digital history, specific tools and technologies. Sharon Leon, associate professor of history and digital humanities at Michigan State University, describes digital public history as having "a much greater sense of shared authority and . . . is much less about winning a methodological argument with a community of scholars" than history more broadly. Leon goes on to note that the "primary difference, however, is that public history is directed at a particular audience. It's not a 'we will build it, they will come, and they might be interested' mentality. Instead, it is 'I am going to do research about you, I'm going to find out the kinds of materials and prior knowledge you bring to the topic, and I'm really going to engage you.'"[5] Clarifying intent and implementation in ways that help and actively engage communities requires constant reflection and self-assessment, and ungrading proves a key way for students to practice this while doing digital history.

Using an ungrading approach this semester meant that deadlines became suggestions and I needed to make some changes to how I've assigned and responded to work in the past. In the end, I eliminated late penalties and meeting attendance requirements, and asked students to build a professional website with a résumé, write three blog posts, and complete a choose-your-own (CYO) digital project. I also asked that they keep up with readings and respond to discussion prompts in Slack in order to build community and connection.[6] The course ended up being fully online, with one Zoom meeting per week. I divided the class into three learning groups to make asynchronous Slack discussions manageable.

While some of the details needed to change, I'd used most of these sorts of assignments before. The biggest difference was that, on the whole, I'd simply be noting if people completed the work (not so much when) and offering them feedback as a group in class meetings and as individuals as they requested it. To facilitate the feedback process, I created three self-reflection Google Forms for the students to complete. After four weeks, they shared with me about their time management, any struggles they were having with the course, something they'd learned about digital history, and any individual feedback that they'd like from me. At the midterm, they completed a similar form, though this one also asked that they assign themselves a grade for the course so far. After each of these, I emailed each student, providing both the feedback they requested and anything else I thought relevant to their specific situation. As part of the midterm response, I let them know what I thought of their proposed grade and of their plans for their work moving forward. The final self-reflection was similar, and all are discussed in more detail in the pages that follow.

As I hoped, the freedom from strict deadlines was a relief for most individuals, and even those who struggled with this reported that their time management mostly improved over the course of the semester. In digital history, as in public history more broadly and many other professions, people often need to be working on a variety of tasks at once that contribute to different projects. Tracking their own assignments and working out how much time they need for each is helpful practice, though I did provide guidelines and reminders. Several said that the course helped them feel better prepared for their careers, and some noted that it helped them to think about digital in new ways. Others discussed how asking for help, listening to their peers, and working together made their work better. It is worth noting that there weren't any group projects in the class, though this is often a feature of public history courses. Students also related key lessons from specific class content in their self-assessments.

The required self-reflection helps people process what they are learning, to be aware of it, and to more consciously build on it in the future. As public historians work in different situations with different groups and communities, reflection helps convert methods to action that serves each individual community or circumstance. Through ungrading, students learn to do some of this as they go along, rather than only making time for it at the end of a process. Likewise, the bulk of this chapter was drafted journal-style once a week during planning and after class meetings so that I could also practice self-reflection.[7]

January 8, 2021—Planning

The term doesn't start until January 19, but I'm already stressed about making this a good semester for everyone. I'm a planner, and normally I have my syllabi mostly done by now and ready to go, but the ever-shifting nature of the current COVID-19 pandemic and the sheer exhaustion from last semester means I do not feel ready.

I took lots of time last summer to update my course expectations (which I used to call policies), and those don't need much tweaking. The concern here is all about the schedule. This is an introduction to digital history course with a public history focus. It is an upper-level undergraduate course that attracts both history majors and non-majors. Some folks will have a basic understanding of historical work and what public history is, but others will not.

The last time I taught it, in spring 2019, I had two big projects. For mid-semester, people had to submit their professional websites and write a personal digital strategy, and at the end of the term, they completed one of two large group projects creating Omeka exhibits for partners. I'll explain more about the first when we get to those parts in the semester and reflect on the second in another venue, but for now I am struggling with the thought that this is just too much to require in a semester that will mostly be taught online.[8]

This spring's course is listed as a web-based hybrid course, and this translates to mostly online with a few in-person meetings. Due to the pandemic, my plan is to begin the course all online and to reserve in-person meetings for optional technology troubleshooting sessions later in the semester. Most weeks we will meet on Tuesday on Zoom, and folks will do small group discussions on Slack in place of the normal Thursday sessions. There are exceptions, which I will explain as I go along. The university is expected to announce any day that it plans to begin all online, and I will email the students at that point and let them know what to expect, something I would have done in any case.[9]

I think that requiring group work on a new technology under these circumstances would potentially set people up for failure. In part, this is because of the lessons I learned last time. So I'm thinking about shifting the plan a bit. I'll have them submit a draft of their professional website for peer review around mid-semester (not sure yet if I'll have them write a personal digital strategy essay) and the final version for the end of term. At the end of the term, I'll have them include an individual project on their website. I'd like to give students a choice of presenting historical information digitally—through a small Omeka exhibit, a short documentary, a podcast, or something else. I've assigned some of this before, but not all of it. I think I'll email some colleagues for their experience in these types of assignments as I'm drafting my own.

A small group of us in the History Department had an informal meeting yesterday to talk through what went well teaching during a pandemic last semester and what we'd like help with for the upcoming term. These meetings and the support of a group have been invaluable to me. The meetings started off the cuff in summer 2020, and yesterday there were six of us chatting. Carrie Streeter, currently ABD from the University of California San Diego and adjuncting for the department this year, used an "ungrading" approach with her U.S. survey courses in the fall. Talking with her about the ways her class did and didn't go well helped me realize that it would be a great approach for this class.

I've done a contract grading assignment for a class before, and the results were mixed.[10] I've been reading about ungrading for a few years now, and while I see the pedagogical appeal, it is a bit scary, too, if I'm honest. But I think that allowing students to estimate their own grade for the class will help them to take ownership of their part of the work required for learning, which is an essential skill for both public and digital history. Working with technology requires experimentation and time that may not be immediately evident from the final product (ditto working with communities in public history work), and folks understandably struggle with this shift away from the flow of their other history courses. It can be hard for people to accept that I factor those efforts into their grades even as it isn't as simple as "an A for effort." The ungrading approach might be just what these students need to help them situate their work as being primarily to learn the material rather than to score points.

Streeter has sent me her assignment details and information, and I'm going to spend time over the next few days looking at them and seeing if I can adapt them in a way that makes sense pedagogically for this class.

January 18—Quick Note

Term starts tomorrow, and I've decided to go all in on the ungrading approach and to have the students in this class self-assess and submit their own grades for the class. I'm finalizing today how I'm going to begin talking with them about this, but overall, I am excited about the prospect.

January 26—Week One: Introductions

Welp, the internet went out halfway through the first class, so it was an auspicious start to the semester. The students rolled with it, and I emailed and reminded them that technology will sometimes just break.

Over the course of the week, I asked them to fill out a syllabus quiz that asks things like What do you like in the syllabus? and What questions do you still have? For this class, I also asked them to fill out a quick survey that asks their major, their level, their computer access, and anything else about the course that makes them nervous.

Several things stood out that I needed to discuss with them today. There were some questions about procedural matters, like if we'd be learning coding for this class and when things would be due. We won't be coding, and my guidelines are for things to be complete at noon. Weekend and midnight due dates encourage a 24/7 work culture that I want to step away from, if possible. At the same time, since folks are self-assessing, they can use whatever guidelines work for them; there are no late penalties, but I strongly encourage work to be completed in order. Several people had questions about the end-of-term CYO research project. I didn't go into too much detail, but I told them they'd need to craft a historical argument and work with primary sources, but they could choose the digital format and the main subject. I will provide more guidance later in the semester.

Nearly everyone responded in time for me to compile notes for our Zoom discussion. Demographically, half the class are seniors and half are applied and public history majors. Other majors include history, history education, art management, anthropology, and communication. I always think it is a benefit to have people from different disciplines in a group, and I shared why with them as well. Different backgrounds means that students will approach problems from various angles, which can only help.

People shared that they hoped to learn to be more comfortable with technology, learn more about historical research; some mentioned specific technology and programs. Students also shared that they were nervous about feeling lost or incompetent, not knowing what to do for the CYO assignment, and only about 25 percent of respondents consider themselves "tech savvy." I let them know that several folks were worried about not knowing what to do or looking incompetent. I said, "If you're feeling this way, even if you didn't write it down, you're not the only one. If you already knew all the things, you wouldn't need the class." I reminded them to reach out to me if they get lost or confused, and I hope they will.

I was surprised and encouraged that more people weren't nervous about the ungrading approach, though of course some were, and we talked about it quite a bit. A few of them had noted that they were excited about it, just as others were nervous, so I opened by asking if folks who were looking forward to it would share a bit about why. I wanted them to hear from one another. One person said they felt like everyone is coming from different places and skill levels and they are looking forward to being evaluated as an individual. Another said they were excited about taking responsibility for their own learning. A couple of others spoke up and said versions of the same. One noted something I'd said last week, which is that you can spend ages learning a digital technology and still have an end product that looks only so-so; the end product doesn't always reveal all that they've learned.

I shared that these reasons are essentially why I chose ungrading. As public historians, they will need to be adaptable to different circumstances, each starting with their own skills, as well as to explain the deep work that goes into products that can appear deceptively simple. Further, in order to do all of this well, they will need to reflect and be self-aware. I have guidelines for when assignments should be completed because I've structured the course intentionally. It should build in a certain way. But if those deadlines don't work for them, they can be flexible. Three times during the course they will submit self-evaluative feedback in response to a set of questions from me. The second time, at midterm, they will propose a grade for themselves so far and provide evidence to support it. I will let them know what grade I think they've earned, also based on the evidence. But one of the great things about the system is that this doesn't really mean anything at this point—it will be a guide. They can still earn something totally different by the end of term.

We also talked through a set of readings for the week. Since we are only meeting once a week, it is hard to compress items to discuss what I'd normally do with more time. But it does help me to home in on what is the most essential. They have another reading and a video on the history of the internet that I asked them to do for their Thursday work.

Next week they will be evaluating digital history projects. They will look at review standards for two journals, evaluate a site (responding in a Google Form), and discuss one aspect of that evaluation in their Slack groups. We will spend time in our Tuesday class session talking about how to evaluate digital history projects, and then they will do it later in the week.

Engagement was pretty good this week. I had twenty individuals come to the Zoom, including one who is auditing the class, and a handful of people both spoke aloud and interacted in the chat. Because there was so much for me to cover, we didn't get to do that as much as I'd like, but it showed great promise for our later discussions.

February 2—Week Three: Getting Going

We didn't meet as a class during week three, but I asked people to evaluate a digital history project and to respond to a Google Form about it as well as to discuss it on Slack in their learning groups. There were extremely high levels of engagement on these things! Of twenty-one students, only three didn't do all of the things, and one of those is auditing the course. This is encouraging. I created a list of about twenty digital history projects, including digitized collections, a historical Twitter reenactment, online exhibits, and digital mapping projects. Some of these were created in the last year, and others are over a decade old. In the Google Form, students noted which project site they reviewed, how they would categorize it, who made it (along with why and when), if it is still being added to, if the site still worked well, and if they'd learned anything from it. In their Slack learning groups, I asked them to share which site they reviewed and either one thing they learned from it or one way that the project could be improved. This got them right in there talking with each other about what they could observe from other projects. They've been introducing themselves to one another already, and I wanted to ask them a question that would be easy to answer and hopefully get them talking to each other. This worked very well; there was quite a bit of back and forth as they compared the sites they'd each looked at and asked each other questions.

Before we move on next week to discuss ways we might define digital public history, this activity got people thinking about some key issues, and we will open the next meeting discussing those. This is also something that they can look back on later in the semester as they plan their own websites and, even later, the CYO projects. They can use these examples to guide what they hope to accomplish. Between this and their Slack conversations with one another, I think we are setting great patterns for the rest of the term.

February 9—Week Four: What Is Digital Public History?

Today we met on Zoom and opened with a quick discussion on the evaluation of digital history projects they did. I asked for a few volunteers to share a key lesson from the experience. Lessons included that passion projects can be great, and putting loads of information/resources out there, even without contemporary web design, isn't necessarily a bad thing; that the best sites made their arguments clear but subtle, and it was evident in the design and organization of materials; and that the web moves fast—dead links and places they couldn't explore were frustrating.

We then turned to the readings. For today I'd asked them to review the National Council on Public History's "About the Field" page, as well as an interview with Sharon Leon by the *Los Angeles Review of Books* from 2016.[11] We spent a lot of time talking about what public history is and isn't, and what digital public history is and isn't, which I'd asked them to prepare for in advance. The discussion was quite lively, and it was great to see folks disagreeing civilly, asking each other for clarification, and engaging further in the chat. For this discussion, the goal was to begin reflecting on how what they are reading integrates with other things they already know (building the sort of self-reflection that is central to ungrading). The goal was not to agree on the definitive definitions; instead, I wanted the students to practice asking the deep questions that will continue to push their work and encourage curiosity. For example, is it public history to use a new tool to do something that historians have long done? Is just creating an online exhibit digital public history? In this latter case, it is definitely digital, but what makes it public—the act of sharing outside an academic text? These questions connect to the continually renegotiated definitions of public history itself that were discussed in the readings. I wanted to push them to ask these complex questions, even if they cannot answer them yet, in order to encourage self-reflection in their future public history work. In this sense, the class session modeled something that often proves essential in public history professional practice. I am very excited to see where this group goes!

Readings for the rest of the week include reflecting on building a personal digital strategy.[12] Next week we will be doing domain and hosting setup with Reclaim Hosting, and so I let them know that there are some resources in our course management system that they should preview. I also talked a bit about the importance of thinking through what their website domain would be and how they wanted to publicly identify themselves. I noted that there are very good reasons why folks should want to be "found" online and to stand out from others with similar names. At the same time, there are very good reasons why people may need to keep their names and images private, and I suggested some work-arounds for that as well. I reminded them that I've had people in the class in the past with these issues, and we've worked around them. I've also had folks who already knew what they wanted to do and wanted to use their site to brand themselves in a particular way that might not always be historically relevant. I told them that this is fine, though they still had to complete the requirements of the class.

I am a bit nervous about doing the Reclaim walkthrough and sign up over Zoom, where I can't physically go to individual machines and help them get through the process.

February 16—Week Five: A Domain of One's Own

I stayed nervous about doing the domain set-up on Zoom, but I think it worked pretty well. We are only thirty minutes after the class and a couple of people have already shared their domain names in the course management system.

Over the past week, as I was confirming links and setting up things to share with the class on this, I found that it seems as if very few of the people from the recent past have maintained their domain and hosting that we set up in class. I'm not sure what this means, really, but it has me thinking: Is teaching this skill obsolete? My instinct is that it isn't, that setting up a website of one's own is foundational to continuing curiosity and confidence in digital history and digital public history work. I know that I've gotten a lot of confidence from being able to do this, from how easy companies like Reclaim make it, and I have also had individuals get jobs in which they were told that they were hired because they could clearly demonstrate those digital skills. But I also know things change so quickly; is it time to rethink requiring a personal website for future iterations of this course?

Review of Early Term Self-Reflections

Knowing that students would be concerned about the ungrading approach and, more importantly, wanting to give them early feedback, I asked them to complete a four-week self-reflection using a Google Form. I asked them to share about their time and engagement committed to the course so far, what is working well, what is challenging, and what they could do to address those challenges, as well as key concepts they've learned so far, and anything they think I should know or that they'd like more feedback on.

Their reflections line up with my observations for the most part. Some expressed really enjoying being able to focus on learning rather than counting points, and they are mostly picking up the key course content points that I'd planned for up till now. There are a couple of people who remain confused, but I genuinely think that is because they haven't been engaging with the class much. I wrote an email to each person in response to their self-reflections with a quick note on whether or not I agreed with their assessments and any tips for improvement that I had. I don't know how well it would work for much larger classes, but taking time out at this point in the term for us to communicate directly one-on-one was valuable.

February 23—Week Six: Omeka

Over the weekend, I emailed and messaged with a few individuals over Slack. They'd started getting notifications about the WordPress Limit Login Attempts plugin that Reclaim includes with its WordPress install. The plug-in shuts down login attempts from IP addresses after so many failures. It is a safety feature to prevent bot hacking. It is a good thing, but all the notifications freaked people out and had them panicking about why someone wanted into their site. This is an entirely understandable reaction! The more times I teach this, the more I have students who are reluctant to put anything online (though it is clear in the course description that we will do so, and I tell them on the first day, in case it is truly a deal breaker for anyone—I also allow aliases). Obviously, these notifications bothered them. I sent out an email to everyone Friday afternoon explaining the issue and posted in Slack that I'd done so. I hope that helped. I think this is one of the complications of doing this online and not meeting together multiple times per week—there's less opportunity for reassurance.

Today I'll be walking them through an Omeka classic installation on their sites, and I'll add a quick update about that after our meeting. Omeka is a free and open-source online platform for creating exhibits and sharing digital collections.

The Omeka installation went well, and like last week, I added a typed walk-through with links to the course management system. Omeka is so great, but it can be a hard sell for students who are used to everything coming more naturally to them. I talked about Omeka's use, benefits, and flexibility, but in general they don't love working with it, despite all that it can do. I don't really know what to do about this, or how to talk about it in a more successful way.

March 2—Week Seven: Organizational Digital Strategy

Today we talked about organizational digital strategies, and they were quite engaged, especially when it came to talking about the ways that different organizations use social media. Before class, they read Adam Koszary's "Seven Broad Statements That May or May Not Help Your Museum Do Social Media," Manuel Charr's "How Do Museum Professionals Harness Social Media for Marketing?" and Josette Souza and Rachel Lee's "How Your Museum Can Use Social Media during COVID-19." At the time the article was published, Koszary was running the surprisingly popular Museum of English Rural Life Twitter account (@TheMERL), though someone else runs the account now, I believe. Koszary used humor and pop culture references to raise the profile of the museum and shares some of the guiding principles of how one might accomplish this in the piece, but he is also careful not to be overly prescriptive.[13] Charr's piece is more general and discusses some of the ways that museums might organize and plan their social media presence, and Souza and Lee's article provides specific examples and insight into museum social media during the global pandemic.[14] I also provided the class with a link to the Library of Congress's organizational digital strategy. They didn't have to read that one, but I encouraged them to skim its structure and bookmark it for future reference.

Through the readings and the class discussion, students realized that there is no single formula for an organization's social media and online presence. We talked about what works in different contexts and emphasized the fact that this needs to be a planned part of at least one person's job. It is time-consuming labor that should be done with reflection and care, and it needs to be compensated. One of the key connections to larger themes of the class and public history work is that it doesn't necessarily matter what the plan is, just that there be a good and thoughtful reason for it. When crafting an organizational digital strategy, those involved should reflect on what they know and are capable of doing, what they can reasonably learn and do, what their stakeholders need from them, and how (or if) they'd like to expand on that.

This segues well into next week's class, where we will be joined by Sarah Calise, an archivist who supervises the social media for their archive. Calise will be able to discuss that experience as well as issues around digital archival work.

March 9—Week Eight: Digital Archiving

Sarah Calise, an archivist at the Gore Center, joined us as a guest speaker.[15] Calise talked with the class about their journey, beginning as a graduate student creating a digital archive of the Forrest Hall Protest Collection. Calise began working with Documenting the Now and learned a lot about consent and intent on digital archiving.[16] Calise shared a mistake they made early on with the Forrest Hall Protest Collection, in which they'd put names to contemporary protest photos with the intent of uplifting their voices and ensuring they got credit for their activism. But after discussions with a variety of people, including folks from Documenting the Now, Calise realized that carceral or university authorities could use those collections to bring harm to the activists whose names were listed and so went back and removed them from the metadata.

This decision wasn't easy; there were questions about photo-blurring techniques, but Calise noted that "these are human beings that we are dealing with," and that it is better to focus on doing no harm now than worrying about the future. Calise would rather ensure that folks are safe now rather than center the content. They acknowledge that this approach could mean information and connections are lost in the future but further argue that contemporary ethics of care for the people involved is the most important thing.

It was so good for the students to hear from a professional in the field, and I think they really enjoyed it. Calise and I set the readings for the week together, and I think it went really well.[17]

March 16—Week Nine: Is It All Too Much?

At the end of week eight, people submitted their midterm reflections, including an assessment of what grade they believe they are earning so far. I look forward to digging into these and seeing how students are doing and how I can help them further.

The university canceled spring break, and I'd planned for class to still meet. I eliminated Slack discussions and reading assignments for the week, and was only going to have a Zotero workshop. I opted to go ahead and cancel our class meeting and provide a written Zotero walk-through on the course management system instead (with links to two different tutorials recorded by others). Zotero, a reference storage and citation manager, is a great program that will be so helpful, but we all needed a break.

Several people are struggling to set their personal website themes, but others have done quite a bit of work in that direction. I admit that I am grappling with taking the time to respond to their evaluations in light of my other responsibilities. Next week, we are coming back together to talk about how they will be doing their peer review of each other's websites and get into using mapping tools.

March 23—Week Ten: Mapping

This week's class involved a lot of me going over things to get started. Between not meeting at all last week and only meeting once a week, finding that balance is difficult. I can write out all the instructions I want, but many of them won't really take it in until I've said it a couple of times. I don't fault them for that; often I'm the same way, but it is something I have to continually reflect on and adapt to throughout the semester.

I encouraged them to keep working and to set up time each week to be working on their website and the "un-essay"/CYO project, and reminded everyone that one of the great things about doing ungrading for this course is that there aren't hard deadlines and there's room for everyone to improve. I want them to have more confidence in assessing where they are truly at, and if they are seriously struggling at mid-semester, there's time to sort it out and finish strong. This is nearly always the case, but it can be hard for students to really take it in when they see those zeros or other poor marks in the course management system gradebook.

For today they were to read about maps, including an article from Andrew Wiseman on "When Maps Lie." I showed them my favorite Hank Green (vlogbrothers) video "42 Amazing Maps." Green's video is from 2013, but he gets through a bunch of information and maps so quickly that demonstrate how arbitrary some of our mapping conventions are.[18] But that doesn't mean we can't learn from maps or have good ones. I also showed them some Esri StoryMaps, which is a program that combines GIS location data with media (photos or videos) and written work to tell a story.[19] From here, they will begin using a digital mapping tool and writing a blog post about their experience.

Everything we're talking about for the rest of the semester should be things that either directly influence their work on their projects or at least offer new ways to be thinking about their public-facing work.

March 30—Week Eleven: Crowdsourcing

After taking a quick glance in the course management system, I can see that over half of them have done their peer reviews and their mapping blog posts. I haven't read either yet, but those are pretty good numbers in all. The goal was to complete peer review by last Thursday and the blog post by today, but since we are ungrading, there's room. I told them that if they aren't ready for peer review, they should ask their partner to wait. I have two folks who still haven't completed their mid-semester reflection, and one of them apparently hasn't started their website at all, or if they have, they haven't shared it anywhere and their partner can't find it. I'm going to ask in class today if anyone else is having this issue and see if I can get this person a new review partner.

I'm set to get my second dose of the Moderna vaccine this afternoon, I have my annual review, and we've had some extended family issues over the last week, so my head is honestly not in it today. I typically write this reflection after class, but I started some of it before class today to help get me in the headspace I need to be in. I need to be the best I can for these students, who are also having a tough semester.

This class is one that people often struggle with because it asks them to think and do things differently than in many other classes, and that difference takes time and effort. In addition to reading and writing, they are also learning digital tools and crafting their learning for more public consumption. At the same time, they might spend hours working with a tool that they ultimately decide not to use again for this class. I'm constantly working on ways to help them see that in many ways, exploration is the point. We learn some jargon and some tools, and we learn that we can really mess things up and that it takes ages to fix a small problem—but that we can fix it! I'm trying to encourage curiosity and connection, but they get down in the best of times, and these aren't the best of times.

Sometimes their complaints are truly because they aren't doing what I ask them to do, not trusting that we aren't doing arbitrary things. I reassure them about that as much as I can, but sometimes I just can't guarantee buy-in. At the same time, some of the students are clearly loving and thriving in the course, and I need to remember that too.

Fewer individuals were in class today, but still a good number, and participation was good. We talked about the different types of crowdsourcing and *Wikipedia* and connected this back to questions of the perils and promises of digital history (How does *Wikipedia* serve in some ways as a peril to overcome?), and we discussed whether participating in crowdsourcing is doing public history.[20] Is creating a crowdsourcing opportunity public history? Some argued that inviting public participation is inherently public history, but others argued that it can depend on who is asking the questions and what will be done with the answers (or the resources and knowledge contributed). We did talk about some of the complications that come from only relying on secondary sources and who gets left out of the narrative of *Wikipedia* as a tertiary source.

I also returned them to the questions, What is digital history? Is all digital history public history? Is there a difference between being a public historian and being a historian in public? These are questions that public historians continue to debate. I don't want to get bogged down in definitions, and I think it is important to acknowledge that our definitions of different work often evolve over time (I know that I define public history slightly differently now than I did when I was first asked the question!), but to practice reflective scholarship, it is also important to keep asking ourselves these questions and thinking through the answers so that we know what we're doing and why. This reflection should ultimately influence actions and create a public history that serves others well. As I've been working through this semester with the students, I've tried to model the practice as I teach the course by sharing my own reflections with them and changing our plans when it would best serve the group.

April 6—Week Twelve: Timelines and Other Data Visualizations

For an in-person version of this course, I'd have one meeting where we talk about the article we read on data visualization and another where we work through a Neatline tutorial.[21] Neatline and TimelineJS are programs for building timeline visualizations on websites. One of the things I've learned from the midterm self-evaluations is that a portion of the students aren't actually doing the walk-through along with me; instead, they are just watching. I've talked about this in class and discussed how important it is to do it together so we can help each other and they can actually get the experience. When we are in a room together, this works pretty well, but apparently online, they aren't doing it. They've reported poor experiences with tools and asked to set up meetings with me where I can walk them through it again. The Neatline tutorial is a little more in-depth, and since we are only meeting once a week, I decided not to fight this battle. Perhaps I'll replace this with something different the next time I teach the course, but I find that communities often want digital timelines, so I'm not sure.

I reserved some class time for general project and website questions, then we talked through the article, and then I shared my screen and talked through some examples on the Neatline and TimelineJS pages. I added a Neatline tutorial by Kristen Mapes to the course management system, and I told them what they'd need in order to try it themselves if they wanted to use one of these tools for their CYO project.[22]

We had a really good discussion on what makes good data visualizations, when to use visualization tools based on research questions and project goals, and when to hire an expert in this type of work. We also talked about pro-quantitative data bias—the idea that some people are more prone to believe an argument if it has numbers as evidence (rather than a narrative argument). They raised great points connecting this to our discussions about maps, and I made sure that we also connected it to museums more broadly. I encouraged them to think about these issues in relation to their projects as well. I told them there are three axes to consider: What topic do they want to make a historical argument about? Do they want to go deeper with a tool they've used a little already or learn a new tool? and What tool is the best fit for their argument? After all, some information is well suited to a Story-Map, but other topics would work better with a podcast.

I also tried to emphasize that the choice between working deeper with a program they know a little and working more shallowly with a new-to-them program is a value-neutral one—either is a great option for work in this class, and this is another reason why self-evaluation works well for us here. It is week twelve, and I worried that most of them would have dropped off or would be too stressed to focus on this class, but I'm really pleased at the high attendance numbers and number of folks who are clearly engaged with the material. At this point in the semester, I have students in both of my undergraduate classes who are logging in, turning off their cameras, and not really following along with the class. I can tell because I stay after for any questions, and they will be the only names in the Zoom room and don't respond when I talk to them. I mention this because it is happening, but I don't think it is that different from a regular semester. No matter what I do—and I will keep trying to avoid this!—there're always people who, for one reason or another, don't engage with the class at this point. At the same time, so many of them are not only hanging in there but are thriving in this environment. I've begun to turn my mind to thinking about how this version of the course will affect the way that I teach it next time, and I'm excited about the possibilities.

April 13—Week Thirteen: Ethics

This week, fourteen of twenty-one people joined our Zoom, which is honestly quite good for this point in the semester, when I'm not taking attendance. Originally, today is when the last blog post would be due, but I cut it a few weeks ago when I realized how behind many folks still were. In a normal semester, I also have two other CYO blogs, but I'd cut those before the term even began. I think they'd get something from another post and exploring another tool, but one more just isn't essential to the overall course goals, and many of them are exploring new-to-them tools in their CYO projects anyway.

    This week they have two sets of readings and two Slack engagement conversations, similar to how we began the term. I reminded them of this assignment last week so that they'd be able to plan accordingly. Readings include things on web accessibility, copyright, social media history-in-photos-style accounts, the possibilities of big data, Netflix algorithms, and Reddit and mapmaking. This is a wide-ranging group of topics that we can never spend enough time on but that touch on issues that have come up so far this term. There are, of course, other ethical considerations, some of which we've already talked about in class—like those in community work—but bringing these threads together to overview ethical considerations in digital history work works well. It also feels important to explicitly name accessibility (both connecting to the internet and being able to use it if you are a person with various abilities), accuracy, crediting work, and algorithm creation and use as ethical considerations—not just talk about them as complicated aspects of the work. We had good discussions and engagement in class today, and I'm looking forward to reading their Slack conversations on these issues as well.

For Slack conversations at this point in the semester, I try to have the jumping-off point be something pretty simple, because I know how worn out everyone is. For the first set of readings—ones we talked about in our meeting today—I ask them to focus on one of the articles and share something that stood out to them about it. Often in our class discussions, I remind them that these points are so good to start from—we notice something and then interrogate *why* we notice it and how it connects to other themes. For the second set, I asked them to note one thing they see in the readings (either specifically in one of them or in the group) that connects back to the ongoing themes of the class. This is a low-stakes jumping-off point that also helps them remember that all the things we are doing have connections, and that talking through them can help to synthesize the information. That's my intention, at least. I'll see where they get to with it.

Next week there's just one set of readings for the second half of the week, and we are going to use class time just to talk through questions and issues they are having with their CYO projects. These will be all different, with each student crafting a historical argument on a subject of their choosing and using a specific technology to share their research. I encouraged them to think about what questions they have and to be ready to share screens if needed. I also noted that they should come even if they don't have questions, because the questions of others might help them out in unforeseen ways.

We took just a bit of time in class today for questions as well, and one student asked about a point in the instructions they'd lost sight of: that I ask that their project have a thesis. They shared a bit about what they wanted to do and wondered how it could have an argument. It was a great opportunity to talk about the nuances of something that is central to a lot of historical work. I said that the project needed to go beyond the desire to simply inform, because "I want people to know about this" isn't an argument, but "It is important for people to know x because of y" is an argument they can use. I connected this to the point I made earlier: that it is good to start with something interesting that you want to share, and then you can dig deeper into why you want to share it, why someone else should care, and what you want them to do with the information. I reminded them of discussions we had earlier in the semester about digital project reviews—What makes a good project? Do we want a subtle hand of presenting information for folks to draw their own conclusions, or do we want to lead them very clearly to specific conclusions? Either requires an argument and intention, because even then the historian selects what sources and evidence to show.

I'm really looking forward to seeing what they do and what we will talk about next week. In the meantime, I reminded them that even though I'm not giving lots of small grades I am reading all their work—they aren't doing it for nothing. In the end, they were relieved not to be graded on every little assignment, so long as they were getting feedback from me and discussion with their peers. I invited them to reach out if they have questions or would like specific feedback, and encouraged them to keep up reading and commenting on their group members' work as well.

April 20—Week Fourteen: CYO Project Workshop

For this week's class, there were no set plans other than things I wanted to remind them about for the end of the semester. I left it open as to their questions about end-of-term planning and the CYO projects. I opened with a reminder to be sure to complete this week's reading and Slack discussion post. Readings this week are about digital storytelling, and I'm hopeful, too, that they will still be able to influence how they are thinking about their projects. The readings have built up to these themes, and we can talk about them with the ones next week if they like.

I also offered general advising comments, some things about the upper-level class I'm teaching next semester, and information about the courses from the new person in the department this year and the one who will be joining us next year. In our department, we have three people who do all the formal advising, and they do a great job, but sometimes there's nothing like talking options over with someone in your major field. I told them that regardless of their major, if they're thinking about more history classes, internships, or graduate school, I'd be glad to talk things over with them anytime.

Then I opened it up for project questions. One student had several questions and was willing for those to serve as a basis for providing several options and reminders about the project, which I was sure to thank them for. This student is creating an Omeka exhibit, and I know several others are as well. Another student shared what they are thinking about for their topic with the group. While I wish this particular student was farther along in their process, I am realistic about this too. It is a solid topic and allowed me to offer additional tips specific for them and generalizable to the rest of the group. There were some other questions on deadlines, number of sources, and number of blog posts. In particular, there were a few questions about citing sources, as I have asked them to do so but recognized that the precise method would vary depending in part on their medium and in part on their preferences.

Students often struggle with answers like "There needs to be enough" rather than being given a set number of primary sources, for example. I talk through this as often as I can, and I acknowledge that it can be stressful for some of them. My hope is that they will see the potential in it as well—they know their subject and its possibilities, and they have opinions on what the best they can do is. Paired with the ungrading approach, I have had fewer of these questions this semester. I don't know if that is because folks are overwhelmed and not thinking ahead and working on stuff, or if it is because they have genuinely embraced the spirit of the course. I suspect it is some of both. Their chosen subject and technical axes are going to determine what "enough" looks like, and I let them know that they can ask me specific questions if they like. At the same time, I reminded them that this is indeed an upper-level history course, and I do have expectations about their capabilities.

I talked through our remaining schedule and provided some reminders. I explained what the CYO project peer-review process should look like, and let them know that while folks have been able to set their schedules a bit, the final project submission and final self-assessment had hard deadlines set by the university for finals week. I may be able to offer some extensions, and I'm willing to do that, but they will need to ask me for them and let me know when they think they can have things completed.

For peer review, the goal is that they will have at least a shell of their CYO project up by next week. They have the same peer-review partners as last time, but instead of completing a form, they will answer three questions in a forum on the course management system. They will note how the person dealt with the last peer review, share one thing they think is particularly strong about the CYO project, and share up to three things they think can be improved in the week before the CYO project is complete. I reminded them that the goal here is to help each other and to actually get feedback.

The feedback forms for their websites around the middle of the semester were a definite success and something I'll carry forward for this class even if I don't keep using the ungrading/self-assessment style. They were able to give each other concrete and directed feedback much more quickly than my doing all of it, allowing me to just respond if I saw anything glaringly absent or incorrect from that. I also reminded them that they can ask me about their peer reviews if they aren't sure about a peer's advice. They were mostly (the exception being the couple of people who aren't active in the class at all anymore) a great combination of diligent and kind in their reviews of each other, which is a good balance. I hope they see them as being as helpful as they actually are.

Next week is our last formal class meeting, and I reminded them of all the places they could ask questions about their remaining work—both of me and of each other. Next week we will be bringing it back and talking about digital history and public history.

April 27—Week Fifteen: Digital History and Public History

I opened our final class meeting with a review of how far I've seen them come over the course of the semester and a discussion about what "finishing strong" means during a pandemic. To me this means finishing at all. Getting something in and not cheating. Everyone's "best" is going to look different right now, and that is the beauty of self-assessment. In fact, I suspect everyone's best often (always?) looks different. This is still an upper-level course, so I'm not saying they shouldn't try; I'm saying that everyone's "try" will get them to a different place.

Our last set of readings today were an article by Andrew Hurley from *The Public Historian* and three blog post responses on *History@Work* on the topic of digital history and public history.[23] On Slack, I asked them to discuss one of the blog responses in particular and what it adds to the discussion. For class, I asked them to be ready to discuss Hurley's argument and the case study he provides. I also let them know that they could discuss any connections between the Hurley piece and the storytelling readings from last week. They are all dealing with a lot of work at the end of the term, not just for this class, and so they weren't as prepared as I'd hoped. In fact, it seemed that most of them weren't able to find the Hurley article, and no one emailed to ask me about it. I appreciate the student who was honest and let me know in class, and some of them found it on JSTOR just fine. Just goes to show that even in an upper-level course, we can make no assumptions. I typically link articles on our course site anyway to avoid this reality, but the link didn't copy and paste the way I thought.

We were still able to talk about some key points. Connecting back to the beginning of the term and Cohen and Rosenzweig's concept of the perils and promises of digital history, I argued that the concept of "if we build it, they will come" is another peril, as described by Hurley when discussing the digital divide. We can do so much with technology, but if people don't have access and training to use it, then what are we doing? The experiences of the last year brought this home to the people in this class in ways that didn't affect the previous course versions. The class also talked a bit about what history is and the role of the word "story" in working with it. I asked what might be helpful and what might be harmful about using "storytelling" to describe what historians do. Just as some digital tools are right for some communities, so, too, is certain language for what historians do. I reminded them that some digital history tools are used to help us do history as it has long been done—just faster or with more data input and output. But there are other digital tools, or other ways of using the same tools, that change the types of history folks can do, share, and experience.

I closed class with another reminder that I'm proud of all they've done so far. I encouraged them to take a moment to appreciate how much they've learned. There are several ways in which this class isn't like their other history classes, and I know that has presented particular challenges. I reminded them of all the ways they have to contact me if they have questions, and asked that they use the final self-reflection as an opportunity to think about all they've learned.

Attendance was a bit down, but participation was strong, with several different voices both on video and in the chat. Most individuals left their cameras off, but enough had them on to allow me to feel as if we were talking rather than me just performing for them. On the whole, this class has far exceeded my modest fear-based expectations, and I can't wait to see their projects and read their reflections. Several waved and thanked me as we closed, and one cheered a bit. I hope they know how much these small tokens mean in such a tough semester.

May 4—Week Sixteen: Finals Week and Conclusions

For finals week, people should post a link to a blog post reflection on their CYO project in the relevant forum on the course management system, complete their last self-reflection, and tell me what grade they earned for the semester. I am very much looking forward to seeing their projects, and I'll include a list of topics and technology types here. This assignment is modeled on the "un-essay," which many professors and teachers use. Several of them had done this sort of CYO project in the past, which helped.

I asked them to focus on a historical argument and choose from a list of options to create a digital history project. The options I gave were a short documentary, an Omeka exhibit, a social media plan and two weeks' worth of content for a history museum or site, a podcast, or a StoryMap. They were permitted to do something else, but they needed to get my approval first. One person asked to do a blog series. I admit that I'd had something slightly more technical in mind, but I also know that blog writing is a particular skill and genre that should be encouraged. It was also relatively late in the process when they asked me this, and they were stressed. It turns out that a few students took this option, even though only one got formal approval.

One student did a creative WordPress site-based exhibit, three did blog sets, three did podcasts, three did StoryMaps (though one of those did two), and nine used Omeka in some way. They also had to write a 500–800-word reflective blog post that linked to or introduced their project and explained their argument/thesis and why they chose the format they did. A few didn't really complete this part of the project, but for those who did, reading them was one of the best parts for me. The subjects of their CYO projects varied so widely that I'm not sure how to summarize them here. The projects themselves also varied in what I'll call objective quality, but the students were all coming at this from different class levels and historical understanding, so that is to be expected. Some of them did truly impressive work.

For the final self-assessment, I asked them several questions. I worried it was too many in addition to the CYO blog post, but I also wanted them to use the opportunity to truly reflect on what they learned and all they accomplished over the course of the semester. I asked the following:

- Talk about what you have committed to the course over all. How would you characterize your learning and engagement with the readings and discussions? If relevant, include any areas that you started out strong but found challenging later in the semester and/or areas that were initially challenging but that you worked through later in the semester. You might also discuss anything that you wish you'd taken better advantage of or more time with for this class and/or anything you're particularly proud of.
- What was the biggest challenge for you with the CYO project?

- What aspect of the CYO project are you the most proud of?
- What is one thing from this class that you will take with you into other classes, your work, and/or your personal digital activities? This can be a small tip or a more generalized lesson. Another way to phrase this question would be: What's something you learned in this class that has impact for you?
- What letter grade would you give yourself for the semester? (Ideally, I would give everyone the grade they give themselves, but I reserve the right to raise or lower grades as appropriate.)
- Briefly, how does your grade recommendation reflect your learning and effort in this course?

As I was crafting these, I consulted my colleague Carrie Streeter, who pointed me to one of Jesse Stommel's final reflection questions along with sharing her own.[24] It really helped me to home in on what I truly wanted to know. I cut a couple of questions and refined a couple of others to come up with my final list. Some instructors don't ask for the proposed grade and then ask for a justification after, but I'm glad that I did, as those brief answers were often quite revealing.

I struggled with how much and whether or not to alter the recommended grades for about eight of the nineteen that submitted them. Roughly half were folks who I thought did better than they did, and half were people who I think overestimated themselves a bit. In the end, I let some stand, lowered a couple, and raised a few more. As a former self-proclaimed overachiever, allowing those who overestimated themselves to stand was much more of a struggle than the opposite. There are a variety of reasons for this concern, and I'm not sure this is the place to dig into them, but in general I am much more concerned with folks who are unable to value their work as highly or who cannot see themselves truly, so I opted to do more raising than lowering.

In the end, though, it isn't the specific grades that are the most important thing, which is why I opted for the ungrading approach in the first place.[25] I did not ask the students' permission, so I have not shared any of their direct words in this chapter. I can say that unequivocally, the majority of them said that they really appreciated the way we conducted the class this semester. Some struggled in the beginning and then really got it later; a minority were never able to set their own deadlines, and their overall learning and project work suffered as a result. Of that minority, though, a couple did note that this was perhaps the most important lesson of the class—that they are responsible for their own learning. At the same time, those who really bought in from the beginning liked leaning in to that lesson as well.

As for me, I still think this method works particularly well for this sort of class—one that is part seminar, part learning and practicing new skills. I will definitely be ungrading again in the fall semester for my upper-level Introduction to Public History course. A couple of these same individuals will be in that class, and so I'm looking forward to learning from them how they will grow over the course of a year with this process. As of right now, that class will be fully in-person again, and I find myself wondering how it will go. I will be rereading the reflections from these students as I prepare the fall's class, and I look forward to making the required changes both in this methodology and in the content.

Overall, I know that for some this emphasis on self-reflection and the conversations that go into ungrading can seem like overthinking, like making things that are straightforward more complicated. But simple isn't always better, and over time this sort of reflection won't require as much work. This connects to grading as well—we inherited these systems that were to give feedback to students in a clear and simple manner, but the current results often aren't what the situation truly calls for. Ungrading, in contrast, can sound way more complicated, like it requires more effort and customization. Perhaps it does at first, and maybe that's not a bad thing. Grades should reflect student learning and should help them grow, and if they aren't doing that, then students don't need them. Likewise, self-reflection should be an impetus for action—action that helps others and improves public history work for communities. Do public historians need grades? For now, I'm not sure that they do.

Notes

1. For the history and discussion of ungrading, see Stommel, "What If We Didn't Grade?" This is a fairly broad overview built on the scholarship of teaching and learning.

2. For more details, see the Doing Digital History: 2016 website at http://history2016.doingdh.org/.

3. For more of my personal digital journey and a preview of some themes I discuss in this class, see Deathridge, "Teaching the Digital Self."

4. Others in my department are doing the same, notably Rwany Sibaja and his Teaching History in the Digital Age course.

5. Dinsman, "Digital in the Humanities." In addition to being an associate professor, Leon is a core faculty member of the Consortium for Critical Diversity in a

Digital Age Research at Michigan State, and was formerly director of public projects at the Roy Rosenzweig Center for History and New Media at George Mason University.

6. Slack is an internet-based chat platform, where people can be grouped together and only approved members can read and interact with posts.

7. As such, most of the following is recorded using present-tense verbs.

8. The personal digital strategy is discussed in some detail in Deathridge, "Teaching the Digital Self."

9. Appalachian State allowed faculty quite a bit of choice in how our spring courses would be offered in the 2020–21 academic year, provided the course format was clear in the registration system for students (in-person, hybrid, or online, and synchronous or asynchronous). In the end, we stayed online all semester at the students' request.

10. Contract grading can vary, but it most often refers to a process in which students determine at the beginning of the semester what grade they want and what they will do to earn it. Sometimes the professor has set this up ("to earn a B+, students must . . ."), and other times each student and the professor work the details out collaboratively. I tried it with the major project assignment, having students determine what a successful group project would look like. It can definitely work well, but when the project is for an outside partner, there's a lot less room for student determination when it comes to the details.

11. National Council on Public History, "About the Field," NCPH, https://ncph.org/what-is-public-history/about-the-field/; Dinsman, "Digital in the Humanities."

12. Posner, "Creating Your Web Presence." This piece is a few years old now, but it brings up key themes and questions for students to consider.

13. Koszary, "Seven Broad Statements."

14. Charr, "How Do Museum Professionals Harness Social Media?"; Souza and Lee, "How Your Museum Can Use Social Media during COVID-19."

15. I'm grateful to the History Department for paying Calise a stipend for their time and work with my class. At the time, Calise was an archivist at the Albert Gore Research Center at Middle Tennessee State University.

16. Later, Calise also worked with Student Activism Now Documented, https://standarchives.com; see also Documenting the Now at www.docnow.io/.

17. Readings for the week included: Agarwal, "Doing Right Online," https://www.historians.org/publications-and-directories/perspectives-on-history/november-2016/doing-right-online-archivists-shape-an-ethics-for-the-digital-age; "Digital Blackness in the Archive: Collecting for the Culture," YouTube (DocNow, May 10, 2018), https://youtu.be/3sKCDuBbiPM; Vavra, "The Right To Be Forgotten: An Archival Perspective"; and Kaplan, "We Are What We Collect."

18. Hank Green, "42 Amazing Maps."

19. For an overview of Esri's ArcGIS StoryMaps, see www.esri.com/en-us/arcgis/products/arcgis-storymaps/overview.

20. See Cohen and Rosenzweig, introduction, for more on the perils and promises of digital history. (This is something we read early in the semester and referred back to several times.)

21. Graham, Milligan, and Weingart, "Principles of Information Visualization."

22. Mapes, "Tutorial."

23. Hurley, "Chasing the Frontiers of Digital Technology"; Kelland, "Digital Community Engagement across the Divides"; Leon, "Access for All"; Young, "Audience Analysis and the Role of the Digital in Community Engagement."

24. See Stommel's self-reflection Google Form for an introductory level digital studies course here: https://docs.google.com/forms/d/e/1FAIpQLSdm6wPw9MaxxkbBlPTNrczneyez5xMVOixP-5N0eG7-bwE_1Q/viewform (accessed June 4, 2021).

25. In an age when college and graduate school cost so much, it would be foolish to say that grades don't matter at all.

Contributors

JULIA BROCK is assistant professor of history at the University of Alabama. She practices, studies, and teaches public history with special interest in museums, digital history, and oral history. Her independent research focus is the post–Civil War U.S. South; her current manuscript focuses on the development of game and fish laws in the Progressive and New Deal eras.

THOMAS CAUVIN is associate professor of public history at the University of Luxembourg, where he leads the Public History as the New Citizen Science of the Past research team. He is the current president of the International Federation for Public History and the author of *Public History: A Textbook of Practice* (2016).

KRISTEN BALDWIN DEATHRIDGE earned a PhD in public history from Middle Tennessee State University in 2012 and is associate professor in the History Department at Appalachian State University. She teaches courses in history, public history, digital history, and historic preservation. Baldwin Deathridge's research centers on community formation and re-formation in relation to the built environment.

JENNIFER DICKEY is professor and coordinator of the public history program at Kennesaw State University in Kennesaw, Georgia. She is the author of *A Tough Little Patch of History: Gone with the Wind and the Politics of Memory* and coeditor of *Museums in a Global Context: National Identity, International Understanding*.

EVAN FAULKENBURY is associate professor of history at SUNY Cortland. He teaches courses on public history, oral history, and U.S. history, and he also facilitates public history internships for undergraduates. He is the author of *Poll Power: The Voter Education Project and the Movement for the Ballot in the American South*. His current book project involves memory, public history, and slavery in America.

TORREN GATSON is assistant professor of history at the University of North Carolina at Greensboro. Gatson is a trained public historian and a scholar of nineteenth- and twentieth-century U.S. and southern history, with an emphasis on the African American built environment and material culture.

ABIGAIL GAUTREAU is assistant professor of history at Grand Valley State University in Allendale, Michigan. She teaches public history, museum studies, U.S. history surveys, and writing history. Her public history work focuses on community engagement and the preservation and interpretation of cultural heritage.

ROMEO GUZMÁN is assistant professor in history at Claremont Graduate University. He is the codirector of the South El Monte Arts Posse and coeditor of

East of East: The Making of Greater El Monte. From 2016 to 2020 he directed the Valley Public History Initiative at Fresno State. For more on his work, please visit romeoguzman.com.

JIM McGRATH is a white academic living and working on the lands of the Massachusett and Pawtucket peoples. He is currently instructional designer at Salem State University and faculty associate in Arizona State University's School of Historical, Philosophical, and Religious Studies. He has worked on several digital public humanities projects, including Mapping Violence, the Rhode Island COVID-19 Archive, and Our Marathon: The Boston Bombing Digital Archive. His writing has appeared in *Doing Public Humanities* (Routledge, 2020), *American Quarterly*, the *Public Historian*, *Digital Humanities Quarterly*, and *Reviews in Digital Humanities*. More information on Jim can be found at his personal website (jimmcgrath.us); he is also on Twitter @JimMc_Grath.

PATRICIA MOONEY-MELVIN is associate professor of history at Loyola University Chicago. She established the public history program at the University of Arkansas at Little Rock and directed the public history program at Loyola in the 1990s. As part of her service to the National Council on Public History, she was president in 1994–95 and chaired the Curriculum Committee from 2000 to 2005.

LINDSEY PASSENGER WIECK is associate professor of history and director of graduate public history at St. Mary's University in San Antonio. She studies urban, Latinx, and twentieth-century U.S. history. She's currently writing a book on how the San Francisco Mission District's growth as a Latino neighborhood set the stage for one of the nation's biggest gentrification battlegrounds.

REBECCA S. WINGO is a scholar of the Indigenous and American West, assistant professor of history, and director of public history at the University of Cincinnati. She has written exactly 2.5 books: *Homesteading the Plains* (with Rick Edwards and Jacob Friefeld), *Digital Community Engagement* (with Jason Heppler and Paul Schadewald), and *Housing the Crows* (in progress).

Bibliography

Abenir, Mark Anthony D., and Carol Ma Hok Ka. "Social Theories and Service Learning: Towards Building an Integrated Service-Learning Sociological Framework." *Journal of Community Engagement and Higher Education* 12, no. 3 (2020): 53–68.

Achenbaum, Andrew W. "Public History's Past, Present, and Prospects." *American Historical Review* 92, no. 5 (1987): 1162–74.

Agarwal, Kritika. "Doing Right Online: Archivists Shape an Ethics for the Digital Age." *Perspectives on History*, November 1, 2016. www.historians.org/publications-and-directories/perspectives-on-history/november-2016/doing-right-online-archivists-shape-an-ethics-for-the-digital-age.

Allison, David B., ed. *Controversial Monuments and Memorials: A Guide for Community Leaders.* Lanham: Rowman & Littlefield, 2018.

———. "From Columbus to Serra and Beyond." In *Controversial Monuments and Memorials: A Guide for Community Leaders*, edited by David B. Allison, 115–23. Lanham: Rowman & Littlefield, 2018.

Allitt, Patrick. *I'm the Teacher, You're the Student: A Semester in the University Classroom.* Philadelphia: University of Pennsylvania Press, 2004.

Amato, Rebecca, Gabrielle Bendiner-Viani, Dipti Desai, Denise D. Meringolo, and Mary Rizzo. "Radical is a Process: Public History Pedagogy in Urban Universities." In *Radical Roots: Public History and a Tradition of Social Justice Activism*, edited by Denise D. Meringolo, 325–60. Amherst, MA: Amherst College Press, 2021. https://doi.org/10.3998/mpub.12366495.

Anderson, Marvin Roger, and Rebecca S. Wingo, "Harvesting History, Remembering Rondo." In *Digital Community Engagement: Partnering Communities with the Academy*, edited by Rebecca S. Wingo, Jason Heppler, and Paul Schadewald, 71–92. Cincinnati: University of Cincinnati Press, 2020.

Appleby, Joyce. "Should We All Become Public Historians?" *Perspectives on History*, March 1, 1997.

Appleby, Joyce, Lynn Hunt, and Margaret Jacob. *Telling the Truth about History.* New York: W.W. Norton, 1994.

Auslander, Mark. "Slavery's Traces: In Search of Ashley's Sack." *Southern Spaces* (blog), November 19, 2016. https://southernspaces.org/2016/slaverys-traces-search-ashleys-sack/.

Banner, James M., Jr. *Being a Historian: An Introduction to the Professional World of History.* New York: Cambridge University Press, 2012.

Barthel-Baucher, Diane. *Cultural Heritage and the Challenge of Sustainability.* Walnut Creek, CA: Left Coast Press, 2012.

Bauer, Shane. "Your Family's Genealogical Records May Have Been Digitized by a Prisoner." *Mother Jones*, August 13, 2015. www.motherjones.com/politics/2015/08/mormon-church-prison-geneology-family-search/.

Beasley, Betsey, and David P. Stein, "Podcasting History." *American Historian*, August 2017, 12–16.

Becker, Carl. "Everyman His Own Historian." *American Historical Review* 37, no. 2 (1932): 221–36.

Belanger, Elizabeth. "Radical Futures: Teaching Public History as Social Justice." In *RadicalRoots: Public History and a Tradition of Social Justice Activism*, edited by Denise D. Meringolo, 295–324. Amherst, MA: Amherst College Press, 2021. https://doi.org/10.3998/mpub.12366495.

Black, Olivia Williams, "The 150-Year War: The Struggle to Create and Control Civil War Memory at Fort Sumter National Monument." *The Public Historian* 38, no. 4 (2016): 149–66.

Bodner, John. *Remaking America: Public Memory, Commemoration, and Patriotism in the Twentieth Century*. Princeton, NJ: Princeton University Press, 1992.

Boyer, Ernest L. *Scholarship Reconsidered: Priorities of the Professoriate*. Edited by Drew Moser, Todd C. Ream, and John M Braxton. San Francisco: Jossey-Bass, 2016.

Boyer, Paul. "Whose History Is It Anyway? Memory, Politics, and Historical Scholarship." In *History Wars: The Enola Gay and Other Battles for the American Past*, edited by Edward T. Linenthal and Tom Englehardt, 115–39. New York: Metropolitan Books, 1996.

Brand, Stewart. *How Buildings Learn: What Happens After They're Built*. New York: Penguin Books, 1995.

Brecher, Jeremy. "A Report on Doing History from Below: The Brass Workers History Project." In *Presenting the Past: Essays on History and the Public*, edited by Susan Porter Benson, Stephen Brier, and Roy Rosenzweig, 267–77. Philadelphia: Temple University Press, 1986.

Brookins, Julia, and Sarah Fenton. *Careers for History Majors*. Washington, DC: American Historical Association, 2019. www.historians.org/teaching-and-learning/why-study-history/careers-for-history-majors.

———. "Statement on Confederate Monuments," August 2017. www.historians.org/news-and-advocacy/aha-advocacy/aha-statement-on-confederate-monuments.

Brown, Vincent. "Mapping a Slave Revolt: Visualizing Spatial History through the Archives of Slavery." *Social Text* 33, no. 4 (December 2015): 134–41.

Brown University Steering Committee on Slavery and Justice. *Slavery and Justice*. Providence, RI: Brown University, 2006. http://brown.edu/Research/Slavery_Justice/documents/SlaveryAndJustice.pdf.

Brundage, W. Fitzhugh, ed. *Where These Memories Grow: History, Memory, and Southern Identity*. Chapel Hill: University of North Carolina Press, 2000.

Cameron, Fiona. "The Politics of Heritage Authorship: The Case of Digital Heritage Collections." In *New Heritage: New Media and Cultural Change*, edited by Yehuda Kaley, Thomas Kvan, and Janice Affleck, 170–84. New York: Routledge, 2008.

Cannady, Shelley. "Tule Lake Today: Internment and Its Legacies." *Boom California* 3, no. 1 (2013): 17–33.

Carter, Rodney G. S. "Of Things Said and Unsaid: Power, Archival Silences, and the Power in Silence." *Archivaria* 61 (Spring 2006): 215–33.

Caswell, Michelle. "Seeing Yourself in History: Community Archives and the Fight against Symbolic Annihilation." *The Public Historian* 36, no. 4 (November 2014): 26–37.

Cauvin, Thomas. "Campo nuevo, iejases iejas: promesas y desafíos de la historia pública." *Hispania Nova* 1 (2020), https://e-revistas.uc3m.es/index.php/HISPNOV/article/view/5365.

———. "New Field, Old Practices: Promises and Challenges of Public History." *Magazen* 2, no. 1, June 2021.

———. *Public History: A Textbook of Practice*. London/New York: Routledge, 2016.

———. "The Rise of Public History: An International Perspective." *Historia Crítica* 68, no. 68 (2018): 3–26.

———. "Undergraduate Public History Teaching: How and Why It Can Change University History Training." *International Public History* 2, no. 1 (2019).

Charr, Manuel. "How Do Museum Professionals Harness Social Media for Marketing?" *MuseumsNext*, July 16, 2019. www.museumnext.com/article/how-do-museum-professionals-harness-social-media-for-marketing/.

Christopher, Tami. "The House of the Seven Gables: A House Museum's Adaptation to Changing Societal Expectations since 1910." In *Defining Memory: Local Museums and the Construction of History in America's Changing Communities*, 2nd ed., edited by, Amy K. Levin and Joshua G. Adair, 59–70. Lanham: Rowman & Littlefield, 2017.

Cifor, Marika, Michelle Caswell, Alda Allina Migoni, and Noah Geraci. "'What We Do Crosses Over to Activism': The Politics and Practice of Community Archives." *The Public Historian* 40, no. 2 (May 2018): 69–95.

Cohen, Daniel J., and Roy Rosenzweig. Introduction to *Digital History: A Guide to Gathering, Preserving, and Presenting the Past on the Web*. George Mason University's Center for History and New Media, 2006.

Colwell, Chip. *Plundered Skulls and Stolen Spirits: Inside the Fight to Reclaim Native America's Culture*. Chicago: University of Chicago Press, 2017.

Conard, Rebecca. "The Pragmatic Roots of Public History Education in the United States." *The Public Historian* 37, no. 1 (2015): 105–20.

———, ed. "Roundtable: Ethics in Practice." Special issue, *The Public Historian* 28, no. 1 (2006).

Conn, Steven. *Do Museums Still Need Objects?* Philadelphia: University of Pennsylvania Press, 2010.

Corbett, Katharine T., and Howard S. (Dick) Miller. "A Shared Inquiry into Shared Inquiry." *The Public Historian* 28, no. 1 (2006): 9–38.

Crosson, David. "Museums and Social Responsibility: A Cautionary Tale." *History News*, July–August 1988, 6–9.

Daley, Matthew Lawrence, and Scott Stabler. "'The World's Greatest Minstrel Show under the Stars': Blackface Minstrels, Community Identity, and the

Lowell Showboat, 1932–1977." *Michigan Historical Review* 44, no. 2 (Fall 2018): 1–35.

Davis, Jack. "A Struggle for Public History: Black and White Claims to Natchez's Past." *The Public Historian* 22, no. 1 (2000): 45–63.

Deathridge, Kristen Baldwin. "Teaching the Digital Self." *History@Work* (blog). National Council on Public History, September 13, 2018. https://ncph.org/history-at-work/teaching-the-digital-self/.

Denson, Andrew. *Monuments to Absence: Cherokee Removal and the Contest over Southern Memory*. Chapel Hill: University of North Carolina Press, 2017.

Diaz, Rose T., and Andrew B. Russell. "Oral Historians: Community Oral History and the Cooperative Ideal." In *Public History: Essays from the Field*, Rev. ed., edited by James B. Gardner and Peter S. LaPaglia. 203–16. Malabar, FA: Krieger, 2004.

Dickey, Jennifer. "'Cameos of History' on the Landscape: The Changes and Challenges of Georgia's Historical Marker Program." *The Public Historian* 42, no. 2 (May 2020): 33–55.

———. "Public History and the Big Tent Theory." *The Public Historian* 40, no. 4 (2018): 37–41.

D'Ignazio, Catherine, and Rahul Bhargarva. "Creative Data Literacy: A Constructionist Approach to Teaching Information Visualization." *Digital Humanities Quarterly* 12, no. 4 (2018). www.digitalhumanities.org/dhq/vol/12/4/000403/000403.html.

Dinsman, Melissa. "The Digital in the Humanities: An Interview with Sharon Leon." *LA Review of Books*, July 10, 2016. https://lareviewofbooks.org/article/the-digital-in-the-humanities-an-interview-with-sharon-m-leon/.

Donovan, Bill, and Ira Harkavy, eds. *Connecting Past and Present: Concepts and Models of Service-Learning in History*. Service Learning in the Disciplines. Washington, DC: American Association for Higher Education, 2000.

Downie, Andrew. *Doctor Socrates: Footballer, Philosopher, Legend*. London: Simon & Schuster, 2018.

Dubois, Laurent. *The Language of the Game: How to Understand Soccer*. New York: Basic Books, 2018.

Elliott, Debbie. "'Why Don't Y'all Let That Die?' Telling the Emmett Till Story in Mississippi." *NPR*, August 28, 2019.

Elsey, Brenda, and Joshua H. Nadel. *Futbolera: A History of Women and Sport in Latin America*. Austin: University of Texas Press, 2020.

Eng, Norman. *Teaching College: The Ultimate Guide to Lecturing, Presenting, and Engaging Students*. Self-published, 2017.

Falk, John H. *Identity and the Museum Visitor Experience*. Walnut Creek, CA: Left Coast Press, 2009.

Farmer, Ashley. "Archiving While Black." *Black Perspectives*, June 18, 2018. www.aaihs.org/archiving-while-black/.

Faulkenbury, Evan. "Practicing History: Why SUNY Cortland Requires Public History." *Perspectives on History* 58, no. 8 (2020): 19–21.

Fetter-Vorm, Jonathan, and Ari Kelman. *Battle Lines: A Graphic History of the Civil War.* New York: Farrar, Strauss and Giroux, 2015.
Figal, Gerald. "Between War and the Tropics: Heritage Tourism in Postwar Okinawa." *The Public Historian* 30, no. 2 (2008): 83–107.
Filene, Benjamin. "Letting Go? Sharing Historical Authority in a User-Generated World." *History News* (Autumn 2001): 7–12.
Finney, Karen. "I'm Black. Robert E. Lee Is My Relative. His Statues Can't Come Down Soon Enough." *Washington Post*, August 15, 2017.
Fleming, John E. "The Impact of Social Movements on the Development of African American Museums." *The Public Historian* 40, no. 3 (August 2018): 44–73.
Frisch, Michael. *A Shared Authority: Essays on the Craft and Meaning of Oral and Public History.* Albany: SUNY Press, 1990.
Galloway, Patricia. "Archives, Power, and History: Dunbar Rowland and the Beginning of the State Archives of Mississippi (1902–1936)." *American Archivist* 69 (2006): 79–116.
García, Michelle. "Beyond Borders: Life in the Middle Space." Lecture given at the Watson Institute of International and Public Affairs, Brown University, January 2020. https://watson.brown.edu/clacs/events/2020/beyond-borders-life-middle-space.
———. "The Border and the American Imagination." *Baffler*, July 2, 2018. https://thebaffler.com/latest/border-imagination-garcia.
Gardner, James B., and Paula Hamilton, eds. *The Oxford Handbook of Public History.* New York: Oxford University Press, 2017.
Gardner, James B., and Peter S. LaPaglia, eds. *Public History: Essays from the Field.* Rev. ed. Malabar, FA: Krieger, 2004.
Glassberg, David. "The Changing Cape: Using History to Engage Coastal Residents in Community Conversations about Climate Change." *George Wright Forum* 34, no. 3 (2017): 285–98.
———. "Public History and the Study of Memory." *The Public Historian* 18, no. 2 (1996): 7–26.
Goodwyn, Wade. "*Come from Away* Musical Tells Story of Resilience after 9/11." NPR's *All Things Considered*, September 8, 2016. www.npr.org/2016/09/08/493157938/come-from-away-musical-tells-story-of-resilience-after-9-11.
Goulding, Cathlin. "Tule Lake: Learning from Places of Exception in a Climate of Fear." *Forum Journal* 31 (Spring 2017): 40–51.
Graham, Shawn, Ian Milligan, and Scott Weingart. "Principles of Information Visualization." In *The Historian's Macroscope: Big Digital History*, Pre-draft. London: Imperial College Press, 2015.
Green, Hank. "42 Amazing Maps." Uploaded by vlogbrothers, September 20, 2013. YouTube video, 3:43. https://www.youtube.com/watch?v=dldHalRY-hY.
Green, Howard. "A Critique of the Professional Public History Movement." *Radical History Review* 25 (1981): 164–71.
Green, James. *Taking History to Heart: The Power of the Past in Building Social Movements.* Amherst: University of Massachusetts Press, 2000.

Greenspan, Anders. *Creating Colonial Williamsburg: The Restoration of Virginia's Eighteenth-Century Capital.* Chapel Hill: University of North Carolina Press, 2002.

Grele, Ronald J. "Whose Public? Whose History? What Is the Goal of a Public Historian?" *The Public Historian* 3, no. 1 (1981): 40–48.

Gutierrez, Paul. "Galaxy Rallies to Beat Fuego in U.S. Open Cup." *Los Angeles Times*, August 7, 2003. www.latimes.com/archives/la-xpm-2003-aug-07-sp-galaxy7-story.html.

Guzmán, Romeo. "Field of Dreams: Migrant Futboleros in Greater Mexico." *Boom California*, June 13, 2018.

Guzmán, Romeo, Carribean Fragoza, Alex Sayf Cummings, and Ryan Reft, eds. *East of East: The Making of Greater El Monte.* New Brunswick, NJ: Rutgers University Press, 2020.

Halifax, Shawn. "McLeod Plantation Historic Site: Sowing Truth and Change." *The Public Historian* 40, no. 3 (2018): 252–77.

Hanna, Karen Buenavista. "Pedagogies in the Flesh: Building an Anti-Racist Decolonized Classroom." *Frontiers: A Journal of Women Studies* 40, no. 1 (2019): 229–44.

Harney, Stefano, and Fred Moten. *The Undercommons: Fugitive Planning and Black Study.* New York: Autonomedia, 2013.

Hartman, Saidiya. "Venus in Two Acts." *Small Axe*, no. 26 (July 2008).

Hayashi, Robert T. "Transfigured Patterns: Contesting Memories at the Manzanar National Historic Site." *The Public Historian* 25, no. 4 (2003): 51–71.

Hayward, Claire. "Waxworks and Wordless Women: The Jack the Ripper Museum." *The Public Historian* 39, no. 2 (2017): 51–57.

Hidalgo, Melissa Mora, and Giovanni Hortúa Vargas. "'Ehhhhh Pu! . . . what?' A Critical Conversation about Mexican Football Fandom and the Word at the Center of a Homophobic Chant." In *Football, Politics and Identity*, edited by James Carr, Daniel Parnell, Paul Widdop, Martin J. Power, and Stephen R. Millar, 126–42. New York: Routledge, 2021.

Hirzy, Ellen Cochran. *Excellence and Equity: Education and the Public Dimension of Museums.* Washington, DC: American Association of Museums, 1992.

Hoffer, Peter Charles. *Past Imperfect: Facts, Fictions, Fraud—American History from Bancroft and Parkman to Ambrose, Bellesiles, Ellis, and Goodwin.* New York: PublicAffairs, 2004.

Holley, Kenan K., dir. "Redemption Song." *Spike Lee's Lil' Joints.* Season 2, episode 3. Aired June 7, 2016, on ESPN.

Horton, James Oliver. "Slavery in American History: An Uncomfortable National Dialogue." In *Slavery and Public History: The Tough Stuff of American Memory*, edited by James Oliver Horton and Lois E. Horton, 35–56. New York: New Press, 2006.

Horton, James Oliver, and Lois E. Horton. *Slavery and Public History: The Tough Stuff of American Memory.* New York: New Press, 2006.

Horwitz, Tony. *Confederates in the Attic: Dispatches from the Unfinished Civil War.* New York: Pantheon Books, 1998.

———. *A Voyage Long and Strange: Rediscovering the New World.* New York: Henry Holt, 2008.

Hurley, Andrew. "Chasing the Frontiers of Digital Technology: Public History Meets the Digital Divide." *The Public Historian* 38, no. 1 (February 2016): 69–88.

Inayatullah, Naeem. "Teaching Is Impossible: A Polemic." In *Pedagogical Journeys in World Politics*, edited by Jamie Frueh, 17–26. New York: Palgrave, 2020.

International Federation for Public History, "Internship and Public History Training." 2021. https://ifph.hypotheses.org/files/2021/03/Internship_-Public-Draft-1.pdf.

Jimerson, Randall J. "Ethical Concerns for Archivists." *The Public Historian* 28, no. 1 (2006): 87–92.

Johnson, G. Wesley. "Editor's Preface." *The Public Historian* 1, no. 1 (1978): 4–10.

Johnson, G. Wesley, and Noel J. Stowe, eds. "The Field of Public History: Planning the Curriculum." Special issue. *The Public Historian* 9, no. 3 (1987).

Johnson, Jessica Marie. "Markup Bodies: Black [Life] Studies and Slavery [Death] Studies at the Digital Crossroads." *Social Text* 36, no. 4 (December 2018): 57–79.

Johnson, Ronald W. "The Historian and Cultural Resource Management." *The Public Historian* 3, no. 2 (Spring 1981): 43–51.

Kahn, Andrew, and Jamelle Bouie. "The Atlantic Slave Trade in Two Minutes." *Slate*, 2015. www.slate.com/articles/life/the_history_of_american_slavery/2015/06/animated_interactive_of_the_history_of_the_atlantic_slave_trade.html.

Kaley, Yehuda, Thomas Kvan, and Janice Affleck, eds. *New Heritage: New Media and Cultural Change.* New York: Routledge, 2008.

Kammen, Michael. *In the Past Lane: Historical Perspectives on American Culture.* New York: Oxford University Press, 1997.

Kaplan, Elizabeth. "We Are What We Collect, We Collect What We Are: Archives and the Construction of Identity." *American Archivist* 63 (Spring/Summer 2000): 126–51.

Katz, Philip M. "Public History Employers—What Do They Want?" *Perspectives on History*, September 1, 2003. www.historians.org/publications-and-directories/perspectives-on-history/september-2003/public-history-employers-what-do-they-want-a-report-on-the-survey.

Kaufman, Ned. "Historic Places and the Diversity Deficit in Heritage Conservation." *CRM: The Journal of Heritage Stewardship* 1, no. 2 (2004): 68–85.

Kean, Hilda, and Paul Martin, eds. *The Public History Reader.* New York: Routledge, 2013.

Kelland, Lara. "Digital Community Engagement across the Divides." *History@Work* (blog). National Council on Public History, April 20, 2016.

Kelleher, Michael. "Images of the Past: Historical Authenticity from Disney to Times Square." *CRM: The Journal of Heritage Stewardship* 1, no. 2 (2004): 6–19.

Kelley, Robert. "Public History: Its Origins, Nature, and Prospects." *The Public Historian* 1, no. 1 (1978): 16–28.

Kelman, Ari. *A Misplaced Massacre: Struggling over the Memory of Sand Creek.* Cambridge, MA: Harvard University Press, 2015.

King, Thomas F. *Cultural Resource Laws and Practice.* Rev. ed. Lanham, MD: AltaMira Press, 2013.

Kohn, Richard H. "History and the Culture Wars: The Case of the Smithsonian Institution's *Enola Gay* Exhibition." *Journal of American History* 82, no. 3 (December 1995): 1036–63.

Koszary, Adam. "Seven Broad Statements That May or May Not Help Your Museum Do Social Media." *Medium*, November 12 2018. https://medium.com/@adamkoszary/seven-broad-statements-that-may-or-may-not-help-your-museum-do-a-bit-better-at-social-media-6173c3b3afoc.

Kriebel, Andy, and Eva Murray. *#MakeoverMonday: Improving How We Visualize and Analyze Data, One Chart at a Time.* Hoboken: Wiley, 2016.

Kytle, Ethan J., and Blain Roberts. *Denmark Vesey's Garden: Slavery and Memory in the Cradle of the Confederacy.* New York: Free Press, 2019.

Landrieu, Mitch. "Speech on the Removal of Confederate Monuments in New Orleans." *New York Times*, May 23, 2017.

Lang, James M. *Small Teaching: Everyday Lessons from the Science of Learning.* San Francisco: Jossey-Bass, 2016.

Lee, Lis Yun. "The Stories We Collect: Promoting Housing as a Human Right at the National Public Housing Museum." *Forum Journal* 31 (Spring 2017): 9–20.

Leon, Sharon. "Access for All." *History@Work* (blog). National Council on Public History, March 2, 2016.

Leon, Warren, and Roy Rosenzweig, eds. *History Museums in the United States: A Critical Assessment.* Urbana: University of Illinois Press, 1989.

Lerner, Gerda. "The Necessity of History and the Professional Historian." *Journal of American History* 69, no. 1 (1982): 7–20.

Levin, Amy K., and Joshua G. Adair, eds. *Defining Memory: Local Museum and the Construction of America's Changing Communities.* 2nd ed. Lanham: Rowman & Littlefield, 2017.

Liddington, Jill. "What Is Public History? Publics and Their Pasts, Meanings, and Practices." *Oral History Review* 30, no. 1 (2002): 83–93.

Linenthal, Edward T., and Tom Englehardt, eds. *History Wars: The Enola Gay and Other Battles for the American Past.* New York: Metropolitan Books, 1996.

Locke, Brandon. "Critical Data Literacy in the Humanities Classroom." August 13, 2018. http://brandontlocke.com/2018/08/13/critical-data-literacy-in-the-humanities-classroom.html.

Loewen, James W. *Lies across America: What Our Historic Sites Get Wrong.* New York: Simon and Schuster, 2019. Originally published in 1999.

Lonetree, Amy. *Decolonizing Museums: Representing Native America in National and Tribal Museums.* Chapel Hill: University of North Carolina Press, 2012.

Lord, Alexandra M. "Finding Connections." *Public Historian* 40, no. 2 (2018): 9–22.

Lowenthal, David. *Possessed by the Past: The Heritage Crusade and the Spoils of History.* New York: Free Press, 1996.

Loza, Mireya. "From Ephemeral to Enduring: The Politics of Record and Exhibiting Bracero Memory." *The Public Historian* 38, no. 2 (2016): 23–41.

Lyon, Cherstin M., Elizabeth M. Nix, and Rebecca K. Shrum. *Introduction to Public History: Interpreting the Past, Engaging Audiences.* Lanham, MD: Rowman and Littlefield, 2017.

Lynton, Ernest A. *Making the Case for Professional Service.* Washington, DC: American Association for Higher Education, 1995.

Lynching in America: Confronting the Legacy of Racial Terror, 3rd ed. Equal Justice Initiative, 2017. https://lynchinginamerica.eji.org/report/.

Maiden, Peter. "Fresno Soccer History." *Community Alliance,* April 7, 2018. https://fresnoalliance.com/fresno-soccer-history/.

Mapes, Kristen. "Tutorial: Neatline for Historical Maps." *Kristen Mapes,* November 13, 2015. www.kristenmapes.com/neatline/.

Martin, Randy. "Linked Fates and Futures: Communities and Campuses as Equitable Partners?" *Public: A Journal of Imagining America* 1, nos. 1 and 2 (March 2014). https://public.imaginingamerica.org/blog/article/linked-fates-and-futures-communities-and-campuses-as-equitable-partners/.

Martinez, Monica Muñoz. *The Injustice Never Leaves You: Anti-Mexican Violence in Texas.* Cambridge, MA: Harvard University Press, 2018.

———. "Lives, Not Metadata: Possibilities and Limits of Mapping Violence." Lecture given at the Institute for the Study of Societal Issues, University of California, Berkeley, March 2019.

———. "Mapping Segregated Histories of Racial Violence." *American Quarterly* 70, no. 3 (September 2018): 657–63.

Meighan, Clement W., and Larry J. Zimmerman. "Debating NAGPRA's Effects." *Archaeology,* February 26, 1999. https://archive.archaeology.org/online/features/native/debate.html.

Melish, Joanne. "Recovering (from) Slavery: Four Struggles to Tell the Truth." In *Slavery and Public History: The Tough Stuff of American Memory,* edited by James Oliver Horton and Lois E. Horton, 103–34. New York: New Press, 2006.

Meringolo, Denise. "A Cry for Help: Collegial Syllabus Revision." *History@Work* (blog). National Council on Public History, March 22, 2014. https://ncph.org/history-at-work/cry-for-help-syllabus-revision/.

———. *Museums, Monuments, and National Parks: Toward a New Genealogy of Public History.* Amherst: University of Massachusetts Press, 2012.

Miles, Tiya. *Tales from the Haunted South: Dark Tourism and Memories of Slavery from the Civil War Era.* Chapel Hill: University of North Carolina Press, 2017.

Miller, Theresa L., Emilie L'Hôte, and Albert Volmert. *Communicating about History: Challenges, Opportunities, and Emerging Recommendations.* Frameworks, August 2020.

Mooney-Melvin, Patricia. "Characteristics of Public History Programs." Curriculum and Training Committee Report prepared for the National Council on Public History, Fall 2005.

———. "Harnessing the Romance of the Past: Preservation, Tourism, and History." *Public Historian* 13, no. 2 (1991): 35–48.

Nadel, Joshua H. *Fútbol! Why Soccer Matters in Latin America.* Gainesville: University Press of Florida, 2014.

National Association for the Advancement of Colored People. *Thirty Years of Lynching in the United States, 1889–1918.* New York: NAACP, 1919.

National Park Service. *How to Apply the National Register Criteria for Evaluation.* National Register Bulletin. Rev. ed. Washington DC: National Park Service, 1997. www.nps.gov/subjects/nationalregister/upload/NRB-15_web508.pdf.

Newfield, Christopher. *Unmaking the Public University: The Forty-Year Assault on the Middle Class.* Cambridge, MA: Harvard University Press, 2008.

O'Donnell, Terence. "Pitfalls along the Path of Public History." In *Presenting the Past: Essays on History and the Public,* edited by Susan Porter Benson, Stephen Brier, and Roy Rosenzweig, 239–44. Philadelphia: Temple University Press, 1986.

Painter, David Lynn, and Courtney Howell. "Community Engagement in the Liberal Arts: How Service Hours and Reflections Influence Course Value." *Journal of Experiential Education* 43, no. 4 (December 2020): 416–30.

Parra, Alvaro. "Punk Flyers from El Monte and the Greater San Gabriel Valley Scene." KCET, July 3, 2014. www.kcet.org/history-society/punk-flyers-from-el-monte-and-the-greater-san-gabriel-valley-scene.

Portelli, Alessandro. "The Peculiarities of Oral History." *History Workshop* 12 (1981): 99–107.

Posner, Miriam. "Creating Your Web Presence: A Primer for Academics." *ProfHacker* (blog). *Chronicle of Higher Education,* February 14, 2011. www.chronicle.com/blogs/profhacker/creating-your-web-presence-a-primer-for-academics.

Rose, Julia. "Interpreting Difficult Knowledge." *AASLH Technical Leaflet* no. 255 (Summer 2011): 1–8.

———. "Three Building Blocks for Developing Ethical Representations of Difficult Histories." *AASLH Technical Leaflet* 264 (Summer 2013): 1–8.

Rosenthal, Gregory Samantha. *Living Queer History: Remembrance and Belonging in a Southern City.* Chapel Hill: University of North Carolina Press, 2021.

Rosenzweig, Roy, and David Thelen. *The Presence of the Past: Popular Uses of History in American Life.* New York: Columbia University Press, 1998.

Rousso, Henry. "Applied History, or the Historian as Miracle-Worker." *The Public Historian* 6, no. 4 (1984): 65–85.

Sayer, Faye. *Public History: A Practical Guide.* New York: Bloomsbury Academic, 2019.

Scarpino, Philip, and Daniel Vivian. *Career Paths in Public History.* Washington, DC: American Historical Association, 2019.

———. *What Do Public History Employers Want? Report of the Joint AASLH-AHA-NCPH-OAH Task Force on Public History Education and Employment.* Washington, DC: American Historical Association, 2017. www.historians.org/about-aha-and-membership/affiliated-societies/national-council-on-public-history/public-history-employer-report-and-survey.

Schön, Donald. *Educating the Professional Practitioner: Toward a New Design for Teaching and Learning in the Professions.* San Francisco: Jossey-Bass, 1987.

———. *The Reflective Practitioner: How Professionals Think in Action.* New York: Basic Books, 1983.

Seavey, Nina Gilden. "Film and Media Producers: Taking History Off the Page and Putting It on the Screen." In *Public History: Essays from the Field*, Rev. ed., edited by James B. Gardner and Peter S. LaPaglia. 117–28. Malabar, FA: Krieger, 2004.

Sergel, Ruth. *See You in the Streets: Art, Action, and Remembering the Triangle Shirtwaist Factory Fire.* Iowa City: University of Iowa Press, 2016.

Serrell, Beverly. *Exhibit Labels: An Interpretive Approach.* 2nd ed. Lanham, MD: Rowman and Littlefield, 2015.

———. *Judging Exhibitions: A Framework for Assessing Excellence.* New York: Routledge, 2017.

Ševčenko, Liz. "Sites of Conscience: New Approaches to Conflicted Memory." *Museum International* 62, no. 1–2 (2010): 20–25.

Ševčenko, Liz, and Maggie Russell-Ciardi, eds. "Sites of Conscience: Opening Historic Sites for Civic Dialogue." Special issue. *Public Historian* 30, no. 1 (2008): 9–15.

Shopes, Linda. "Oral History and Community Involvement: The Baltimore Neighborhood Heritage Project." In *Presenting the Past: Essays on History and the Public*, edited by Susan Porter Benson, Stephen Brier, and Roy Rosenzweig, 249–63. Philadelphia: Temple University Press, 1986.

Shulman, Lee S. "Signature Pedagogies in the Professions." *Daedalus* 143, no. 3 (2005): 52–59.

Simon, Nina. *The Art of Relevance.* Santa Cruz: Museum 2.0, 2016.

———. *The Participatory Museum.* Santa Cruz: Museum 2.0, 2010.

Smulyan, Susan, ed. *Doing Public Humanities.* New York: Routledge, 2020.

Society of American Archivists. "Using Archives: A Guide to Effective Research." Updated March 26, 2016. www2.archivists.org/usingarchives.

———. "What Are Archives?" Updated September 12, 2016. www2.archivists.org/about-archives.

Souza, Josette, and Rachel Lee. "How Your Museum Can Use Social Media during COVID-19." American Alliance of Museums, March 24, 2020. www.aam-us.org/2020/03/24/how-your-museum-can-use-social-media-during-covid-19/.

Spock, Daniel. "A Practical Guide to Personal Connectivity." *History News*, Autumn 2008, 11–12.

Stanton, Cathy. "What Is Public History? Redux." *Public History News* 27, no. 4 (2007).

Stearns, Peter N. "Why Study History?" American Historical Association, 1998. www.historians.org/about-aha-and-membership/aha-history-and-archives/historical-archives/why-study-history-(1998).

Stein, Marc. *Queer Public History: Essays on Scholarly Activism.* Berkeley: University of California Press, 2022.

Stoecker, Randy. *Liberating Service Learning and the Rest of Higher Education Civic Engagement.* Philadelphia: Temple University Press, 2016.

Stommel, Jesse. "What If We Didn't Grade? A Bibliography." March 3, 2020. www.jessestommel.com/ungrading-a-bibliography/.

Stowe, Noel J. "Public History Curriculum: Illustrating Reflective Practice." *The Public Historian* 28, no. 1 (2006): 39–65.

Straus, Emily E., and Dawn M. Eckenrode. "Engaging Past and Present: Service-Learning in the College History Classroom." *History Teacher* 47, no. 2 (February 2014): 253–66.

SUNY Cortland Department of History. "Why Study History?" September 22, 2020, web.archive.org/web/20200922013955/https://www2.cortland.edu/departments/history/docs/History%20Skills%20-%20SUNY%20Cortland.pdf.

Tang, GVGK. "We Need to Talk about Public History's Columbusing Problem." *History@Work* (blog). National Council on Public History, June 25, 2020. https://ncph.org/history-at-work/we-need-to-talk-about-public-historys-columbusing-problem/.

Tell, David. "Remembering Emmett Till in Money, Mississippi." *Places Journal*, April 2019.

Thomas, Adam Adrian. "From Theory to Practice to Problem: Teaching Public History with a Real Client." *International Public History* 2, no. 1 (2019).

Tilden, Freeman. *Interpreting Our Heritage*. Edited by R. Bruce Craig. 4th ed. Chapel Hill: University of North Carolina Press, 2007.

Tise, Larry E. "Jacques Cousteau, the U.S.S. *Monitor*, and the Philosophy and Practice of Public History." *The Public Historian* 5, no. 1 (1983): 31–45.

Tramposch, William. "Mickey and the Muses." *History News*, Winter 1998, 10–16.

Trifone, Nicole. "Half the History." *Trend and Tradition*, Winter 2019. www.colonialwilliamsburg.org/trend-tradition-magazine/trend-tradition-winter-2019/half-history/.

Trouille, David. "Association Football to Fútbol: Ethnic Succession and the History of Chicago-Area Soccer since 1920." *Soccer and Society* 10, no. 6 (2009): 795–822.

Trouillot, Michel-Rolph. *Silencing the Past: Power and the Production of History*. Boston: Beacon Press, 1995.

Tsutsui, Laura. "'Roots and Routes' Event Highlights Valley's Soccer History, and Looks to Its Future." KVPR, April 23, 2019. www.kvpr.org/community/2019-04-23/roots-and-routes-event-highlights-valleys-soccer-history-and-looks-to-its-future.

Tyler, Norman, Ilene R. Tyler, and Ted J. Ligibel. *Historic Preservation: An Introduction to Its History, Principles, and Practice*. New York: W. W. Norton, 1999.

Tyrell, Ian. *Historians in Public: The Practice of American History*. Chicago: University of Chicago Press, 2005.

Tyx, Daniel Blue. "Signs and Blunders: The Fight to Commemorate a Massacre by the Texas Rangers." *Texas Observer*, November 26, 2018.

Vagnone, Franklin D., and Deborah E. Ryan. *Anarchist's Guide to Historic House Museums*. Walnut Creek, CA: Left Coast Press, 2016.

Vavra, Ashley. "The Right to Be Forgotten: An Archival Perspective." *American Archivist* 81 (Spring/Summer 2018): 100–11.

Vlach, John Michael. "The Last Great Taboo Subject: Exhibiting Slavery at the Library of Congress." In *Slavery and Public History: The Tough Stuff of American Memory*, edited by James Oliver Horton and Lois E. Horton, 57–74. New York: New Press, 2006.

Wallace, Michael. *Mickey Mouse History and Other Essays on American Memory*. Philadelphia: Temple University Press, 1996.

———. "Visiting the Past: History Museums in the United States." *Radical History Review* 25 (1981): 63–96.

Weible, Robert. "Defining Public History: Is It Possible? Is It Necessary? *Perspectives on History*, March 1, 2008. www.historians.org/publications-and-directories/perspectives-on-history/march-2008/defining-public-history-is-it-possible-is-it-necessary.

Wells-Barnett, Ida B. *The Red Record: Tabulated Statistics and Alleged Causes of Lynching in the United States.* Chicago, 1895. www.gutenberg.org/files/14977/14977-h/14977-h.htm.

Weyenth, Robert. "History He Wrote: Murder, Politics, and the Challenges of Public History in a Community with a Secret." *The Public Historian* 16, no. 2 (1994): 51–73.

Whisnant, Anne Mitchell, Marla R. Miller, Gary B. Nash, and David Thelen. *Imperiled Promise: The State of History in the National Park Service*. Bloomington, IN: Organization of American Historians, 2011.

White, Richard. "What Is Spatial History?" *Spatial History Lab*, February 1, 2010, 1–6.

"Why Should You Study History?" Department of History. University of Wisconsin–Madison. https://history.wisc.edu/undergraduate-program/history-careers/why-history/.

Williams, Melvin. "My First Love." Interview by Juan Fonseca. Edited by Marisela Hernandez. *Tropics of Meta*, May 7, 2019. https://tropicsofmeta.com/2019/05/07/melvin-williams-my-first-love/.

Wineburg, Sam. *Historical Thinking and Other Unnatural Acts: Charting the Future of Teaching the Past*. Philadelphia: Temple University Press, 2001.

Wingo, Rebecca S., Jason Heppler, and Paul Schadewald, eds. *Digital Community Engagement: Partnering Communities with the Academy*. Cincinnati: University of Cincinnati Press, 2020.

Wingo, Rebecca, and Amy Sullivan. "Remembering Rondo: An Inside View of a History Harvest." *Perspectives on History*, March 2017. www.historians.org/publications-and-directories/perspectives-on-history/march-2017/remembering-rondo-an-inside-view-of-a-history-harvest.

Winks, Robin W. *The Historian as Detective: Essays on Evidence*. New York: Harper and Row, 1969.

Winters, Mary-Frances. *Inclusive Conversations: Fostering Equity, Empathy and Belonging across Difference*. San Francisco: Berrett-Koehler, 2020.

Wiseman, Andrew. "When Maps Lie: Tips from a Geographer on How to Avoid Being Fooled." *Bloomberg CityLab*, June 25, 2015. www.citylab.com/design/2015/06/when-maps-lie/396761/.

Woodward, C. Vann. "On Believing What One Reads: The Dangers of Popular Revisionism." In *The Historian as Detective: Essays on Evidence*, edited by Robin W. Winks, 30–31. New York: Harper and Row, 1969.

Young, Kerri. "Audience Analysis and the Role of the Digital in Community Engagement." *History@Work* (blog). National Council on Public History, March 22, 2016.

Index

anthropology, 4
archives, 4, 65, 113–114, 128–131, 152–155, 163–165, 178–179, 237–238
assignments, 32, 43, 46–50, 63, 64, 69–71, 72–74, 81, 85–86, 89–90, 122, 125, 129–130, 137, 140, 147, 151–152, 158–160, 247–250

blogs, 22–23, 43–44

class time, 57–58, 61–67, 71–74, 75, 78–89, 102–105, 123–139, 146–152, 172–177, 180–186, 193–199, 206–222, 230–250
Colonial Williamsburg, 80
community partnerships, 2–3, 4–5, 22, 58–60, 64–65, 73–74, 78, 81, 121–122, 155–166, 171–172, 186–188, 192, 195–199, 211–220
Confederate monuments, 43, 61, 82
course objectives, 103, 115, 145, 169, 225–226
COVID-19, 41, 54–55, 139–141, 163
Cultural Resource Management, 138

digital public history, 105–118, 225–228, 232–250

environmental history, 28
equity, 75, 84
ethics, 31–32, 242–244

field trips, 49, 68–69, 127–128, 131, 177–178
films, 67

grading, 225, 227–228, 229, 231–232, 235
graduate courses, 18–33, 76, 191–192
graduate programs, 13–15, 18–20, 85–86
guest speakers, 105, 205–206, 208, 209–211, 213–214

Harriet Tubman Home, 68–69
heritage tourism, 28–29
historic preservation, 4, 122, 132–137
history departments, 1, 4–5, 58–59

inclusivity, 75, 79, 82, 85, 90–92
internships, 15, 210–211

job market, 36, 72

library science, 4, 19

media, 30–31
memory, 30, 82–83
museums, 4, 84–85, 125–127

National Council on Public History (NCPH), 1, 2, 14–15, 72
National Park Service, 182–183, 185
National Register of Historic Places, 134–137

oral history, 30–31, 47–48, 66–67, 148–151, 153

professors, 24–25, 41–45, 52–55, 76–77, 192
public historians, 5–6, 25–26, 36, 38–39, 133–134, 144–145, 189–192

public history: definitions of, 2, 11–12, 40–41, 60, 125, 145, 198, 202–204, 206–208, 233–234; pedagogical context of, 1–2, 18, 27

readings, 23, 25–28, 39–40, 41–43, 45–46, 62, 77, 79–89, 98, 105–109, 124, 126, 128, 130, 131, 133, 135, 137, 138, 147–149, 174, 176–177, 180–181, 191, 206–209
reflective practice, 6, 13, 15–18, 27–28, 32–33, 90–92
roadside historic markers, 59, 65–66, 174–175

service learning and community engagement, 3
social justice, 31, 93–96
social media, 236–237
students, 21–33, 45–47, 57–58, 61–74, 78–89, 95, 109–114, 123–140, 146–166, 172–188, 192–199, 206–222, 230–250
syllabi, 36–40, 52–54, 60, 77–78, 98, 102–103, 123–124, 147, 191, 205–206, 225–226, 228–229, 230

teamwork, 19–20, 51, 64–66, 69–71, 89–92, 96–97, 155–166, 175–181, 186–188
The Public Historian, 13, 14, 62
Tilden, Freeman, 29, 79, 179, 209
tours, 21
Trouillot, Michel-Rolph, 29, 206–207

undergraduate courses, 58–59, 93–95, 99–102, 121–122, 126, 168–171
urban planning, 4

WordPress, 43–44, 48–49
writing, 19–20

Printed in the USA
CPSIA information can be obtained
at www.ICGtesting.com
LVHW092346031023
760074LV00004B/157